Countryside Recreation

Sue Glyptis

Series Editor: **Brian S. Duffield**

Longman

in association with
Institute of Leisure and Amenity Management

Longman Group Ltd
Westgate House, The High,
Harlow, Essex CM20 1YR
Telephone (01279) 442601
Faximile (01279) 444501

First published 1991

Reprinted 1992, 1993, 1994, 1995

A catalogue record for this book is available form the British Library

ISBN 0-582-05035-9

Printed and bound at Bell and Bain, Glasgow

Contents

Contents

Dedication
For Valerie and David Liddle, in memory of Bill.

Acknowledgements

My thanks are due first and foremost to Brian Duffield who, as Series Editor, initially encouraged me to write this book, and who has waited patiently for its completion. In easing my time pressure he added to his own, and for that I am deeply grateful. I am grateful to Longman for commissioning the book, and to the editorial and production staff for their professional services.

At Loughborough University of Technology many colleagues and friends have provided encouragement and direct assistance. I am grateful to Professor Clyde Williams, Head of the Department of Physical Education and Sports Science, for providing a supportive environment for research and writing, and for not asking about the progress of this book when the answer would have been embarrassing! Within the Recreation Management group, Dr Ian Henry and Dr Tess Kay have taken a particular interest in the project, and have tolerated my periodic disappearances at times when it has inconvenienced them. Michael Collins, Director of the Institute of Sport and Recreation Planning and Management within the Department, injected enthusiasm throughout, and supplied far more source materials than I could keep up with! I am grateful too for the interest shown by the postgraduate students of the 1989–90 MSc course in Recreation Management, who at least found some justice in the fact that, while they were writing their dissertations, their Director of Studies was struggling to write her own. Staff in the Department's general office gave good humoured encouragement throughout. I am particularly indebted to Beverley Colburn and Janet Gutteridge, both for their general support and friendship, and for typing the tables.

Further afield, Professor J. Allan Patmore of the University of Hull provided helpful comments on the initial outline. Mrs Jean Tallantire, Senior Regional Officer of the Sports Council Yorkshire and Humberside Region, shared a wealth of knowledge about countryside issues and management approaches. If I had written down everything she said, this would be a much better book, and I hope that she will one day write her own. When the likelihood of my ever getting the book started or finished seemed remote, Dave and Rosemary Chambers demanded weekly telephone reports to get me back on course, and my father and stepmother endured several postponements of holiday!

Needless to say, the inadequacies of the book are mine alone; but, to all who have helped, my heartfelt thanks for making it less inadequate than it could have been.

Sue Glyptis   Loughborough
                                                         November 1990

Introduction

Countryside recreation is one of the most popular forms of contemporary out-of-home leisure activity, engaged in by some 18 million people (two-fifths of the population) in England and Wales on a typical summer Sunday (*Countryside Commission 1985a*). Its growth has been essentially a twentieth century, and especially post-war, phenomenon, fuelled principally by the widespread availability of personal transport, coupled with increased leisure time and disposable income. Indeed, in terms of volume, there are signs that the level of activity has passed its peak; since the late 1970s, numbers participating have stabilized or even decreased slightly. Nonetheless, participation remains high, and grows ever more diverse: the range of countryside activities continues to expand as new technology, the quest for challenge and adventure, and the demand for individual, as opposed to team, sports combine to foster new pursuits, such as jet-skiing, parascending, hang gliding and micro-light flying.

Encouraging and catering for such large and varied demands, and their attendant transport and facility requirements, would be complicated enough if the countryside were specially set aside as a national public playground with no competing uses. In reality, recreation has no such exclusive claims; indeed, in most places it is a latecomer and an interloper to the rural scene.

Nonetheless, the countryside has long been cherished as a place of rest and recreation. It serves both as setting and as focus. For many people, the countryside is *context*, a setting in which to walk, climb, ride, sail, canoe or ski. Each activity has its preferred places and treasured sites although, as we shall see, such preference brings no guarantee of protected or exclusive use. For other people, to be in the countryside, to view its scenic splendour and to savour its tranquillity, are recreation enough: the countryside itself is the *object* of the recreation experience.

Whether central or contextual to our recreation, the British countryside is treasure indeed. Its inherent variety of landscape, habitat and human heritage provides a resource of incomparable beauty, diversity and potential, ranging from rugged peak, windswept moor and exposed cliff to rolling down, lush meadow and sluggish stream. Nor does its appeal derive from physical characteristics alone. Two centuries as a nation of town dwellers have done little to dispel the English attachment to the countryside as a vital symbol of national identity, and as a vision of perfection:

> All of us—even those who rarely step outside our towns—cherish somewhere in our souls the same vision of our real homeland: a rural vision . . . . . virtually all of us know and value the world's most celebrated landscape and cherish rural England's patchwork quilt of fields, downs and woods, separated by thick hedgerows, mossy banks, sunken lanes and sparkling streams. For hundreds of years, our English countryside has given us such ideas as we have had of what paradise might be like . . . . . our countryside has knitted itself into our idea of ourselves as a nation as thoroughly as it has delighted and amazed strangers who have travelled from the far corners of the earth with no other purpose than to feast their eyes upon it *(Shoard 1980, p.9)*.

Clarity of vision, though, can obscure complexities and changes in reality. In the present context, the complexities are twofold. Firstly, though we may claim a romantic attachment to the countryside as national symbol, we can make no such claim for it as national property. Far from being a resource of the nation, it is very much the preserve of the private landowner. Eighty seven per cent of the land of the United Kingdom lies in private hands *(Shoard 1987, p.120)*; a decade ago, the richest one per cent of Britain's population owned 52 per cent of all personally owned land, and the next two–five per cent owned a further 22 per cent *(Royal Commission on the Distribution of Income and Wealth 1979, p.151)*. Secondly, even where there is access for public enjoyment, recreation is rarely the sole or prime user of the country-side. Instead, it sits alongside other, generally prior, activities, notably farming, forestry, mineral extraction, water supply, defence require-ments, and conservation, sometimes harmoniously, sometimes not. For a resource widely held to portray the character of the nation, the British countryside is a remarkably private and multi-purpose place.

This complex arena is far from static. The changes are both physical and cultural, and the two are intertwined. Indeed, the countryside is all too often romanticized as being nature untarnished by the hand of humankind, when in fact its present day appearance and special character derive primarily from the farming customs of our forebears. The main changes in prospect for the 1990s are agricultural and demographic. The agricultural revolution of the post-war years, fuelled by technological transformation and government subsidies, has produced bigger farms, greater output and larger farm profits. It has also produced unwanted food surpluses, and in Britain and other EEC countries there are now pressures to reduce subsidies to farmers and to extensify farming practices. As part of this agricultural counterrevolution millions of hectares will become uneconomic to farm, and surplus land will become available for other uses including, perhaps, recreation.

Demographic trends have also switched. After decades of out-migration from the countryside, the 1980s have seen a net inflow of population to small towns and villages in rural areas, a trend which is set to continue as early retirees, commuters and high-technology industries are more free-floating, and no longer tied to towns and cities. While at the extremes, therefore, urban and rural areas remain geographically distinct, much of the rural scene, in southern Britain in particular, is becoming progressively urbanized, and development pressures are intense. Culturally, even more so than physically, urban and rural stereotypes are being eroded, as counter-urbanization brings into the countryside incomers who are affluent, mobile, articulate and accustomed to urban standards of service provision. Even residents in the remotest rural areas are not the isolated self-contained communities of the past; they have access to urban aspirations and values via the media. Rural Britain is urban Britain in all but appearance.

The countryside, then, is no single or static resource, not does countryside recreation take any one form. Overall, countryside visiting is one of the most popular forms of out-of-home recreation. The sheer scale and diversity of usage pose management issues in their own right, and all the more so because peak demand is concentrated sharply into popular times and favoured places. The task of planning and managing countryside recreation, however, is even more challenging, embracing the issue of public access to a predominantly private resource; the relationship between recreation, other rural land uses, and the changing rural economy; the impact of recreation on conservation; and the compatibility or conflict between different forms of recreational pursuits. The requirements of the various countryside users, their implications for recreation, the complex web of agencies and provisions which have sought to develop and manage countryside recreation, and the effectiveness with which they have done so are the concerns of this book.

The aims of the text are:

1 To develop an understanding of the evolution and contemporary significance of countryside recreation, and the factors affecting access to countryside recreation opportunities.

2 To examine the countryside as a recreation resource, its diversity, and the competing claims with which recreation must co-exist.

3 To embrace the respective roles of the public, private and voluntary sectors in the provision and management of countryside recreation opportunities, and in providing a service to visitors.

4 To discuss the scale, nature and diversity of contemporary demands, and their relationship with social and economic trends.

5 To identify key contemporary planning and management issues and, through illustrative examples. to discuss possible solutions.

The book deals almost entirely with Great Britain, and mainly with England and Wales, because differences in land ownership and planning systems render many overseas comparisons inappropriate — or, at least, difficult to do justice to in the confines of a short text.

Chapter 1 outlines the nature of countryside resources, their ownership and prime usage, and the problems and prospects for recreational access. Chapter 2 places contemporary recreational usage in historical context, and charts the emergence and present system of planning provisions for countryside recreation. Chapter 3 gives a more detailed account of the role of central and local government, statutory agencies, and the voluntary sector. Chapter 4 examines special measures taken to protect certain categories of resources and to promote others for recreational use. In Chapter 5, attention switches to demand and usage, including problems of demand measurement, and management information needs. Chapter 6 links demand and supply issues, examining the range and effectiveness of planning and management approaches currently employed to provide access, facilities and services to visitors. Finally, Chapter 7 provides a brief appraisal of the extent to which countryside recreation has been encouraged or encumbered to date, and of the planning and management challenges that lie ahead.

1 The countryside as a resource for recreation

Definitions and delimitations

The countryside is familiar in everyday parlance and in common experience, but elusive of firm delineation. For the purposes of this book, countryside will refer simply but plainly to land beyond the urban edge. Such an approach will suit most, though not all, of the agencies involved in the planning and provision of countryside recreation. A comprehensive appraisal of recreational resources and strategic need would embrace the whole spectrum of outdoor recreation spaces, from private garden and street corner playground at the local scale, through urban parks, urban fringe parks and regional parks, to national parks and remote wilderness. For the most part, however, the planning framework which has evolved, and the agencies charged with implementing it, have split the open space hierarchy into discrete parts. By far the most accessible parts are within the urban fabric. Indeed, urban parks consume the largest single share of the recreation revenue budgets of most local authorities, and a critical appraisal of their recreational significance and potential, to build upon the excellent review by the *Tourism and Recreation Research Unit (1983a)* is long overdue. By far the largest part of the open space spectrum, however, in areal terms, lies beyond the urban edge; that 80 per cent of our land surface classed as countryside is the concern of this book.

Competing claims

Many forms of recreation enjoy the sole use of facilities and resources designed, allocated and managed specifically for them—sports centres, playing fields, theatres, concert halls, restaurants, pubs and the like. Countryside recreation is very different; it is but an add-on to a rural scene whose character has been formed by the interplay of natural forces and human intervention over many centuries—'all evolved as a varied and harmonious whole by a long living-together of man and nature in a gentle climate' (*Fairbrother 1972, p.13*). The contemporary complexion and usage of the countryside derive largely from a dominant agricultural regime. Much that is currently cherished in countryside landscape — both upland and lowland — is a landscape of traditional husbandry. Modern farming, however, has done much to change the face of the British countryside, and to threaten treasured landscapes. Further changes are in prospect in the 1990s as a slick farming system racing full-speed into ever greater productivity is being thrown into reverse gear by the imposition of quotas and the withdrawal of subsidies for surpluses. For recreation, there are both penalties and possibilities in prospect.

Agricultural use

Though geology and climate can claim the prime creative role in shaping the countryside and in defining its broad landscape and vegeta-tion forms, it is farming which has defined its detailed land use and visual character. Over 70 per cent of the land surface of England is farmed. Little of the countryside is the true wilderness of undisturbed nature. The fields, woods, hedgerows, ditches and leafy lanes of the homely, more gentle rural scene are but the happy outcome of human intervention, the aesthetic bonus of a purely utilitarian purpose. No less artificial are the distinctive field systems, barns and stone walling of our upland valleys which, with dense cultivated woodlands on the steep valley sides, complement open fell, bare mountain and moorland to complete our classic upland landscapes. But the vastness and timeless-ness of the open country, and the intricacies of its more local and intimate form, can be deceptive. Whilst our image of rurality remains unblemished, the realities of changing technology and the changing political economy of farming have wrought many changes upon the rural scene, mostly to date to the detriment of recreation.

The post-war years have witnessed an agricultural revolution, charac-terized by four main changes. Firstly, the development and widespread use of larger and more sophisticated farm machinery has led to the enlargement and standardization of farm units. In many areas tradi-tional crop and livestock rotation has been replaced by intensive monoculture. This is nowhere more evident than in the arable lands of eastern England, where large-scale amalgamation of fields has produced a prairie environment with single fields stretching for up to 200 hectares (*Lean 1989a*) — a landscape of logic, but of little aesthetic appeal. *Newby (1988, p.74)* put it unpoetically but not inaccurately: 'large tracts of lowland countryside now possess the rational geometry of the accountant's spreadsheet'. Over England and Wales as a whole, estimates show that between 1946 and 1974 as many as a quarter of all hedgerows (190,000 kilometres) were removed (*Shoard 1980*). The county of Norfolk lost 45 per cent of its hedgerows (13,700 kilometres) between 1946 and 1970 (*Newby 1988*). Not only is the visual character of the countryside transformed, but there is a drastic deple-tion of habitat for flora and fauna. More recently, the rate of hedgerow destruction has accelerated: between 1969 and 1980 the average loss was 4,670 kilometres per year; between 1980 and 1985 it was 6,400 kilometres per year (*Lean 1989a*).

Secondly, new, more intensive stock-rearing practices have developed, including the rearing of stock indoors, and the chemical treatment of pastures. Thirdly, the use of stronger and more varied pesticides and fertilizers on land under crops has depleted wildlife and dislodged the balance of nature in local habitats. Fourthly, advances in technology and in chemistry have led to an expansion of land under cultivation, with a concomitant loss of economically marginal but aesthetically and ecologically prized habitats, such as hedgerows, copses, heath and moor. Major changes have been wrought by the draining of wetlands, the clearance of broadleaved woodlands, and the ploughing of moorland. The North York Moors National Park, whose character and uniqueness lie in its sweeping expanses of heather moorland, illustrates the rapidity and extent of change. Since the park was designated in 1952, as much as 25 per cent of the moorland has been converted to forest or to improved agricultural land, and 88 per cent of the moorland which remains is technically convertible (*North York Moors National Park Committee, 1982; Parry et al.1982*). Some has legal protection as common land, but much remains vulnerable to change. Departures from traditional management practice pose a further threat to moorland. Controlled burning of the heather has hitherto been carried out on a 10–15 year cycle, to permit young growth for sheep to graze. With the widespread withdrawal of sheep from the moors this practice has declined, resulting in large expanses of old heather which pose a fire threat and tend to burn indiscriminately, resulting in bracken encroachment at a rate of approximately 120 hectares per annum. Lord Porchester examined similar changes on Exmoor (1977). In the uplands generally, the extent of semi-natural vegetation remained virtually unchanged in the hundred years to 1967; between 1967 and 1978 its rate of shrinkage increased eleven-fold (*Countryside Commission 1983a*).

Overall, then, the farming trends of the recent past have had profound effects on the visual (and social) landscape of the countryside depleting the intimacy of scale and detail of character of many lowland areas, and the openness and characteristic vegetation of the uplands. Far from being custodian of a traditional rural scene, the farming community has been the prime agent of change, and with devastating effect: 'The countryside may be the repository of our "heritage", but it is also the countryside of tower silos, asbestos barns, up-rooted hedgerows, ploughed-up moorland, burning stubble, pesticides, factory farming and genetic engineering' (*Newby 1988, p.2*).

As we enter the 1990s, however, much of the basic impetus for agribusiness has been removed. What made the development of an ever more productive farm economy economically desirable, as well as technically possible, was a complex system of annual price reviews, subsidies and support payments to farmers, which has now been substantially withdrawn. These were provided first as part of national policy, and provided more recently under the Common Agricultural Policy (CAP) of the EEC. Tax allowances, and the exemption of virtually all farm developments from the rigours of normal planning control have also encouraged farm investments.

British farming, however, is now suffering from the excesses of its own success. The systems of intervention payments have, in a sense, created an industry independent of its market, and in EEC countries generally the output of virtually all major farm commodities greatly exceeds demand, resulting in surplus stocks of butter, skim milk powder, beef and cereals. By the end of 1986 these 'intervention stocks' had built up a total book value of 11.4 billion ECUs (one European Currency Unit = approximately £0.75); their real value, however, was only 3.4 billion ECUs, due to falling world prices for major commodities (*Countryside Commission 1987a*).

With these problems on the horizon, the EEC first introduced milk quotas in 1984 and suggested in a Green Paper on the future of the CAP that ten per cent of the Community's farmland might be "set aside", by paying farmers not to produce on 'environmentally sensitive' land. Indeed, in 1987 there followed an encouraging step towards integrating farming practice with conservation needs, in the designation in England and Wales of six Environmentally Sensitive Areas (ESAs), modelled on the early success of an experimental management scheme established in 1985 in the Halvergate area of the Broads, eastern England's last remaining stretch of open grazing marsh. In 1980 a scheme to drain and improve the area was proposed for grant-aid from the Ministry of Agriculture, Fisheries and Food. When it was refused on environmental grounds, the farming organizations demanded compensation for not proceeding. The Experimental Broads Grazing Marshes Conversion Scheme was the outcome, funded by the Countryside Commission and the Ministry of Agriculture, Fisheries and Food (MAFF). It sought to retain permanent grassland with grazing stock in the marshes of the central Broads; to manage farmland effectively while conserving a unique landscape, and to re-establish grassland in former grazing areas converted to arable use. The scheme attracted a high rate of take-up: in its first two years over 90 per cent of the eligible land area was included.

Overall, the ESA scheme heralds the greening of farming policy, albeit at a price. It provides financial assistance to farmers and landowners who undertake to promote practices which maintain and enhance environmental features and the special character of the countryside, and specifically helps to protect, under special guidelines, landscape, wildlife and historical features. It gives income support to retain the viability of traditionally run farms. It limits the conversion of land to high yielding and unwanted crops; and it encourages lower input – lower output farming. To the first six ESAs — West Cornwall (West Penwith), the Cambrian Mountains, Pennine Dales (Swaledale and Dentdale), Somerset Levels and Moors, South Downs and Norfolk Broads — were added 12 more later the same year. Other European countries are also offering environmental incentives to farmers (*Bureau Européen de Recherches 1990*).

For the future, the issues remain clear, the solutions more clouded:

> the long term prospect for EC agriculture is that technological progress already in train will continue to push up yields and output faster than any growth in demand for food within the Community . . . . . either a substantial amount of land could come out of food production in the UK, or the intensity of production could generally be reduced, or a combination of these courses could be pursued (*Countryside Commission 1987a, p.11*).

Estimates vary of the likely extent of transfer of rural land out of agricultural production. Edwards (1986) calculates that, with productivity rising at approximately two per cent per annum and demand increasing modestly, the UK could remain 80 per cent self-sufficient in food production in the year 2000, and yet afford to lose 23 per cent (four million hectares) of its agricultural land area to other uses. How much change of use actually takes place, of course, will depend on the policies adopted and the response of the farming community (*Carruthers 1986; M. Bell 1986, 1987*). A shift of emphasis from maximizing food production towards reaping the wider benefits of farming was embodied in the *Agriculture Act 1986 (section 17)*, which required that agricultural policy should achieve a reasonable balance between maintaining a stable farming industry; safeguarding the social and economic interests of rural areas; conserving and enhancing the natural beauty of the countryside; and promoting the enjoyment of the public (*Countryside Commission 1989a*). Possible policy measures and their likely agricultural and environmental impact were outlined by the Countryside Commission earlier (*1987b*), namely price restraints, further quotas on production, constraints on inputs, especially fertilizer, lower input farming in the forms of extensification, more organic farming, concentration on rare breeds, and land retirement or diversion. The Commission has urged that any form of land diversion policy should be resourced and managed in such a way that not only the most marginal and unattractive land be reallocated, but that diversion is aimed at 'creative' uses, including new woodland, wildlife reserves, public amenity and recreation and improved access (*Countryside Commission 1987c*). Specific incentives for positive conservation management are given to farmers in the form of the Countryside Premium for Set-aside Land (*Countryside Commission 1989b*); this is available for land set aside as permanent fallow under the MAFF Set-aside scheme, particularly where there is potential for environmental improvement or quiet enjoyment.

Possible options to match different timescales are shown in Table 1.1. These have been further encouraged since 1987 by the Alternative Land Use and Rural Enterprise package (ALURE), to assist with such projects as farm-based tourism and the conversion of redundant buildings. How tempting these alternatives will be to the farming community remains to be seen. In principle, there is scope for recreation to gain—both in terms of visual and environmental improvements to the farmed countryside, and possible new facility provision for tourists and day visitors. The Countryside Commission is optimistic: 'In the 1960s and 70s, the public "invasion" of the countryside was interpreted as a threat. Today, with many agricultural products in surplus, the patterns of British agriculture and rural enterprise will have to respond to significant changes in economic demand. In this light, public interest in enjoying the countryside becomes an opportunity' (*Countryside Commission 1987b, p.8*). In practice, limitations are likely to be imposed by farmers' understandable reluctance to be diverted from the business and the farm practices they know best, by a lack of capital and entrepreneurial skills to develop recreation facilities, and by residents' resistance, particularly among the nouveaux-rustiques recently settled in the green belt, to the building of sports halls, squash courts and golf driving ranges (*Elson 1989a*); furthermore, the opportunities for viable recreational alternatives will be far greater in the urban fringe than in the National Parks and remoter countryside (*Patmore 1987*).

Table 1.1   Options for diversifying land use: illustrative examples

| Land use with bias towards | *Length of time for which land allotted* | | |
	Short term (up to 5 years)	Medium term (5–10 years)	Long term (more than 10 years)
Agriculture	Rotational fallow	Alternative crops Organic farming	Lower input farming including new permanent grassland
Landscape and wildlife conservation	Headland fallow Small scale conservation planting and management	Integration of conservation into agricultural systems, including ESAs	New nature reserves New woodlands
Recreation and alternative enterprises	Picnic sites and other public access measures	Rights of way improvements	New country parks New woodlands Urban or urban-induced users

Source: Countryside Commission 1987b

Forestry
As with farming, so too with forestry, its relationship to recreation can be positive or negative. Like farming, much of the relevance of forestry to the present purpose is contextual: as a major component of the landscape it can enhance or offend the visual element of countryside

appreciation. In addition, there is a more direct recreational role, with some of our woodland and forest offering an attractive and appropriate setting for recreational activities in their own right (*Richardson 1970*).

The origins of managed forest, and much of its rationale today, have little to do with recreation and amenity. From the outset, the prime task of the Forestry Commission, established under the Forestry Act 1919, was to replace the nation's timber stocks, which had been greatly depleted in the First World War (*Thompson 1971*). The Second World War served only to reinforce that strategic need. Thus the priority for many decades has been the planting of swift growing conifers, mainly in the uplands, to sustain the supply of softwood. That need is still argued, because Britain imports 90 per cent of its timber, and has only ten per cent of its land area (approximately 22.7 million hectares) under forest. Indeed, in recent years, forest expansion has received fresh impetus. The Forestry Commission proposed in 1979 to double the rate of afforestation by planting an additional 1.5 million hectares by the year 2025. The bulk of the Commission's own efforts now goes into the planting of the next rotation of trees in its existing forests; the majority of the new afforestation is being developed by private interests. Virtually all new woodland in Great Britain is grant-aided by the Forestry Commission, under the Woodland Grant Scheme. By 1986–87 some 8,000 hectares a year were in new private planting, compared with only 1,000 hectares a year in new public ownership planting (*Travis 1990*).

Where farming and commercial afforestation have gained ground, semi-natural woodland has often lost. Estimates by the Nature Conservancy Council show that some 30–50 per cent of all ancient semi-natural woodland in Great Britain has been lost since 1947 (*Newby 1988*). Much woodland has suffered a similar fate to that of the heather moorlands; after clearance for grazing, former woodlands on valley sides have become overrun with bracken and gorse.

In 1985, the Forestry Commission launched a policy for broadleaved woodlands, with plans to arrest their depletion and degeneration (*Forestry Commission 1985*). In practice, however, the bulk of the Commission's own new planting is coniferous, albeit more sensitive to local relief in its design considerations than much of the earlier planting aptly described by *Fairbrother (1972, p.132)*:

> Crude and unnatural patterns of straight lines and sharp angles on flowing hills, block planting of geometric patches of forest on bare hillsides, chequerboard arrangements of different species, straight rows of trees ruled up and down slopes and extraction roads like wounds slashed across hills . . . . . blanket planting in small scale scenery smothering the landscape in a uniform dark fleece of trees.

Much of the recent government enthusiasm for forest expansion is linked to uncertainties about the future of farming, and the prospect of cultivating trees as an alternative crop (*S. Bell, 1986*). In 1989 the government announced its wish to raise levels of new planting to

33,000 hectares per annum (*Countryside Commission 1987c*).
Agencies with a conservation and amenity role, principally the Countryside Commission, have given cautious welcome to such a prospect,
seeking assurance that forest developments will be planned with
environmental and public interests to the fore. The Commission is a
strong advocate of multi-purpose forestry—to produce timber, whilst
also improving the landscape, creating and sustaining wildlife habitats,
facilitating public access and providing specific recreation sites. In years
to come this commitment will find expression in a new National Forest
in the Midlands, based on the existing Charnwood and Needwood
Forests, which will offer a blend of woods, fields, towns and villages
(*Countryside Commission 1989i*).

Quarrying and mining
Whilst nor widespread in their spatial incidence, mining and quarrying
have significant local impacts, usually negative in a visual sense, and
positive in terms of local employment opportunities. Classic examples
include the limestone quarries at Eldon Hill in the Peak District, and
those at Ribblesdale in the Yorkshire Dales, with working faces well over
a kilometre long, and the china clay works at Lee Moor on Dartmoor.
Market demands and the changing technology of extraction combine to
concentrate production in a smaller number of larger and more capital
intensive sites, thus sparing the broader spread of sites, but heightening
the risk of visual intrusion—and perhaps the duration of active extraction—at the working sites.

Water resources
Water resources, both linear and enclosed, are a vital ingredient of the
countryside scene, whether for purely visual pleasure or for the direct
support of recreational activities. Like the land, though, most water
resources have other prime uses, notably water supply, drainage, flood
control, transport, and sewage and waste disposal. Until 1989 that
range of functions - together with recreation and amenity—was largely
the responsibility of the Regional Water Authorities in England and
Wales, constituted under the 1973 Water Act, and funded through the
water rates. Under the 1989 Water Act, however, the water industry
was reorganized and substantially privatized. The utility functions of
water supply and sewage disposal were transferred to ten private water
companies. The regulatory and environmental responsibilities were
vested in a new National Rivers Authority, established as an independent watchdog in protecting the water environment in England and
Wales, and with the task of 'balancing the legitimate needs of all water
users against the need to protect and improve the environment'
(*National Rivers Authority undated, p.3*). Among its responsibilities is
'the promotion of recreational activities such as boating, fishing and
walking by rivers' (*ibid., p.2*). The work of the Authority is considered
more fully in Chapter 3.
   Inland water comprises a variety of natural and artificial resources:

rivers and lakes on the one hand, and canals, reservoirs and flooded gravel pits on the other. Navigable rivers support many forms of boating and cruising as well as riparian recreations; non navigable rivers support mainly angling and informal bank-side recreation. Lakes are rare outside the Lake District and the Norfolk Broads, though some—notably Windermere and Lake Bala, North Wales—experience intense pressures and varieties of use.

Artificial water bodies support a range of recreational uses. Indeed, for many, including much of the canal network, recreation is the major user. Faced with a canal system largely unwanted for its original commercial purpose and incurring a growing deficit, the government of the mid 1960s decided to maintain the network for pleasure cruising, and to develop its use for private boating, hire boats, angling and towpath recreation. Thus the 1968 Transport Act required that the British Waterways Board, the agency responsible for maintaining the canal system, should develop the recreational potential of its properties.

Artificial enclosed water bodies comprise mainly water supply reservoirs, regulatory and canal feeder reservoirs, and wet gravel pits, many offering access for recreation. For long, recreation was regarded as too risky a use for water supply reservoirs, and the threat of pollution effectively thwarted recreational access, except in a few cases for fishing and birdwatching from the lakeshore. Since the Second World War, however, improved treatment procedures and the increasing demand for water have meant that much of our water supply has been taken from rivers known to be polluted already, and passed through modern purification plants. This, together with a decrease in use of isolated impounding reservoirs, has helped to change attitudes towards public access to water supply reservoirs. In the late 1970s there were 531 water supply reservoirs of two hectares or more in England and Wales, 89 per cent of which had recreational use on the water surface itself or the adjoining land (*Tanner 1977*).

As with many other developments in the countryside, the scale of reservoirs has tended to increase in recent years. *MacEwen and MacEwen (1987)* note that at the time of designation, the national parks contained 118 water supply reservoirs; in the years since designation, 19 further reservoirs have been built, in total occupying virtually half the area of the original 118. Largest of all (1,086 hectares) is Kielder Reservoir in Northumberland, the largest artificial lake in Europe, conceived at a time when demand for water in the north east was rising rapidly and destined to be in deficit by the end of the century (*Northumbrian Water Authority 1978*). Between conception and completion, however, came industrial collapse, and the projected demand proved to be a substantial over-estimate (*France 1984*).

Wet gravel pits, the flooded remains of former sand and gravel extractions, are another important category of artifical inland water area. They are found mainly in the Thames and Trent valleys. For many, recreation is the sole use, and an excellent way of continuing to exploit a resource whilst giving reason to upgrade its appearance. Examples include the Cotswold Water Park in Gloucestershire and the Colne Valley Park west of London.

The natural aquatic environment comprises rivers, lakes, estuaries, coastal waters, and water stored naturally beneath the ground. These, like the dry land that surrounds them, serve a multitude of purposes. Along with purpose-built reservoirs, they are a source of water supply for domestic and industrial use. Either naturally or with suitable adaptations and installations, they provide land drainage and flood defence. They support commercial and recreational fisheries. On major rivers navigation is an important function. They have considerable conservation value, not only for water based wildlife, but also for flora and fauna on associated land. They also offer a valuable recreational resource.

The coast is an important recreation resource in its own right, especially in an island where no-one resides more than 120 kilometres from the sea. It offers rich contrasts of scenery and of recreational potential, ranging from built-up resort towns to remote bays and inlets; like the countryside, the coast supports a wide variety of commercial uses and considerable conservation interest. Recreational use varies not only along the coast, but also across it, in the different but interdependent environments of open water, beach and shore. For long, the recreational impact on the coast was channelled effectively into the urban resorts, both by the attractions specially provided, and by the public transport network—essentially the railway routes—on which all but a few users depended. More recently, recreational interest has spread to the entire coast, as car ownership has fostered the freedom to roam, and interests have shifted away from main holidays spent in serviced accommodation in traditional resorts to day visits and short breaks using informal accommodation.

Military training

Over a fifth of a million hectares of Britain (227,320 hectares in 1985, according to *Shoard 1987, p.119*) is owned by the Ministry of Defence (MOD) and used for artillery ranges and other forms of military training. Indeed, the space demands of the MOD continue to increase with the increasing range and firing power of new weapons: in 1986, the MOD was seeking an additional 20,000 hectares (*MacEwen and MacEwen 1987*). Few countryside uses create such controversy, particularly in the national parks. Quite apart from ethical and aesthetic objections, military use generates noise and disturbance to people and wildlife from live firing ammunition and the use of helicopters and low flying aircraft, leaves unexploded missiles in live firing areas which are also public access land, and scars the ground with shell and mortar fire. Public access, of course, is completely debarred from much military training ground, and time-restricted in the rest.

Critics scorn not merely the presence and practices of the military, but also the processes by which extensions of activity are permitted. As

MacEwen and MacEwen (1987) point out, whereas for mineral extraction each new development has to be justified and fully argued, the MOD is required to produce no such evidence in support of its claims of military necessity. Indeed, as the *Countryside Commission* stated in its *Annual Report for 1984–85*, the Property Services Agency has explicitly adopted the stance that 'the defence of the realm . . . . . will override all other considerations' (*Countryside Commission 1985b, p.27*). *The UK Centre for Economic and Environmental Development (1990)* argues strongly that the MOD's need for land should be subjected to independent scrutiny. The Centre also states that the MOD has tended to over-estimate its need for land for live firing, a claim supported by *Mercer (1990)*: 'figures show that the average use by the military of firing ranges in Dartmoor is considerably less than half the need they say that they have'.

The rural economy and residential use

Though for most the countryside might be playground and showcase, 20 per cent of the population actually lives in the countryside, and many people work there. Indeed, rural communities and the facilities they sustain are crucial elements of the public enjoyment of the countryside — picturesque villages, vernacular architecture, local crafts and customs, village church, village green, and village pub are all part of the appeal of the countryside: 'the English like landscapes compartmented into small scenes furnished with belfried church towers, half-timbered thatched cottages, rutted lanes, rookeried elms, lich gates and stiles' (*Lowenthal and Prince 1965*). Public interest, in turn, creates vital income for rural communities.

The juxtaposition of resident and recreationist, however, is not without sensitivities. Long-standing residents and those who work on the land or in other local employment will tend to view the rural existence with a mixture of pride and pragmatism: the pride of attachment to a small community and to a characteristic (sometimes harsh, sometimes picturesque) environment, and the pragmatism of going about their business and carrying out their routines. A degree of recreational use will be welcomed and will leave them flattered and unruffled. Large scale visitor invasions — both in the form of people and tourist facilities — can, however, cause resentment, changing the physical and visual character of the village, causing congestion and inconvenience to local people in streets, shops and pubs, and casting the indigenous population into the role of rustic showpieces rather than ordinary folk following ordinary routines. These effects are well documented (see, for example, *Bouquet and Winter 1987*).

Recreation, of course, may be a merely transient irritation. There are conflicts enough in contemporary rural communities between the indigenous population and recent incomers. Recent studies in a range of rural areas highlight the resistances and conflicts which can occur (*Glyptis 1987a, 1987b*). In remote Swaledale, for example, many community activities are sustained by a small nucleus of enthusiasts, often from the same family, and with the support of that family over many generations: eleven of the nineteen members of the brass band in one Swaledale village, for example, came from the same family. In such close-knit communities it can be difficult for newcomers to 'break in', become involved in activities, and become accepted by local people. In the rapidly expanding villages of Berkshire, by contrast, the scale of inmigration has been such that traditional villagers feel swamped and threatened, as incomers assert urban values and lifestyles, and seek to organize and take over every aspect of village life.

Levels of recreational activity and aspiration in new communities can be very high (*Glyptis 1987, Elson 1989b, 1990*). *Elson (1980b,p.56*) concluded from studies of new housing areas in Berkshire and Hampshire that there was:

> A youthful and resourceful group within the population with modern tastes. The surveys record high levels of participation, especially in activities such as swimming, keep fit, badminton, cycling and tennis . . . . . There is heavy use of community halls, and local play spaces if provided. Use of the nearby countryside is also popular. Where specific provisions are made, for example, tennis or squash courts, participation in the activity doubles . . . . . if on-site provision is not made as part of a development, the impacts on pre-existing off-site facilities are considerable.

In the 1980s half a million city dwellers moved to the countryside, and the trend of counter-urbanization is set to continue to at least the turn of the century. Overall, population growth will be modest, but with longer life expectancy, the purchase of homes by younger people, and the trend towards smaller households, the Department of the Environment estimates that a further two million homes will be needed in the 1990s; Berkshire, one of the counties of fastest growth, has twice the number of houses already than thirty years ago. Builders estimate that they will need an additional 73,000 hectares of land for house-building in the 1990s (*Lean 1989b*).

It is not necessarily the case, though, that locals want preservation and newcomers want 'progress'. In many villages long-established residents aspire (and have been actively fund-raising) to provide better community facilities for their youngsters, but this has been resolutely opposed by incomers who want to preserve their new-found rural paradise exactly as they found it. Newcomers also tend to be more exclusive than indigenous residents about exercising their proprietorial rights. As *McLaughlin (1989, pp.77–78)* put it, 'country folk have been replaced by folk who live in the countryside . . . . . they do not particularly want to see change. Or, if they do, they want to see it at the appropriate scale, which is small or preferably in the next county'.

As with farming, so too with village life. Its demise would be disastrous for the people directly affected, and disastrous too for the maintenance and appearance of the countryside. The future of the countryside, and its protection and appeal as a recreational environment, depend not on isolated policies for conserving its flora and fauna and for promoting public access, but on a sound and related social and economic strategy to sustain village and farm communities.

Conservation

To conserve that which we cherish has long been a vital concern in the countryside, and ever more so in recent years with the dramatic changes and pressures in farming and forestry practice. Conservation retains its roots and its everyday energy in the ardent amenity claims of voluntary endeavour and pressure groups. The first government recognition of the need came in 1947 from the Ministry of Town and Country Planning, a need since reinforced in the remit of various national agencies and in legislation. The need has come to permeate politics and the mind of the public at large, as the fragility of the environment has become ever more plain.

Conservation policy has embraced a mixture of designation and permeation, with an emphasis on the first. From the outset, official concern was to identify key conservation areas:

> To preserve and maintain as part of the nation's natural heritage places which can be regarded as reservoirs for the main types of community and kinds of wild plants and animals represented in this country, both common and rare, typical and unusual, as well as places which contain physical features of special or outstanding interest. These places must be chosen so far as possible to enable comparisons to be made between primitive or relatively undisturbed communities and the modifications introduced by varying degrees of human interference; typical and atypical physical conditions; distinctive characteristics imposed upon communities and species by differences in geographical position, physiography, climate, geology and soil, both within the main physical regions and in the transitional zones between them; the behaviour of species or communities living within and at the margins of their geographical distribution or their ecological tolerance (*Ministry of Town and Country Planning 1947, para. 50*).

Many sites, being obviously unique or clearly threatened, were readily designated as National Nature Reserves; others of more modest interest became Sites of Special Scientific Interest. The more major task of a comprehensive conservation review was the work of a decade and an army of specialists. *A Nature Conservation Review (Ratcliffe 1977)* describes the ecological features of over 700 sites in Great Britain, classified into major habitat groups, identifying the criteria by which each site can be adjudged in terms of nature conservation value. A four-point grading system for site quality is used, and the objective of the review was clear: 'Since many sites are both irreplaceable and severely at risk, serious and permanent loss is imminent if adequate safeguards are not taken or maintained. Present concern in the Review has thus been to identify these irreplaceable sites before it is too late' (*Ratcliffe 1977, pp.3–4*).

Seven main types of sites were considered: coastlands; woodlands; lowland grasslands, heaths and scrub; open waters; peatlands; upland grassland and heaths; and artificial ecosystems. Criteria used for assessing and selecting sites included size (ie the viability of the unit for conservation management), diversity, naturalness, rarity, fragility, typicalness, availability of recorded history, position within an ecological or geological unit, potential value, and intrinsic appeal.

Patmore (1983) noted that 'active conservation' through some kind of special designation applied to two-fifths of the area of England and Wales, though of course identification alone is no guarantee of protection. Furthermore, in the remaining three-fifths of the country, and at detailed site level within the two-fifths, protection may be minimal. Hence the Nature Conservancy Council (1984) could catalogue a 'stark assessment of the dwindling heritage of nature', charting dramatic losses in virtually every type of habitat over the past fifty to sixty years: only three per cent of lowland herb-rich meadows and of upland limestone pavements left undamaged; 71–77 per cent of chalk lowland lost between 1934 and 1972; 46 per cent of broadleaved woodlands in 23 counties of England and Wales lost between 1937 and 1983; 30 per cent of upland grasslands, heaths and blanket bogs lost or significantly damaged between 1950 and 1980 due to conifer afforestation; agricultural improvement or reclamation of hill land; burning and overgrazing of moors; and damage to lakes and rivers by pollution, water abstraction, land drainage and acidification.

The *Review* concentrated on grade one and two key sites. Grade one sites were deemed to be of international or national (Great Britain) importance, equivalent to National Nature Reserves (many already designated as such), and essential to safeguard if Britain was to have an adequate basis for conserving a balanced representation of ecosystems and the most important examples of wildlife and habitat. Grade two sites were deemed to be of equivalent, or only slightly inferior, merit, but to duplicate or offer alternative sites to those classed as grade one.

Recreation

If defining countryside recreation is difficult, measuring the amount of land available for its use is virtually impossible. Attempts have been few and far between, but that of *Burton and Wibberley (1965)* at least remains indicative. They estimated that approximately 1.2 million hectares of England and Wales were 'rural land available for public recreation', about eight per cent of the total area. Changes have occurred since, notably a profusion of country parks and picnic sites, and some gains and losses through additional or extinguished access agreements, though the outcome is probably little different in absolute areal terms.

A simple figure, in any case, serves little purpose beyond the purely statistical. What matters is not merely the amount of land available for recreation, but its location in relation to centres of demand and access systems, its suitability for different types and volumes of recreational activity, and the relative priority that management can attach to recreation as opposed to other uses. Recreation, furthermore, is rarely the sole user. Nor is it usually a permanent or continuous use: demand is periodic, concentrated into particular days of the week, and times of the year. Even at peak usage, demands on a specific site or area may be intense or inconsequential. In essence the entire countryside is a recreational resource, affording amenity in at least the visual sense. Within it though, there are favoured sites and areas of especial scenic attraction; areas where direct public access is permitted and others where it is prevented; and sites managed wholly or partly with recreation specifically in mind. Recreational use creates not so much a blanket coverage as a clearly etched pattern of nodes and corridors, an interdependent system of focal attractions and linear access routes.

Following the work of *Clawson and Knetsch (1966)*, countryside recreation is often categorized into two or three broad types. Though several activities are hard to pigeon-hole, the basic conceptual distinction is a valuable organizing device, both intellectually and managerially:

> Our classification is a three-fold one . . . . . At one extreme . . . . . are the *user-oriented areas* . . . . . Their most important characteristic is their ready accessibility to users . . . . . *Resource-based areas* are at the other extreme. Their dominant characteristic is their outstanding physical resources . . . . . *Intermediate areas* lie between these extremes, both geographically and in terms of use.

Hence, for resource-based recreation, the character and conservation of the countryside are paramount concerns; for user-oriented recreation, the needs to cater and design for the activity and to provide opportunities in readily accessible places are more important than location *per se*: indeed, in some instances the more appropriate emphasis may be entertainment *within* the countryside, rather than enjoyment *of* it.

Assessing recreational attractiveness

The recreational attractiveness of a given site or stretch of countryside rests rightly with the beholder. Individual users will rate the resource in accordance with their own aesthetic preferences, experiences, expectations, and recreational interests. That which is to one user a stark, forbidding crag may be to another a cherished and challenging climbing face; perception and purpose are closely intertwined. Whilst recognizing the essentially personal nature of preference, however, the planning of the countryside could, in principle, be assisted by systematic evaluations of the attractiveness and potential of different areas, and numerous approaches have been tested. They are broadly of two sorts, the first addressing the evaluation of landscape, the second assessing the capability of the countryside to accommodate particular ranges of recreational activity.

Landscape evaluation is valuable in principle but beset with practical problems. The issues of subjectivity and individual preference have already been alluded to, but the complications run deeper. The key attributes of landscape are by no means easy to identify and prioritize, nor are they readily quantified or ranked on a scale of attractiveness. Indeed, as a composite resource, landscape defies disassemblage into constituent parts, such as beauty, ruggedness, flatness, wildness, serenity, and so forth: for attractiveness lies in the integrated whole rather than the imprint of its individual elements. It can also lie as much in the transient as in the tangible: 'the appearance of any landscape is affected by transient conditions of weather, lighting, diurnal and seasonal changes, and the presence of people, animals and vehicles. It is difficult to include such transients in landscape studies, but they can be surprisingly dominant' (*Unwin 1975, p.130*). Such are the difficulties, and the disillusionment with some of the pioneer approaches that recent appraisals are few (*Landscape Research Group 1987*). Overall, the basic approaches have been of two types, one based on the judgements of 'experts', the other on the canvassing of public opinions. Both are fraught with difficulty. *Appleton (1975, p.122)* aired the apprehension about reliance upon the expert: the 'absence of aesthetic theory brings the professional down to the same plane as the man in the street. His only distinction now is a personal taste, the "normality" of which has been made suspect by his training'. One of the earliest 'expert' approaches—and probably the most widely used in a planning context, was an appraisal of the quality of the coastline by *J. A. Steers (1944)*. Subsequent attempts have generally addressed smaller areas and taken more complex approaches (for example, *Fines, 1968; Linton, 1968; Blacksell and Gilg 1975; Robinson et al. 1976; Dearden 1980*), amenable in most cases to the computer processing of results and the transferability of method to other sites.

Statistical rigour, however, can lead little refinement to aesthetic appreciation, and many of the more complex appraisals, albeit intriguing in their own right, served only to convey a spurious quantification of an essentially qualitative subject. In that respect, what *Appleton (1975, p123)* wrote of geographers is true of all who seek to codify landscape quality:

> Today's geographers are better equipped technically than their predecessors, but too often they lack the capacity to breathe life into what they have created . . . . . This breathing-in of life — literally inspiration — can easily be thwarted by such a meticulous *over*-concern with method and technique that, when the old-fashioned subjective appraisal of artistic, sensitive man is snuffed out, we have no flame left to set anything on fire.

Nonetheless, appraisals of this kind were used widely in the formulation of development policies in the county structure plans of the 1970s (*Penning-Rowsell 1975*).

Other studies (eg *Lee 1990*) have used members of the public as judges, some seeking a fairly superficial rating of scenic preferences, others to understand the amalgam of emotional reactions experienced

by the observers (*Kaplan et al. 1972*), and their histories of experience
and expectations. As *Lee (1990, p.39)* summarized: 'A high quality
landscape is one that evinces many positive feelings — eg warmth,
security, relaxation, freedom or happiness. A low quality one evinces
expressions of claustrophobia, insecurity, gloom, anxiety and so on'.

The evaluation of recreational potential was pioneered by *Duffield
and Owen (1970)* in Scotland. Using two by two kilometres squares
from the Ordnance Survey National Grid as units of assessment, they
produced four assessments of land capability for recreation, one each
for land-based recreation, water-based recreation, scenic quality, and
ecological significance. Each assessment was based on desk research on
a number of predefined dimensions. Capability for land-based recreation was judged, for example, on suitability for camping and caravanning, picnicking, pony trekking, walking and hiking, game shooting,
rock climbing and skiing. Criteria of suitability were predefined for each
of these activities. Recreational capability overall was measured by the
simple cumulative score of the number of criteria that could be met in
each square. Related approaches have been taken by *Hockin et al
(1977)* and *Hogg (1977)*. Methodologically, these appraisals suffer the
same shortcomings as landscape evaluation, not least because most
have been limited by research resources to a desk appraisal rather than
field observation, and therefore constrained to readily available data on
a narrow range of activities.

In practice, therefore, the contribution of evaluation studies to
landscape and recreation planning has been disappointingly limited.
For all their pitfalls, they do lend a comparative judgement of resource
capability, and can at least identify for planners an order of priority in
seeking places to conserve or develop. Furthermore, with ratings based
on straightforward area grids, they can be linked easily to related data
on centres of demand, population characteristics, indices of accessibility, and the like. More pragmatically, it must be admitted of course
that many of the major resource evaluation decisions, such as the designation of national parks, had already taken place prior to any systematic appraisals of quality. However, such appraisals could now be of
enormous benefit in the future use and conservation of the countryside,
particularly if applied to the integrated planning and management of
defined areas such as National Parks. As *Lee (1990, p.38)* asserted, 'If
landscape appreciation is in the eye of the beholder . . . . . there are very
strong reasons for taking public preferences into account in the
planning process'.

Ownership and access

Acknowledging the attractiveness of the countryside is easy enough;
affording access to it is infinitely harder. As we have seen, most of the
countryside is privately owned, by a mixture of large landowners—the
titled and untitled barons referred to by *Shoard (1987)* — and a multitude of small owner-occupier farmers. To make the matter more
complex still, there are signs that land ownership is gradually becoming

concentrated in the hands of fewer people rather than spreading more widely.

Even public ownership, however, is no guarantee of public access. Britain's largest landowner, the Forestry Commission, has priorities other than recreational, and has plans to sell off considerable amounts of land, as permitted under the 1981 Forestry Act and urged by the government ever since. Most of the property of the former Regional Water Authorities has now been transferred to private water companies established under the 1989 Water Act; provision for recreation is likely to be precluded in many instances, and geared solely to profit in others. The Ministry of Defence shows no sign of relinquishing its hold over vast stretches of open country, nor of reducing its usage of the training grounds allocated. Public access for recreation is therefore debarred in many areas, and time-constrained in others. Neither on public nor privately owned land is recreation a strong claimant. Access is allowed on strictly limited terms, and through a curious mixture of law and licence. As *Allison (1986, p.109)* remarked, 'There are very fluid relations between law and custom. Many rights established by custom and convention are taken as the basis of law'.

Sidaway (1986, p.26) classified the use of land for recreation into four convenient categories:

1 Use as of right with legislative origin (*de jure* access).
2 Use as of right with non-legislative origin (*de jure* access).
3 Permissive use (*de jure* or *de facto* depending on circumstance).
4 Use without permission (*de facto* use—'trespass').

Use as of right is considered further below. Sidaway explained the other categories as follows:

> Permissive use enables use to be made of the land subject to the owner's express consent, but without creating a right which is binding on future owners . . . . . Use without permission, such as *de facto* use, is, in effect, trespass and it can be restricted at any time. *De facto* use, in certain circumstances, may mature into *de jure* use. Understandably, landowners are often reluctant to move from *de facto* to *de jure* as such a change increases the landowner's liability for any injury and . . . . . the owner is no longer free to terminate the use.

Therefore, while the establishment of *de jure* access gives the firm assurance of access for recreation, in practice any attempt to increase or force the conversion of *de facto* to *de jure* access would be likely to result in the loss of some *de facto* access altogether. The same can be true of formal access agreements: 'on some of our estates in the Peak District it is best for us to lie low because the landowners allow that degree of informal access at will which the public needs. If we went to them for formal agreements, the attitudes would harden. We would gain less than we lost. Indeed, we might lose what we have got' (*Michael Dower, Peak District National Park Officer, 1986a, p.96*).

In open country there is freedom to wander more extensively, open country for this purpose being defined by the 1949 National Parks and

Access to the Countryside Act as any area consisting 'wholly or predominantly of mountain, moor, heath, down, cliff or foreshore (including bank, barrier, dune, beach, flat or other land adjacent to the foreshore)'. This definition was extended in the 1968 Countryside Act to include woodlands, rivers, canals and lakes, though, as *Sidaway (1986)* pointed out, the facility to enter into access agreements in such areas has not been widely followed up.

Much access over open country takes place informally, without intervention by the owners, and with no disadvantage to farmer or user. The more popular areas, however, attracting larger numbers of visitors, require closer regulation. This can be achieved by means of 'access agreements' and 'management agreements'.

Access agreements apply only to open country. The agreement, made between the local planning authority and those having an interest in the land, allows the public to wander at will on foot over the area covered by the agreement for the purposes of quiet enjoyment. The planning authority may make annual payments to the owners for maintaining the agreement, may issue bylaws relating to its use, and may appoint rangers to work with the public and to look after the land. Agreements may include restrictions on public access for special reasons, for example, to prevent exceptional fire risk, protect wildlife, and permit specific activities such as shooting on a defined number of days. In practice the facility to make access agreements has not been widely used. According to *MacEwen and MacEwen (1987)*, only 98 such agreements have been reached in England and Wales. Sixty per cent of all access agreements are in the Peak District, where agreements now cover some 197 square kilometres (*Sidaway 1986*).

Management agreements, permitted under *section 39* of the *1981 Wildlife and Countryside Act*, can apply to any type of landscape in the countryside. Like access agreements they are made between local planning authorities and those with an interest in the land. Their purpose is to manage the land in the interests of conservation and the enhancement of natural beauty, to promote public enjoyment, or both, and the local planning authority may make payments to support appropriate management, including payments in kind, such as facilities and wardening services.

In general, then, open countryside does not mean open access. In England and Wales there is no such right of access unless there is a specific indication to the contrary. Nor does common land mean common property. This will be debated more fully in Chapter 4, but suffice it to note for the present purpose that the public has a right of access to only 20 per cent of our 607,000 hectares of common.

Over the lowland countryside, the right of access is broadly synonymous with public rights of way, a resource amounting to some 193,000 kilometres of footpaths, bridleways and byways in England and Wales as a whole (*Countryside Commission 1987b*). The paths network has evolved over many centuries in relation to local and national needs, some specifically planned, but many the outcome of years of journeying from cottage and farm to village, and acquiring the legal status of rights of way from long histories of use. The *1949 National Parks and Access to the Countryside Act* required all county councils in England and Wales to identify their rights of way and prepare definitive maps. Provision was made for objections to be placed, but once entered onto the definitive maps, the rights of way were to run in perpetuity, their status to be upheld in the courts. For a path to become a right of way it had to have been used by the public for at least twenty years without interference from the landowner. County councils were further required to assert and protect the public right of passage along all paths. That right, however, 'does not extend to activities such as standing still on a highway and flapping an umbrella to interfere with grouse shooting, or timing racehorses with a stopwatch, although it is permissible to rest on a highway for a reasonable period' (*Collins 1984, p.143*). The mode of passage depends on the type of highway: footpaths may be used on foot only; bridleways may be used on foot, horseback, leading a horse, or on a bicycle, provided cyclists give way to walkers and horse riders. 'Byways', open to all kinds of traffic, were defined by the *1981 Wildlife and Countryside Act* as 'a highway over which the public have a right of way for vehicular and all other kinds of traffic, but which is used by the public mainly for the purposes for which foortpaths and bridleways are used'.

The legal entitlement is the right to pass and repass without deviation. Footpaths and bridleways are classed as 'highways'. As highway authorities, counties have the duty to maintain rights of way, and they may create entirely new paths or re-route existing ones. Owners of land over which rights of way pass have an obligation not to impede those rights by obstacles or cultivation. Significantly, recreational need is not a test for the classification of a highway: under the *1980 Highways Act* recreational access is not a consideration as to whether a right of way is needed or can be closed or diverted.

The extent of the path network, and its present condition, vary from county to county. In Scotland and Northern Ireland, separate provisions apply, and public footpaths and bridleways are less common. In Scotland, local planning authorities may create paths, divert existing ones, or close them, but no definitive maps are required. In Northern Ireland similar provisions apply as a result of the *1983 Access to the Countryside (Northern Ireland) Order*; in this particular instance the more formalized arrangements thereby introduced could actually be to the detriment of public access, as landowners have hitherto taken a relaxed and generally welcoming attitude to public use on a casual basis.

The rights of way system is clearly the principal gateway to the countryside. The network, though, is far from being as complete and convenient as possible. Many paths are difficult to find, ploughed over, obstructed and left in poor order by landowners: others are so accessible and well used that they are eroded, poorly drained and in need of repair. Some local authorities have been slow to complete their definitive maps and to assert public rights. In several cases access is possible but genuinely inconvenient from the landowner's point of view because routes interfere with present farming practice; in others rights are unused because paths lack interest in route or in destination.

Access to water

Generally the Crown owns the soil of the seashore and the beds of estuaries and tidal navigable rivers. The public enjoys certain common law rights of access to the foreshore and seashore (between high and low water marks at ordinary tides):

> Public rights at common law over the seashore are limited to fishing, navigation and ancillary rights; walking, bathing and beachcombing, though tolerated by the Crown, give no legal rights to the public. The right to use the seashore for bathing may be claimed by custom or prescription, but such a right must be exercised 'decently'. A local authority may make bylaws regulating sea bathing under the *Public Health Act 1936*, or by means of a private Act (*Collins 1984, p.147*).

The state of dress (or undress) permitted on beaches and elsewhere under the law is outlined by *Hirst and Coleman (1983)*.

Many recreational pursuits require access to water (eg fishing) or passage through water (eg boating, canoeing, water-skiing, windsurfing); in either case, they need access also across adjacent land. The right to fish is usually associated with the bed of a river which, generally, is owned to midstream by the owner of the bank (the riparian owner). Rights of navigation are considerably more complicated, and have been the subject of several recent studies (most notably *Telling and Smith 1985*).

Except with evidence to the contrary, tidal stretches of rivers are deemed to be 'arms of the sea' and, as such open for public navigation. Non-tidal rivers, by contrast, are normally regarded as the property of the riparian owners, and afford no general right of public navigation. A public right of navigation, however, may have arisen through common law or by statute. A common law right can arise in one of three ways. The first is by ancient or immemorial user, that is to say public navigation has taken place since 'time immemorial'; in practice, this is taken to mean that navigation has taken place uncontested by, and without the express permission of, the owner for as long as anyone can remember. The second source of a common law right is the owner's express dedication of a stretch of river for public navigation. The third source is implied dedication, a status of some contention as it involves inferring from the fact that usage has occurred uncontested for a substantial period of years that the riparian owner *intended* to dedicate usage.

Statutory rights of navigation have generally arisen under private Acts of Parliament, principally in the seventeenth and eighteenth centuries, which authorized entrepreneurs to carry out improvements to rivers. In many cases this resulted in hitherto physically unnavigable stretches being made navigable. Such statutes may be repealed by subsequent Act of Parliament. Many statutory navigations were in fact transferred to the ownership of the British Waterways Board, whereupon previous statutory entitlements generally ceased to have effect; however, the Board may permit any use of a river that was permissible under former statutory rights, and so in practice 'the rivers under the Board's control may thus be regarded as a special category of statutory navigation' (*Telling and Smith 1985, p.5*).

In tidal waters there is a public right to navigate at will, together with some associated rights for anchoring, mooring and grounding. There is no associated right to enter the land of the riparian owner, to moor to the bank above the normal level of the tide, or to tow from the banks, unless such rights are provided for under separate statute or custom. In non-tidal rivers the banks and bed are generally the property of the riparian owner, and the right of navigation is simply the right to pass and repass.

For statutory navigations, the rights of navigators and land owners are set out in each particular statute. In such cases the bed and the banks may or may not have been acquired by the navigation authority under the statute; if not, then there is no automatic guarantee that a statutory right of navigation carries with it a right to fix moorings or to enter the adjacent land, although such practices may take place by custom. Similarly, although the promoters of statutory navigations generally provided towpaths, they did not necessarily acquire the freehold of the land, in which case the navigation authority has only the right (and duty) to maintain it in an adequate state for use as a public towing path. Towing paths originated, of course, as exactly that, and not as a general public amenity. In practice, though, many have become public rights of way through long usage, and many appear on the county council definitive maps.

Canoeing complicates the issue of navigational access. Canoe touring and white water canoeing require access to long stretches of water and to many different sites. Most such stretches offer no right of navigation, having been physically unnavigable in the past. The problem is compounded by the fact that many of the favoured stretches are valuable fisheries, under the control of private clubs and individuals who have purchased private property rights, often at considerable expense, and who resist the canoeists, both as trespassers *per se*, and as alleged causes of disturbance to the fishery and the anglers.

Access to lakes, reservoirs and flooded gravel pits generally depends on permissive or *de facto* access. In most cases access relies on a permissive system, involving leases, licences or day tickets. Often the controlling rights are allocated to clubs or organizations, though this can preclude access for casual and unaffiliated participants. *Sidaway et al (1986, p.17)* identified an informal but widely held pecking order of recreational pursuits:

An informal hierarchy of permissive users appears to be favoured by many public authorities and private landowners, in which angling is almost universally encouraged, and dinghy sailing and boardsailing may be permitted, while the claims of other users (eg. water-skiing and other 'noisy' watersports) are perceived as being illegitimate or undesirable. Conservationists often ally themselves with private landowners, water authorities and anglers to exclude other recreational users.

Conclusion

The key themes of this chapter have been the variety of the countryside resource, its essentially private nature, the prime land uses, and the interplay of recreation with these competing demands. We have established that little of the 'natural' resource we cherish in the countryside is unmarked by human endeavour, and that little of the countryside would remain in its present form if patterns of ownership and management were radically altered. In scenic terms, the British countryside is characterized not only by complexity but also by change. It is not so much the mosaic of a single snapshot, but a kaleidoscope of shifting patterns which change continually over time, according to economic, social and political impetus. In that sense, the nature of the countryside resource is not merely the assemblage of its physical elements, but a changing and changeable resource ever 'expanding and contracting in response to human effort and behaviour' (*Zimmerman 1951, p. 7*).

The countryside is a multi-purpose resource, in which policy for any single use will have repercussions for others; in the case of recreation, so dependent on other uses which cause it to fail or flourish, that interdependence is particularly crucial. Policy makers have recently come to recognize that the recreational resource is not merely those special places set aside and managed primarily with recreation in mind, but the entire countryside:

> Since 1968, policy on public enjoyment of the countryside has centred very largely on the development and management of a limited number of facilities. These have included country parks, picnic sites and long distance routes. The time has now come for a broader approach. An appreciation is needed of the opportunities that the wider countryside offers for public enjoyment and a reconciliation of these opportunities with agricultural, economic and conservation objectives (*Countryside Commission 1987b, p. 15*).

Linked with that recognition must be two related approaches. The first is to recognize recreation as an important rural land use, and an important contributor to an integrated social, economic and conservation strategy for the countryside. The second is to keep human needs to the fore, not to the detriment of the natural environment, but as the prime raison détre for wishing to conserve it. As *Newby (1988, p. 108)* put it:

> Today it sometimes seems that more attention is given to the effect of pesticides on butterflies than on farm workers, or that the only endangered species in the countryside are of the non-human kind. More concern has now been expressed over how to preserve the countryside than how to allow

it to develop in ways which benefit the whole spectrum of the rural population. This is not to argue for some kind of environmental philistinism. It is not, in any case, a question of conservation *versus* community development, but of how the two can be brought together.

Beauty and variety, then, encapsulate the value of the countryside as a resource for recreation, for 'The importance of the countryside for recreation lies in the huge variety of opportunities it offers to people of all ages, capacities and skills. From peaceful walks and picnics to challenging pursuits like mountaineering, the countryside is a never-ending source of inspiration and pleasure' (*Countryside Commission 1987, p.6*).

2 Countryside recreation: participation and planning in historical context

In less than a hundred years, and predominantly in the last thirty, countryside recreation has been transformed from a minority to a mass activity. The planning response has tended to adjust to, rather than anticipate, public demand. This chapter charts briefly the origins and emergence of public interest in the countryside, outlines the pressures brought to bear on an evolving planning system, and discusses the main planning provisions and legislation which shape countryside recreation policy today.

Pre-nineteenth century

For centuries, recreational use of the land was the private preserve of a privileged few. The Norman kings established huge tracts of 'forest' land for hunting, covering one-third of England by the middle of the twelfth century (Darby 1951). Other major landowners had similar preserves. Smaller game parks were created in association with the large country houses developed from the early 16th century, though fashions shifted in the 18th century in favour of elegant schemes of formal landscape design, led by eminent landscape gardeners such as Humphry Repton and Lancelot (Capability) Brown. Many schemes were very extensive — over 970 hectares at Woburn, for example, and nearly 1,100 at Blenheim.

While the large landowners retained game and shooting rights over their estates and used them primarily for personal pleasure, access to land for lesser mortals was much more restricted, and rarely recreational. Commoners had access for the purposes of grazing, fishing and gathering wood, but recreational use of the commons was unknown. The only recreational use of open space recognizable as such took place on village greens, established primarily as a place of protection for the livestock of the village, but which came to accommodate the village archery butts and a training and social role for the community (Thorpe 1949).

Nineteenth century changes

Until the mid 19th century the majority of people lived in rural areas and worked on the land. They placed little demand upon it, though, for leisure, other than for such simple pastimes as going for walks and picking flowers *(Pimlott 1947)*. Urbanization created the need, but industrialization for long stifled its expression. By the mid 19th century more than half the population of England lived in urban areas, and by 1911 more than four-fifths — a rather higher proportion than today — did so. Living and working conditions deprived the new urban dwellers of time, means and inclination for leisure, and with high density terraced housing crammed more than twenty four to the hectare, space for recreation was a low priority. Time for leisure for most working families was confined to Christmas Day, Easter Day and, perhaps, Whitsuntide as public holidays; *Sir John Lubbock's Bank Holiday Act of 1871* allowed for four public holidays per year. Throughout Victorian times, therefore, recreation for the majority was at best an escape from the city on occasional day excursions and more frequent resort to the urban parks and pleasure grounds established, almost literrally, as 'lungs' of the cities *(Chadwick 1966; Cartwright 1977)*. Outings were channelled, both by routeway and by the lure of special excursion fares, to the coastal resorts rather than the broader countryside.

Prior to the First World War, then, recreational demands upon the countryside were few. Most were pleasures of the large landowners, catered for on their own private property. While the working population had time and energy only for rest rather than recreational exertions, though, there had developed a growing interest in scenic heritage and in walking and rambling among the professional and intellectual classes. Travel was given early impetus by religious pilgrimages, and by 'resorting' to mineral springs and spa towns. Inspired by the writings of Wordsworth, Rousseau and others, wealthy Victorians began to explore the Lake District, the Scottish Highlands, and the Swiss Alps. By the end of the 19th century, great expanses of upland countryside were in use for field sports, notably grouse shooting and deer stalking. The urban transformation of England precipitated concerns for countryside conservation, concerns addressed most vociferously through individual initiative and focused mainly on the uplands. In 1865, Britain's first national conservation group, the Commons, Open Spaces and Footpaths Preservation Society, was formed; several cities in northern England had earlier had their own local societies. Much of the initial concern came to a head in the Lake District, but events there had parallels in other parts of the country.

As early as 1810 Wordsworth had written in his travel book, *Guide to the Lakes*, (de Selincourt 1970), that 'the Lake District should be deemed a sort of national property in which every man has a right and interest who has an eye to perceive and a heart to enjoy'; a few decades later, though, the prospect of the nation actually coming to look at the

Lake District evoked a more elitist stance. Objecting to the proposed extension of the railway from Kendal to Windermere, he wrote:

> A vivid perception of romantic scenery is neither inherent in mankind nor a necessary consequence of even a comprehensive education . . . . . Rocks and mountains, torrents and wide spread waters . . '. . cannot in their finer relations to the human mind, be comprehended without opportunities of culture in some degree habitual . . . . . Persons in that condition, when upon holiday, or on a Sunday after having attended divine worship (would be better off making) little excursions with their wives and children among the neighbouring fields within reach of their own urban dwellings *(Margetson 1969)*.

It was not only Wordsworth who extended a cool welcome to the townspeople:

> A great steam monster ploughs up our lake and disgorges multitudes upon the pier; the excursion trains bring thousands of curious, vulgar people . . . . . the donkeys in our streets increase and multiply a hundred fold . . . . . our hills are darkened by swarms of tourists; our lawns are picnicked upon twenty at a time *(James Payne*, writing about Ambleside, quoted in *Margetson 1969)*.

Such resistance resulted in the formation of the Lake District Defence Society in 1883, which successfully opposed the penetration of the railway into Borrowdale. Twelve years later its founder, Canon Rawnsley, joined with Robert Hunter and Octavia Hill to found The National Trust for Places of Historic Interest and Natural Beauty, which sought to protect property through the acquisition of land and buildings by gift or purchase.

Legislation came first in Scotland, with the passing in 1884 of *James Bryce's Access to the Mountains Bill*. This was prompted not only by domestic demand for access and amenity, but was given added impetus by anti-American sentiment following the purchase of large tracts of grouse moor and deer forest by American millionaires. The key clause of the Bill stated that: 'no owner or occupier of uncultivated mountains or moorland shall be entitled to exlude any person from walking or being on such land for the purpose of recreation or artistic study, or to molest him in so walking or being'.

The campaign for access

In the last quarter of the nineteenth century mobility had increased, not least through the widespread ownership of bicycles. The Cyclists' Touring Club was founded in 1878. Between the First and Second World Wars time for leisure increased and transport improved. Holidays had become more widespread and, after the passing of the *1938 Holidays with Pay Act*, the majority of workers received paid time off work. Growing mobility allowed less wealthy people to venture into the countryside. Walking and rambling interests developed rapidly, and the new recreationalists, demanding the freedom to roam, quickly came into conflict with established users, especially in the Peak District, where walkers clashed with long-established shooting interests. According to *Lowerson (1980)*, by the 1930s there were over half a million regular country walkers, including some 10,000 ramblers using the Peak District on summer weekends. Virtually three-quarters of the open moorland comprising the Peak were enclosed under private ownership, and used for only a few weeks a year for grouse shooting; such was the state of public access in an area which had half the population of England and Wales living within 80 kilometres *(Donnelly 1986)*. At the instigation of radical groups such as the British Workers' Sports Federation and the Ramblers' Rights Movement, mass trespass was encouraged as a means of gaining public attention. The most famous took place on Sunday 24 April 1932, when several hundred ramblers invaded Kinder Scout, part of the Duke of Devonshire's grouse moors. In the scuffles that ensued, six of the leaders were arrested on the grounds of unlawful assembly and breach of the peace and five subsequently imprisoned *(Cook 1974; Hill 1980)*. An evocative account, both of the skirmishes and their broader context, is given by *Shercliff (1987)*.

Pressures for access and amenity thus originated from (though rarely intertwined) two separate strata of society *(Donnelly 1986)*. On the one hand, the Romantic movement, inspired by the search for the sublime of the Lakes school of poets, gave rise to walking as a popular middle class pursuit in the 19th century, and the creation of several gentlemen's rambling clubs. On the other hand, the working class interest was prompted by the desire to escape from the town, and by the urge to *regain* recreational access to land which they perceived had been lost to them — land which, prior to enclosure and the creation of private hunting grounds, had been largely open for public use.

Car ownership transformed personal mobility, at first just for the fortunate (and adventurous!) few. In 1907, there were 32,000 private cars in Britain, and by 1919 109,000. Twenty years later, at the start of the Second World War, the number had reached two millions. *Newby (1988, p.115)* portrayed the recreational effect in the Home Counties cynically but not wholly unkindly: 'Accessibility by car reduced the countryside to a series of medieval churches, cream teas and quaint rustic features'. The real explosion of mass car ownership has occurred since — with profound ramifications for the readiness with which people can travel into the countryside, and the complete freedom of range with which they can do so.

The pressures on the countryside were not merely recreational. Earlier in impact and much more tangible in form were the growth and spread of the suburbs, as preference for lower density housing became matched by possibility. The fast and formless sprawl which resulted played a major part in prompting the development of the physical planning system. The need for urban containment gained its first statutory recognition where the problem was most acute, with the passing of the *1938 Green Belt (London and Home Counties) Act*. Physical planning on a more general scale had to await the creation of the Ministry of Town and Country Planning in 1943.

In the early decades of the present century amenity concerns arose with much greater fervour in private than in government circles. In 1926 several local amenity groups merged to form the Council for the Preservation of Rural England (since 1970, the Council for the Protection of Rural England, CPRE), which was to take a leading role in arguing the case for special measures to protect the scenic heritage. Similar Councils for Scotland and Wales followed in 1927 and 1928. The concerns were honest, but undeniably elitist: 'To be sure the countryside needed to be preserved for 'the nation', but it also needed to be protected *from* 'the public'. Only a self-appointed minority possessed the enlightenment needed to appreciate the countryside fully' *(Newby 1988, p.115)*. Continuing interest in the recreational use of the countryside was signalled by the formation of the Youth Hostels Association in 1930.

The path toward government action was significantly advanced by the National Parks Committee of Inquiry, set up in 1929 to 'consider and report if it is desirable and feasible to establish one or more National Parks in Great Britain with a view to the preservation of natural characteristics including flora and fauna, and to the improvement of recreational facilities for the people'. The Committee, chaired by Christopher Addison, recommended the establishment of nature reserves and nature sanctuaries, to be funded and administered nationally. That national commitment was portentous:

> There are in this country areas of peculiar interest to the Nation as a whole — typical stretches of coastline, mountainous regions, moor and downs, riverbanks and fen. These areas constitute an important national asset and the Nation cannot afford to take any risk that they will be destroyed or subjected to disorderly development *(Report of the National Parks Committee 1931, para. 14)*.

The more pressing concerns of the 1930s, however, left amenity issues in abeyance. The CPRE sought legislation that would safeguard the whole of the countryside, and campaigned for special protective status for the wildest and most beautiful areas. In 1936 it established the Standing Committee on National Parks (SCNP), later (1977) to become the Council for National Parks. In the foreword to a pamphlet by *John Dower (SCNP 1938), Professor G.M. Trevelyan* presented an impassioned case for National Parks, deftly interwoven with other concerns of the day:

> The Government is at present engaged on a Health Campaign. It undertakes to assist the health of the nation and to find playing fields for the dwellers in the vast cities to play cricket and football. But it is no less essential, for any national health scheme, to preserve for the nation walking grounds and regions where young and old can enjoy the sight of unspoiled nature. And it is not a question of physical exercise only, it is also a question of spiritual exercise and enjoyment. It is a question of spiritual values. Without vision the people perish and without sight of the beauty of nature

the spiritual power of the British people will be atrophied *(Cherry 1975, p.15).*

A further report, by the Committee on Land Utilization in Rural Areas (Scott Committee) in 1942, kept the issues alive and advocated more positive measures — the creation of a Footpaths Commission, and the establishment of National Parks in which the main land use would be recreation. The crucial step came three years later. John Dower's report to the Minister of Town and Country Planning, 'the most important document in British National Parks history' *(Council for National Parks 1986a),* urged the view that National Parks should be truly national, provided for the nation and by the nation. A National Park should be:

> An extensive area of beautiful and relatively wild country in which, for the nation's benefit and by appropriate national decision and action:
> (a) the characteristic landscape beauty is strictly preserved;
> (b) access and facilities for public open-air enjoyment are amply provided;
> (c) wildlife and buildings and places of architectural and historic interest are suitably protected; while
> (d) established farm use is effectively maintained
> *(Dower 1945, p.6).*

1945 onwards: legislation, mobility and mass demand

The end of the Second World War heralded not only mass mobility and greatly increased leisure time, but also a new optimism, a concern to protect the finest of British landscapes, and the mood for positive action. The *1947 Town and Country Planning Act* initiated a comprehensive physical planning system, geared predominantly to urban imperatives, but also allowing local authorities to submit to the Minister proposals for the designation of Areas of Great Landscape, Historic or Scientific Value. For amenity interests further principles were to be established through a committee chaired by Sir Arthur Hobhouse. That committee's report *(Report of the National Parks Committee 1947)* closely followed Dower's recommendations and proposed that 12 National Parks should be established, each with its own park committee as the statutory planning authority. Ten of the twelve were subsequently approved.

The political climate was opportune, for the National Park proposals were in line with more general social reforms of the post-war Labour government constructing its welfare state. Lewis Silkin MP, in introducing the Bill, said 'This is not just a Bill. It is . . . . . a people's charter for the open air, for the hikers and the ramblers for everyone who loves to get out into the open air and enjoy the countryside. Without it they are fettered, deprived of their powers of access and facilities needed to make holidays enjoyable. With it the countryside is theirs to preserve, to cherish, to enjoy and make their own' *(Hansard, 31 March 1949, col. 1485).* The *1949 National Parks and Access to the Countryside Act* paved the way for designating the Parks, and established a specific agency, the National Parks Commission, to ensure the preservation and enhancement of natural beauty and provision of opportunities for open air recreation within them. The legislation, though, was weaker than the campaigners had hoped for. The Commission was merely an advisory body, not the executive organization proposed by Dower and Hobhouse. Furthermore, the parks were not given their own statutory planning authorities:

> The executive bodies were only in two cases—the Boards for the Peak and the Lakes—anywhere near the pioneers' ideal in constitution or indepen-dent status: the others were Committees of County Councils, often fragmented into different counties within a single Park. Boards and Committees had a majority of local authority nominees, and consequently (by Government reaction to this) no annual money from Government *(Dower 1986b, p.15).*

Nor did the Act afford legal access to open land. It did, however, allow local authorities to enter into access agreements with landowners, and required highway authorities to produce definitive maps of rights of way. It also established powers for designating Areas of Outstanding Natural Beauty (AsONB) and creating Long Distance Footpaths. Two years later, the formation of the Nature Conservancy (now Nature Conservancy Council) forged 'the great divide' *(MacEwen and MacEwen 1982, p.16)* between landscape protection and nature conservation, but provided for further forms of designation for areas of particular scientific significance, notably National Nature Reserves and Sites of Special Scientific Interest.

These early conservation measures could not have anticipated the upsurge in recreational demand that mass car ownership was to bring, or the transformation of its character. Nor would the potential for conflict between the twin National Park roles of landscape protection and recreation provision, and between these and normal farm use, have been apparent. Emerging trends, though, were signalled early on by the new National Parks Commission:

> We are living in an age of transformation when, for the first time, a prepon-derantly urban population largely unfamiliar with rural life has acquired a considerable amount of leisure with the opportunity of using that leisure to satisfy the instinctive and wholesome desire to leave the city for the country. We cannot prevent this influx of town into country, nor on a long view of the healthy development of our nation, should we desire to prevent it *(National Parks Commission Third Report, 1952).*

Thus the dominant concern shifted away from scenic heritage to the growth of recreation.

If the access campaigners of the 1930s shook the elitism of country-side recreation, mass car ownership firmly subdued it. Passive forms of recreation—sightseeing and touring—grew dramatically; and the demand for many forms of active recreation grew faster still. The real effects began to be felt in the 1960s, when a combination of burgeoning demand and concern for the amenity areas under greatest pressure led to further conferences and government action, this time with a greater emphasis on positive provision for recreation. The initial focus, inspired by Max Nicholson of the Nature Conservancy, and presided over by the Duke of Edinburgh, was a series of 'Countryside in 1970' conferences held from 1963. Dominant concerns of the conferences were the volume of recreational use of the countryside, its likely further growth, and the potential for conflict between different types of usage, an incursion most powerfully portrayed by *Dower (1965, p.5)*:

> Three great waves have broken across the face of Britain since 1800. First, the sudden growth of dark industrial towns. Second, the thrusting movement along far-flung railways. Third, the sprawl of car-based surburbs. Now we see, under the guise of a modest word, the surge of a fourth wave which could be more powerful than all the others. The modest word is leisure.

In February 1966 the key issues and possible provisions were outlined in the government White Paper, *Leisure in the Countryside, England and Wales (Minister of Land and Natural Resources/Secretary of State for Wales 1966)*. The diagnosis was clear:

> Given that townspeople ought to be able to spend their leisure in the country if they want to; that they will have more leisure; and that in future they will be able to buy cars and boats and otherwise spend money on their weekends and holidays, the problem is to enable them to enjoy their leisure without harm to those who live and work in the country, and without spoiling what they go to the countryside to seek.

Policy hitherto was largely unstated beyond the confines of the National Parks, and it had viewed the recreationist much more as walker than as motorist. *Nan Fairbrother (1972, p.101)* light-heartedly but appropriately stated the case for the new recreationists:

> The less articulate need better representation, for though there are lively groups for preserving every aspect of our rural past, and protecting everything from birds to mountains, yet we also need equally articulate groups for what will be the main body of future users — a Council for Better Caravan Sites, societies for More and More Attractive Car Parks, for Country Playgrounds, for Motoring for Pleasure, and for Enjoying the Countryside Without Feeling Virtuous.

Provisions to meet some of these needs were embraced in the subsequent *1968 Countryside Act* which in essence extended the concern for recreation and conservation beyond the confines of the designated areas to the entire countryside. This was reflected in the replacement of the National Parks Commission by the Countryside Commission, with wider powers, and in the provision for new types of recreational attraction in the form of Country Parks.

The general tenor of both White Paper and Act was optimistic. Recreation was to be welcomed:

> Whatever changes may come in leisure habits, and however much our towns may be made more fit for living, a very large number of people will probably

continue to spend a large part of their free time in their motor cars, visiting the countryside and the coast . . . . . This movement away from the towns in leisure time is constantly growing: and it is taking place in mid week as well as at weekends, and in spring, autumn and winter as well as summer. No one would want to halt the process. *(Minister of Land and Natural Resources/Secretary of State for Wales 1966).*

The last sentiment was more in tune with hope than reality. However, in government circles recreation continued to be debated as a need to be welcomed, not a threat to be averted. In 1971 the House of Lords established a Select Committee on Sport and Leisure, 'to consider the demand for facilities for participation in sport and in the enjoyment of leisure out-of-doors, and to examine what impediments may exist to the fuller use of existing facilities or the development of new ones, and how they might be removed' *(House of Lords Select Committee 1973, p. ii).*

The Committee affirmed its belief that leisure was a public good; recreation provision should be regarded as 'part of the general fabric of the social services . . . . . one of the community's everyday needs' *(House of Lords Select Committee 1973, para. 67).* Demand was not merely to be accepted, but encouraged: 'The Committee . . . . . do not believe demand to be the only important factor governing the provision of facilities . . . . . the authorities cannot be content with satisfying identifiable demand. They must go further, in an effort to meet latent demand' *(para. 61).*

A Countryside Review Committee was set up in 1974 by the Secretary of State for the Environment to review the state of the countryside and the pressures upon it; to examine the effect of existing policies in containing, modifying or accepting the pressures; and to consider, in the light of other major policy objectives (eg for agriculture) whether any changes of policy or practice were needed to reconcile the the different objectives where they conflicted with the conservation of the countryside, the enhancement of its natural beauty, or public enjoyment. The Committee took the view, characteristic of the decade, that opportunities for countryside recreation should be regarded as an important ingredient of community welfare. Three possible policy approaches were identified:

> The first is essentially defensive — to conserve the rural environment, by guiding the demand for recreation into the least damaging channels. This is the low-cost approach. For the time being, present economic constraints will often dictate its use. The second type of policy is reactive. This still revolves around existing demand, but seeks to provide better outlets and facilities for visitors to the countryside. The continuing programme of country parks and picnic sites is an obvious example. The third possibility is to stimulate demand, as a deliberate act of policy, both expanding opportunities and assisting a wider cross-section of the public to 'discover' recreation in the countryside. *(Countryside Review Committee 1977, para. 17).*

The welfare ethos was to be further underpinned. The White Paper, *Sport and Recreation*, albeit more urban in focus, urged particular attention to the needs of non participants and disadvantaged groups (*Department of the Environment 1975*).

Environmental concerns came to the fore again at the beginning of the 1980s, with a reassertion of the need to protect the countryside from continuing urban demands and from high-technology agriculture. Further conservation measures were introduced in the *1981 Wildlife and Countryside Act*. Its passage through parliament was far from straightforward; the Bill attracted some 1,120 proposed amendments.

The main provisions of the Act of relevance to the present purpose were threefold. Firstly, the Nature Conservancy Council (NCC) was given the duty to inform the landowners, local planning authority, and Secretary of State for the Environment of any area of land deemed to be of special interest by virtue of its flora, fauna, or geological or physiographical features; with Sites of Special Scientific Interest (SSSI) in Britain located on the properties of 40,000 different landowners this was to become an onerous task. Secondly, the Act required that, when an improvement grant was refused on conservation grounds, the farmer should be paid compensation by the objecting authority, ie the county planning authority in the case of National Parks, and the Nature Conservancy in the case of SSSIs. Not surprisingly, this met with considerable hostility from the conservation movement. Precedent, though, had already been established. In 1977 Lord Porchester, reporting on the loss of moorland on Exmoor, proposed the introduction of Moorland Conservation Orders to make compensation payments to oblige farmers not to improve moorland where voluntary agreements could not be reached. Thirdly, within the National Parks, land that had not been in agricultural use for twenty years was not to be converted to such use. However, if owners notified the local planning authority of their intention to pursue such uses, then they many proceed unimpeded, so long as:

(i) the planning authority granted consent;
(ii) the planning authority failed to respond within three months; or
(iii) the planning authority had refused consent, but twelve months had elapsed.

Conservation thus became a very contested and costly business.

The case of West Sedgemoor illustrates the Act at work. In 1982 the Nature Conservancy proposed to designate 1,000 hectares of the Somerset Levels as an SSSI. The area, which floods annually, comprises lush grazing meadows, based on a rich peaty loam, is an important refuge for migrant and breeding birds, and supports a rich variety of flora, mammals and amphibians. MAFF and the Country Landowners' Association supported the designation of a smaller area, but the NCC proceeded to implement its initial proposal. Securing the necessary agreements with farmers cost £170–£225 per hectare, resulting in a total cost of £150,000 per annum (at 1983 prices) for conserving the area. *Newby (1988)* identified two fundamental problems: firstly, it would be cheaper to purchase the   nd than to be making annual compensation payments indefinitely; secondly, a farmer occupying an SSSI has only to *threaten* to change its use or its management in order to receive guaranteed compensation.

The NCC received a substantial budget increase following the 1981 Act, but its resources were to remain thinly stretched. By 1986, 392 management agreements had been entered into, at an annual cost of £2 million; consultants to the NCC estimate that the eventual cost could run to £31 million annually, plus £52 million in lump sum payments *(Newby 1988)*.

Throughout the 1980s further policy developments and legislative changes affected specific sectors of countryside recreation and particular categories of resources, and these are addressed in later chapters. Overall, the evolution of measures concerned with the preservation and enjoyment of scenic heritage has been a fascinating interplay of politics, professionals and pressure groups. *Sandbach (1978)* recalled the actors and actions involved in the campaign for a Lake District National Park and *Sheail (1975)* referred to the National Parks generally. More recently, *Cherry (1985, p.12)* summed up the processes and the products as follows:

> Powerful pressure groups, sometimes though not always with professional support, have articulated a community demand and claimed the allegiance of sectional interests, to which the political system has had to respond. It has often been a confused scene, with compromise and 'fudge', exaggerated claims, political pragmatism, high hopes and faded dreams. The situation has rarely been static or emotionally calm for very long, but inevitably public action has been belated, with the consequence that legislation and new powers have tended to deal with yesterday's problems. The *1949 Act* met the needs of the 1930s; the *1968 Act* addressed the questions of that decade; and the *1981 Act* reverted to issues reminiscent of the 1920s.

The basic planning need was aptly diagnosed by the *Countryside Review Committee (1977)*, which stressed that promoting access to recreational opportunities for welfare reasons would generate more demand and more pressures:

> This means that leisure activities must be channelled, if a real measure of enjoyment is to be retained . . . . . the chief aim should be to offer such a range of planned and organized choice that people's needs channel themselves, so that dispersal of demand comes about both naturally and unobtrusively. This can best be achieved by developing a network of co-ordinated sites specifically designed to spread and absorb demand; and, with proper management, the countryside should be able to accommodate the pressures likely to be put upon it in the next twenty-five years. Indeed, what alternative strategy is there? Not laissez-faire, certainly; only cruder measures of restriction. *(Countryside Review Committee 1977, para. 131)*.

With responsibilities for provision fragmented between many different agencies with varying objectives, the reality of provision is much more piecemeal. Those agencies, and their roles and responsibilities, are the subject of Chapter 3.

3 Planners, policy makers, providers and pressure groups

Countryside recreation provision is neither a single nor a separable field of policy. It embraces a multiplicity of activities, and almost always impinges upon or is influenced by related policy areas. That diffuseness is mirrored in the complex mosaic of organizations with powers, responsibilities and interests in the field. They exist in the public, voluntary and private sectors, and operate at national, regional and local level. A complete compendium would serve little purpose. Rather the aim of this chapter is to introduce the main agencies which have countryside recreation as a substantial part of their function, to outline their objectives and activities, and discuss key recent developments in their work.

Far more organizations are omitted than included. The chapter concentrates wholly on public and voluntary sector organizations, as these are the principal spheres from which policy emanates. The place of the private sector, in welcoming or resisting those policies is a thread which runs through many other parts of the book. The prime private sector role is that of landowner, farmer and custodian, and much of that role is exercised individually, by specific owners. On key issues it finds a collective voice, most notably through the Country Landowners' Association and the National Farmers' Union. Further private sector roles are those of developer and protector, the first mainly in the form of investment in recreation facilities in the countryside which will lend a commercial profit, the second in the form of corporate contributions to pollution control and environmental improvements of the kind harnessed through Groundwork Trusts. These are discussed in Chapter 6.

Within the public sector, there are omissions at both national and local level. The former include English Heritage, not a countryside recreation agency as such, but custodian of ancient monuments and many heritage sites and historic buildings. At local level, there is no specific treatment of the work of county and district councils. They provide the overall local planning framework and have the power to make provision for recreation. Those powers are not confined to the countryside and, partly for that reason, the local authority contribution to countryside recreation provision, though huge, is hard to separate from their wider recreational remit. Examples of local authority work are referred to elsewhere, particularly Chapter 6. Suffice it to note for the moment that the local authorities are the prime public sector 'doers' of work on the ground, albeit often assisted, encouraged, grant-aided and cajoled by the various national agencies.

Within the voluntary sector detailed attention is confined to two national organizations. Others, such as the Council for the Protection of Rural England, the Byways and Bridleways Trust and the Open Spaces Society are referred to elsewhere in the book.

The public sector

The Countryside Commission
The single national agency with countryside conservation and recreation as its core purpose is the Countryside Commission, established under the 1968 Countryside Act and replacing the former National Parks Commission. It carries twin responsibilities: firstly, for the conservation of natural beauty in England and Wales; and, secondly, to encourage the provision and improvement of facilities and access for recreation in the countryside. A separate Countryside Commission for Scotland was established under the *1967 Countryside (Scotland) Act.* The twin functions for recreation and conservation are seen as complementary: 'In promoting conservation of the landscape, we try to ensure that the countryside will remain a pleasure and a delight to visit and live in. In encouraging provision for recreation, we help to ensure that the countryside is accessible to those who want to enjoy it' *(Countryside Commission 1983b, p.5).* The Commission owns no land and manages no facilities. It is an advisory body, achieving its work through collaboration, explanation and persuasion with other agencies, including public authorities, voluntary bodies, and private organizations and individuals. The interdependence of the Commission's tasks, and of the Commission with other partners, is summed up in a recent policy document *(Countryside Commission 1987b, p.4):* 'This policy statement sets out how the public's enjoyment of the countryside can best be met and how it can be harnessed to the conservation on which that enjoyment ultimately depends. It is not a task for the Commission alone, but for every individual and organisation with a concern for the well-being of our rural heritage'.

Members of the Commission (the Commissioners) are appointed by the Secretary of State for the Environment and the Secretary of State for Wales. At the time of writing there are twelve Commissioners, a separate Committee for Wales, and approximately 150 staff at the Commission's headquarters office at John Dower House, Cheltenham, seven regional offices for England, and the Office for Wales. In April 1991, however, the Commission's work in Wales will be combined with that of the Nature Conservancy Council to form a new Countryside Council for Wales. A similar merger will replace the Countryside Commission for Scotland with Scottish National Heritage.

For its first fourteen years the Countryside Commission was part of the Department of the Environment, though not always in harmony with its sister departments and ministries. This was evident, for example, in conflicting grant-aid policies, where the Commission might fund a conservation project for a given area, and MAFF might give grants for its reclamation for farming. Furthermore, as *Blunden and Curry (1985)* have noted, the Commission was often marginalized in affairs quite central to its remit. This was most notably so in the drafting of the *1981 Wildlife and Countryside Bill*. The Commission was not consulted until after the public consultation period, whereas the Country Landowners' Association and the National Farmers' Union were much more centrally involved from the outset. Since 1982 the Commission has been an independent body, grant-aided by the Department of the Environment. Its budget for the financial year 1990 – 91 is £25.1 million.

The Commission's work is of seven main types:

1 Promoting understanding of the countryside, and of issues affecting it, to the public at large, to decision-makers, and to those who influence its appearance and recreational value.

2 Research, aimed at establishing factual data on landscape change and countryside usage, and on the impact and management of different uses.

3 Experimental work to develop, test and demonstrate new methods of management for conservation and recreation.

4 Policy advice to government departments, statutory agencies and others whose activities affect the countryside.

5 Advice on management techniques for conservation and recreation to any organization involved in countryside management.

6 Designation. The Commission has the power to designate areas of scenic quality as National Parks or Areas of Outstanding Natural Beauty, and to designate Long Distance Paths (recently renamed National Trails) for walkers and riders. It also encourages local authorities to define areas of outstanding coastal scenery as Heritage Coasts.

7 Grant aid to local authorities, voluntary bodies, landowners, farmers and others to encourage action to promote conservation and recreation. In 1988 – 89, 65 per cent of the Commission's total expenditure of £20,937,781 was spent on grant aid. The apportionment of that £13.7 million between different categories of work is shown in Table 3.1.

Independent status brought a new style of working. In 1982 the Commission published a prospectus for consultation, setting out issues, current policies and priorities. Its first five-year plan *(Countryside Commission 1983b)* was based on the responses and several assumptions. The first assumption was that the economy — and personal incomes — would grow only slowly. The fast growth of high technology industries would, however, have marked impacts on working patterns and on employment and residential locations. The second was that development pressures would intensify with the drift from cities to small towns and villages, and with the splintering of the population into larger numbers of small households. Demand for building land would therefore continue, posing threats to the rural environment, agriculture, and conservation. The third was a concern for developments in agriculture, poised at that time between the greater productivity and considerable landscape changes wrought by new technology, the increasing EEC concern about food surpluses and trading problems, and a spreading sympathy for conservation practices. The fourth concerned forestry, where modest growth in commercial planting was anticipated, particularly in the uplands, together with an increasing interest in broadleaved woodlands. The fifth assumption was that public interest in conservation would increase, and that conservation would become more visible in the political arena. The sixth was that leisure time would increase, through shorter working weeks, longer holidays, earlier retirement, and unemployment. Demand for recreation in the countryside would therefore grow.

Table 3.1   Work supported by Countryside Commission grants 1988–89

	£	% of total
Amenity tree planting and woodland management	3,096,347	22.6
Countryside advisory services	378,471	2.8
Land acquisition	262,278	1.9
Access/management agreements	290,411	2.1
Recreation sites	1,225,855	9.0
Ranger and warden services	2,875,101	21.0
National Trails	642,970	4.7
Recreation paths and bridleways	570,529	4.2
Coast and countryside management	1,785,902	13.0
Information and visitor services	926,047	6.8
Voluntary work	414,715	3.0
Other	1,227,041	8.6
Total grants given	13,695,667	

Source: Countryside Commission Annual Report 1988–1989

In 1986–87, under the banner 'Recreation 2000', the Commission undertook a more wide-ranging review of its remit towards public enjoyment of the countryside. The outcome is summarized in two policy documents, *Policies for Enjoying the Countryside* and *Enjoying the Countryside — Priorities for Action (Countryside Commission 1987b, 1987d)*. The proposed priorities were based on three concerns: the continuing popularity of the countryside to the population at large; the changing demands being placed upon the countryside; and the persistence of certain problems of recreational use. The key problems were diagnosed as lack of public awareness of rights and opportunities for countryside use; lack of access, especially due to the poor state of the rights of way system; and conflicts of interest between different users. The key changes were the extensification of farming, outlined in Chapter 1, related prospects for conservation and recreation, and the increase in rural tourism.

The Commission does not embrace all forms of countryside recreation in its work. Rather it will:

> focus attention on the informal aspects of enjoying the countryside. Concentrate on facilities available to the general public, recognising that those activities organised into clubs or competitive activities are primarily the concern of the Sports Councils and the bodies represented on the Central Council for Physical Recreation. Give priority to recreational activities that do not cause significant disturbance to others, recognising that comparative tranquillity is one of the main attractions of the countryside. Urge local authorities to ensure that places are available for more noisy activities *(Countyside Commission 1987d, p.4)*.

Seven objectives, that first referring to people, the other six to places, *(Countryside Commission 1987d)* stemmed from Recreation 2000:

> 1 'To ensure that the general public is more aware of the opportunities for recreation in the countryside and has the confidence, ability and understanding to enjoy it in a considerate way' *(p.5)*. Experiments were to be established to evaluate new methods of achieving this. Two main methods of promoting awareness were proposed. The first was to make more use of local media, especially local radio and newspapers, to provide information to the public and to create a network of countryside correspondents. The second was to bring countryside information into the town, in the form of countryside recreation bureaux:

>> A glance inside any tourist information centre shows how diligently commercial undertakings advertise their attractions to the public. Yet these 'pay-at-the-gate' establishments constitute only a small minority of countryside attractions. Woods, lakes, riversides and villages offer a vast range of venues for free enjoyment, but many people are unaware of them. Even some country parks, created with public funds, put little effort into advertising where they are and what they offer *(Countryside Commission 1987b, p.11)*.

Additionally, further use was to be made of existing information networks, such as libraries, tourist information centres, and Citizens' Advice Bureaux, and neighbourhood and local countryside information packs produced for distribution through pubs, shops, garages, schools and estate agents. To increase understanding the Commission proposed to continue promoting codes of practice, notably the Country Code (summarizing people's responsibilities in the countryside), the Countryside Access Charter (summarizing their rights), and the Ploughing Code which advises farmers and landowners of their responsibilities regarding rights of way *(Countryside Commission et al. 1986)*. To create confidence and ability the Commission proposed to experiment with town-based events to welcome people into the countryside and equip them with appropriate confidence and skills; to encourage transport operators, site managers and local authorities to collaborate in the routing, pricing and promotion of public transport to the countryside; and to encourage the provision of adequate basic overnight accommodation, including camping and bunkhouse barns on long distance routes and in the remoter countryside. Participation has also been positively encouraged through Gateway experiments, discussed in Chapter 6.

2 'To promote networks of well-signposted and maintained routes throughout the countryside, giving ready access from towns, linking points of interest in the countryside, and co-ordinated with accommodation, car parks, publicity and guides' *(p.8)*. The Commission regards the rights of way network as 'the single most important means by which the public can enjoy the countryside' *(p.8)* and proposes to encourage the development and implementation of local rights of way strategies. These might encompass an appraisal of the recreational potential of the rights of way in a locality, a clarification of legal status and actual usability, consideration of potential improvements to the network, ways of publicising its availability, and means of harnessing people and finance to maintain it. To give fresh impetus in areas where rights of way issues have lain dormant the Commission recommends that local authorities might appoint access or rights of way managers, and make other appointments to ensure effective liaison with local interest groups and the enforcement of legal powers to secure the public right of passage.

3 'To develop further long distance routes, together with paths, accommodation and publicity linked to them' *(p.10)*. The intention is to create routes through attractive areas, which allow people to make extensive journeys on foot, horseback or bicycle, as far as possible on routes not available to vehicles. Routes will be based predominantly on existing rights of way which are capable of improvement and which offer tourist potential. More detailed recommendations, issued in 1988 *(Countryside Commission 1988)*, are discussed in Chapter 4.

4 'To provide and manage appropriate access to wider areas of countryside' *(p.11)*. The Commission has several approaches to access. It promotes the use of access agreements and management agreements for existing resources of open land and water. It encourages the creation of new resources, especially multi-purpose forest near towns and cities, and small open spaces for recreation, especially where opportunities arise from the reorganization of farming. It is also concerned to secure public access to common land, and will occasionally contribute to the purchase of key sites where public access is deemed paramount.

5 'To develop and manage selected recreation sites (ie land and water managed primarily for recreation)' *(p.12)*, in areas of high demand, where there are attractive sites or sites capable of restoration, and within easy reach by public transport. The role of Country Parks is discussed in Chapter 4.

6 'Rural communities to develop facilities which promote the public enjoyment of the countryside and, in so doing, to enhance their own social and economic life' *(p.12)*. Here the Commission seeks to stimulate local community action and interest in conserving the countryside, and helping to promote public access and enjoyment.

7 'National parks, heritage coasts and areas of outstanding natural beauty to contribute to countryside recreation opportunities in ways that sustain and enhance their particular character' *(p.13)*. The Commission offers to support

recreation schemes devised by the National Parks Authorities and the Broads Authority which are consistent with local character, especially any which apply to open land and rights of way, and involve local communities.

Overall, these provisions reflect a reorientation of recreation-related work of the Commission. Both integration and strategy play far stronger parts than before. Integration is evident, for example, in the impetus given to the linking of rights of way provision to recreational access to the wider countryside, and the linking of supply to demand through better, urban based information and transport services. Strategy is evident in the linking of diagnosis to prescription, the proposals for involving partner agencies, the recognition that recreation repercusses onto conservation and the social and economic character of rural areas. It is also evident in the defining of specific targets for achievement for the Commission itself for the next five years and to the year 2000.

Increasingly, the Commission emphasises the need for a sustainable and multi-purpose countryside, and the need for a planning system to guide development, maintain a clear urban – rural divide, and protect areas of special environmental importance. Countryside planning, it argues, should be based on a number of guiding principles *(Countryside Commission 1989c)*:

1 Natural beauty and landscape diversity should be maintained, particularly in view of the 'increasing uniformity and 'suburbanisation' of the countryside' *(p.11)*. To this end, local authorities and developers are urged to undertake detailed landscape assessments.
2 New countryside should be created wherever possible, such as country parks, green wedges, new woodland, paths and pocket parks.
3 Green belts should play a more positive role to enhance the beauty of the countryside close to towns, and to increase opportunities for public enjoyment.
4 Maximum environmental benefits should be secured from development which has to take place in the countryside, such as community woodland attached to new housing developments.
5 New housing should make a positive contribution to the rural scene.
6 Rural enterprise developed harmoniously with the countryside should be welcomed.
7 Major development should be strictly controlled, and executed to the highest possible design standards, and not be located at all in the National Parks, Broads, New Forest, Areas of Outstanding Natural Beauty or Heritage Coasts unless of over-riding national importance and impossible to locate elsewhere. Particular concern is expressed over road construction, open-cast coal mining, and leisure and tourism developments which are unsympathetic to the countryside in scale, type or appearance — schemes which are 'imposed on the countryside rather than being part of it' *(p.16)*.

These principles are evident in the Commission's most recent policy pronouncement *(1990a)*, which takes the form of a ten-point agenda for the 1990s:

1 'Conservation means creation as well as preservation' — while conserva-

tion requires the protection of key sites, it does not imply blanket fossilization; good conservation practice should preserve the best of the existing heritage, and create, through positive and managed change, a more beautiful countryside for the future.

2 'Cherish the wild places' — even the remotest countryside is under threat and so measures are needed to 'defend, and where possible, extend' areas of wild country, especially in the National Parks.

3 'Conserve through farming' — information and incentives should be given to farmers to maintain a beautiful, accessible and environmentally healthy countryside.

4 'Create a new face for forestry' — stressing a multi-purpose approach to forests, and promoting a new national forest and local community forests.

5 'Make the countryside more accessible' — a well-maintained and well-known path system is essential. The countryside should be made as widely available as possible, the health benefits of countryside recreation should be promoted, and public commitment to conservation should be harnessed.

6 'Avert damage from visitor pressure' — to minimize adverse environmental impacts, recreation and tourism developments and activities must be compatible with the needs of conservation.

7 'Set a new direction for transport' — minimize adverse environmental, atmospheric and aesthetic impacts of roads and traffic.

8 'Establish a new role for planning', moving away from a preoccupation with built development towards the proper integration of environmental improvement.

9 'Build on popular support' — to capitalize upon the growing public interest in conservation, and to harness individual and corporate effort.

10 'Government must give the policy lead' — both at national and at European level, the Commission looks to government to assert the importance of the countryside and create appropriate mechanisms and incentives to meet the above objectives.

Success in translating principles into policy, and policy into action on the ground, is hard to measure, not least for an agency whose work so clearly interacts with and depends upon the activities of others, and many of whose targets are neither visible nor short term. Certainly the shift to quasi-autonomous status in 1982 signalled a more strategic and consultative way of working, and a more integrated view of countryside access, environment and economy. For long the Commission's efforts focused on special places, essentially the 'managed' countryside. The more genuine commitment to the wider countryside that emerged in the 1980s is welcome indeed, but it makes the Commission's bargaining stance, as landless lobbyist rather than owner or executive, all the harder. The greening of politics and public, however, provide cause for optimism for the Commission's work, and its adoption of explicit policy principles and targets provides a clearer framework for action in the future.

The Forestry Commission

The Forestry Commission is the government agency responsible to MAFF for forestry in Britain. It was first established by the *1919 Forestry Act* to remedy the severe depletion of the nation's timber stocks experienced during the First World War. Its headquarters are in Edinburgh, and its regional organization comprises seven Conservancies. Under the *1967 Forestry Act* the Commission has duties to promote the interests of forestry, establish and maintain adequate reserves of growing trees, produce and supply timber, and develop the recreational potential of its forests. It is also required to strike a balance between its forestry functions and the conservation of nature and features of special interest.

The Commission, therefore, is not just a timber producer but a manager of land for multiple use. It provides grant aid to private forestry, regulates tree-felling, and can enter into forestry dedication covenants with private owners, whereby owners receive a grant in return for managing dedicated woodland in accordance with the Commission's advice, adopting sound forestry practice and integrating it with the needs of agriculture, conservation and public access. Through a system of felling licences, introduced in the *1951 Forestry Act*, the Commission has considerable influence over private forestry. Generally trees greater than ten centimetres in diameter cannot be felled without a licence, and the licence would normally require that replanting take place. Tree Preservation Orders, introduced by the *1947 Town and Country Planning Act*, enable local planning authorities to prevent owners from felling or damaging individual trees or groups of trees.

Given its initial purpose of building up timber stocks, for long the Commission's focus was on fast growing conifers, for decades planted with little regard for appearance, often imposing upon rolling countryside a brutal geometry insensitive to contour and form. Faced with growing public criticism, the Commission began in the mid-1960s to lend greater weight to landscaping *(Crowe 1966)*. Greater emphasis was placed on mixed planting schemes, maintaining shrub layers and ground flora, seasonal successions of colour, regular thinning and replanting, incorporating water and other habitats, providing lines of movement for people and animals, and exploiting prominent views. Now, as mature forests are progressively felled and restocked, opportunities are taken to modify them to suit people's needs more closely *(Scott 1990)*.

Recreational use first emerged more as a spin-off than a strategy, though the Commission encouraged it from the outset in its management of the New Forest *(Small 1979)*, and by the early designation of a number of Forest Parks, the first in Argyll (1935), Snowdonia (1937) and the Forest of Dean (1938). Forest Parks now extend over 182,000 hectares, mainly in mountainous country with substantial tracts of unplanted land.

More recently, recreation has become a more pervasive function, extending well beyond the special Forest Parks. The 1972 White Paper, *Forestry Policy (MAFF 1972)*, put forward recreation as one of the main justifications for additional planting. Provision reflected changing fortunes. In the 1970s the Commission introduced modest recreational facilities to many of its properties, and developed a number of more ambitious projects. Usage soared accordingly, from 15 million day visits in 1970 to 24 million in 1976 *(Patmore 1983, p.196)*. Provisions included car parks, picnic places, toilets, information centres, viewpoints, guided walks and nature trails. Budget restrictions, however, arrested further progress. By 1981, the Commission's budget for recreation confined its efforts to maintaining existing provisions and developing revenue-raising schemes. Nonetheless, the resource available for recreation and the finances committed to it are substantial. The Commission's estate amounts to 0.9 million hectares, and its spending on recreation in 1987–88 was nearly £5 million *(Scott 1990)*.

The total woodland resource of Great Britain is approximately 22.7 million hectares. By 1989 specific recreation provisions made by the Forestry Commission comprised 14 forest drives, 732 car parks (with 20,000 spaces), 621 picnic sites, 540 forest walks, 126 forest trails, 54 bridle tracks, 40 wayfaring courses, and 21 visitor centres *(Travis 1990)*. In addition awareness of its properties for recreation and tourism is being promoted as part of a recently launched 'Great Britain . . . . . Great Forests' programme, being piloted initially in seven Forest Districts throughout Britain.

The Commission in its turn encourages private owners to consider allowing public access. Jointly with the Countryside Commission it is currently promoting the establishment of community woods in the Central Scotland Woodland Project and, with the Countryside Commission, in Tyne and Wear, South Staffordshire and East London.

Recreational developments are designed to integrate with the forest environment and with conservation interests, and to be compatible with local authority plans and priorities *(Forestry Commission 1987)*. Due account is also taken of the priority rights of lessors and tenants.

There is no lack of demand for recreation from day visitors. According to *Scott (1990)*, woodlands attract some 170 million adult visits per year. In Forestry Commission forests, public access on foot is permitted free of charge as long as it is compatible with management needs and the protection of the forest, and not an infringement of the law. Indeed, the Commission has recently encouraged the Ramblers' Association to join with them in surveying the 9,600 kilometres of existing footpaths and routes, and to propose new ones *(Forestry Commission 1988)*. Charges are made for car parking, the use of visitor centres and other facilities where it is not prohibitively expensive to collect the charge.

For its prime purpose of harvesting timber and managing forests, the Commission has constructed 16,000 kilometres of forest roads. These afford public access on foot. In particularly scenic forests a small number have been specially designated as Forest Drives, some operated as toll roads. On other roads, public access by car is normally prohibited, except for access to car parks, camping sites and picnic places.

Wildlife contributes considerably to the recreational attractions of forests. Where appropriate the Commission provides hides and viewing points, and special facilities such as the otter hide at Kylerhea in Skye, deer and goat parks in Galloway, a bird trail in Thetford Forest, and a raptor viewing point on Haldon Hill, near Exeter.

Although the main demand is from day visitors, the Commission offers camping and caravan sites for staying visitors where it is financially viable. There are presently 38 camping sites. It also manages self-catering accommodation, mostly in the form of forest cabins.

The recreational value of forests is by no means restricted to informal recreation. Operating under accepted codes of practice, the Commission offers facilities for field sports such as fishing and shooting, including deer stalking. Where possible these are made available on the basis of day permits as well as for club members. Permits are also available in many areas for horse riding, pony trekking, field archery and sailing. Charges are made where considered appropriate. Another popular use, to which the forest environment is particularly well suited, is orienteering, which is provided and managed through the British Orienteering Federation, the governing body of the sport in 43 forest locations.

Nor are sporting pursuits confined to the tranquil and environmentally undemanding. The Commission's forests provide a crucial resource for Britain's motor sports. Over seventy car rallies per year are held on Forestry Commission land, ranging from minor events covering less than 80 kilometres and lasting under three hours, to major rallies such as the RAC Lombard which extends across Britain. Routes for all rallying events are agreed with the Royal Automobile Club and operated under strict control. The Commission recognizes that these activities may conflict in some ways with the quiet enjoyment of the forests, and, more enduringly, with environmental protection, but without access to these areas Britain would be unable to stage international events. Indeed, the events are made particularly challenging and exciting by the complex and winding routeways in forest areas, often over difficult terrain *(Forestry Commission 1988)*.

The National Rivers Authority

Until 1989, apart from a few local exceptions, water supply, sewage treatment, flood protection, pollution control, associated conservation issues, and much water-related recreation provision were a public sector responsibility, largely that of ten Regional Water Authorities. Under the *Water Act 1989*, however, responsibilities were divided, with the utilities moving to private sector control. The regulatory functions were transferred to the new National Rivers Authority, a watchdog agency to ensure the responsible use and management of water resources.

The Act provides for the Authority to have a Board of between eight and 15 members appointed by the Government to direct its overall policy. The Authority reports to the Secretary of State for the Environment and has close links with the Welsh Office and MAFF as the departments responsible for government policy on flood defence and fisheries. It is partly self-financing, generating income from local authorities for flood defence works and from charges for water abstraction licences. Any deficit is met by a government grant. The Authority's budget for 1989 – 90 was £355 million, 70 per cent of which came from charging schemes and 30 per cent from government grant (National Rivers Authority 1990). Half of the total was spent on flood defence, 20 per cent on water resources, and 15 per cent on pollution control. Fisheries management accounted for five per cent (£15 million) and recreation and conservation for 0.7 per cent (£2.5 million).

Figure 3.1   National Rivers Authority Regions

The Authority employs 6,500 staff, and operates through 10 regional offices, based on river catchment areas (Fig. 3.1). Each region has three statutory specialist committees. A Regional Rivers Advisory Committee, with members drawn from agriculture, industry, conservation, sport, recreation and commerce, advises the Authority on river basin management. A Regional Fisheries Advisory Committee, including representatives from angling, fish farming and commercial fisheries, advises on the Authority's fisheries functions. A Regional Flood Defence Committee has responsibilities for flood defence and land drainage. Its responsibilities include monitoring water quality, controlling pollution, and regulating discharges into rivers, lakes and the sea; safeguarding water resources for public supply; providing effective flood forecasting and defences; maintaining and developing fisheries in inland water; conserving the water environment and protecting it as an amenity; and promoting recreational activity. In its prospectus *(National Rivers Authority undated)*, the Authority describes itself as 'the strongest environmental protection agency in Europe'.

Only 17 of the 6,500 staff are classed as recreation staff. However, the Authority seeks to 'actively encourage all the recreational possibilities within the nation's aquatic environment' *(ibid., p.11)* and aims to provide information sheets and booklets outlining the amenities of specific rivers and sites. It is required to maintain fish stocks and ensure the wellbeing of salmon, trout, freshwater and eel fisheries, and it regulates their use through a licensing system and through measures to prevent poaching. In three of its regions — Anglian, Southern and Thames — the National Rivers Authority is also the navigation authority. In these areas it aims to improve and maintain inland waterways and their facilities for use by the public, and it can make and enforce bylaws to regulate river users to ensure safe and enjoyable use.

The privatized water supply and sewage companies have broadly the same conservation duties as their Regional Water Authority predecessors. The National Rivers Authority has two additional duties. Firstly, it is required to consult the Nature Conservancy Council when considering applications for drainage and discharge consents, and abstraction or impoundment licences which could affect SSSIs. Secondly, it has a duty to promote the conservation of flora and fauna. The privatized water companies may fully exploit the potential of reservoirs and other water bodies for recreation, and although conservation bodies argued that preservation of the natural environment should be an over-riding consideration, this was not incorporated into the new Act. Much of the recreation work of the National Rivers Authority is concerned with managing, letting and leasing fishing rights. Rod licences issued in 1989–90 generated an income of £1.28 million. It also controls several major rafting and canoeing facilities, including the National White Water Centre on the Afon Treweryn, and the artificial canoe slalom on the Ouse at Cardington. The

Authority seeks to reconcile the interests of different user groups, for example by forming management agreements with canoeing bodies, convening angling and canoeing liaison groups and, in the Welsh region, funding a project officer jointly with several other agencies to produce a management plan to reconcile conflicts of use on the River Wye.

The water companies own approximately 182,000 hectares of land, most of which are needed for water-gathering. Some, however, is likely to be sold, with development prospects in mind. Under the *1989 Act*, however, the private water companies may not sell any area of land in a National Park, Area of Outstanding Natural Beauty or Site of Special Scientific Interest unless the Secretary of State for the Environment is assured that adequate safeguards will be made through covenants or management agreements for the environmental, wildlife and access value of the land. In appropriate circumstances the Secretary of State may, as an alternative, direct that the land be offered for sale in the first instance to a suitable amenity body, such as the National Trust. Landholdings outside these specially designated areas have no such discretionary protection by the Secretary of State.

British Waterways

British Waterways is responsible for operating and maintaining an extensive network of canals, rivers and reservoirs which it owns or acts as the navigation authority. The British Waterways Board comprises between six and eleven members, appointed by the Secretary of State for the Environment. It employs approximately 2,600 staff in a headquarters base and six regions. Its property portfolio amounts to £271 million *(British Waterways 1990a)*. The Board was established under the 1962 Transport Act, as a nationalized industry 'to provide services and facilities on the inland water-ways in their ownership or management subject to such terms, conditions and charges as they think fit' *(British Waterways 1989, p.1)*. Initially the prime concern was promoting freight usage, but only a small number of larger waterways are now used and being further developed for freight carrying. In any case, the potential for wider recreational use of the waterways system was soon recognized, in the 1967 White Paper, *British Waterways: Recreation and Amenity.* (Ministry of Transport 1967). This led to statutory recognition of the Board's role in leisure and tourism in the *1968 Transport Act*, and to specific powers and duties.

The Board owns or manages 3,200 kilometres of waterways and 90 reservoirs. The linear waterways are classified into three types. Commercial waterways, amounting to 570 kilometres, are to be available principally for the commercial carriage of freight. Cruising waterways (1875 kilometres) are to be available principally for cruising, angling and other forms of recreation. Remainder waterways (809 kilometres) may be developed and managed, eliminated, or disposed of in the most economical manner possible. British Waterways has the duty to maintain the commercial and cruising waterways for public use. It may also acquire and develop land adjacent to such waterways, and manage caravan and camping sites to provide services and facilities for amenity and recreation. Local authorities have powers to assist British Waterways in maintaining and improving the waterways for recreational access and use.

The *1968 Act* also established the Inland Waterways Amenity Advisory Council (IWAAC) as an independent body to advise British Waterways and the Department of Transport on the amenity and recreational uses of the waterways. IWAAC is frequently called upon to advise on matters of safety, licensing and mooring fees, and customer services.

Subsequent Acts made further provisions for recreation. The *1971 British Waterways Act* required that all pleasure boats using or moored on the river navigations controlled by the Board must be registered and be liable for fees. British Waterways may make bylaws to control navigation, prohibit unauthorised waterskiing, and require pleasure boats to be appropriately licensed.

Recreation was brought into greater prominence in 1984, when the Department of the Environment revised the Board's objectives. Despite the fact that the system came into being in the late 18th and 19th centuries as 'the motorways of the Industrial Revolution' *(British Waterways 1989, p.1)* it was recognised that this function was becoming progressively extinct. As the Department of the Environment stated:

> The greater part of the network is unlikely to be suitable for freight transport and should be managed imaginatively for the purposes of leisure, recreation, amenity, conservation (and land drainage as necessary). Public use and enjoyment of the waterways should be enhanced including where practicable that of the disabled.
>
> Opportunities to expand and develop profitable activities (in conjuction with the private sector where possible) should be pursued in ways which would increase the Board's resources. Charges should be kept under review, with the aim of maximising revenue.˙Maintenance standards should be appropriate to the use . . . . . and the prospects of use, of the various stretches of each waterway *(British Waterways 1989, p.5)*.

To this end, the Board encourages private investment in developments on the inland waterways, and also seeks to work in partnership with public and voluntary sector agencies.

Both volume and variety of recreational use are considerable, for 26 million people live within 8 kilometres of a British Waterways river or canal *(British Waterways 1990b)*. In 1986 the inland waterways attracted recreational use amounting to 119 million user days, 20.2 million of which comprised paying customers (Table 3.2). In 1989, total use was estimated at 130 million informal visits and 25 million additional visits for priced activities.

Table 3.2   Leisure activities on the inland waterways: actual and potential markets

	No. of adults taking part 1986	No. not taking part but had seriously considered doing so
Walking/informal recreation	4,830,000	1,290,000
Angling	770,000	1,140,000
Trip boats	500,000	4,200,000
Private boating	400,000	3,130,000
Unpowered boating	400,000	1,530,000
Hire boating	140,000	9,260,000

Source: British Waterways, 1989

The inland waterways provide an important resource for angling and British Waterways is the country's largest single owner of fishing rights. As well as the canals, fishing is also available on 40 reservoirs and over 480 kilometres of river. Most of the network is suitable for coarse fishing, and a few waters have been developed for game fishing. In addition to the 770,000 regular adult anglers identified in surveys undertaken for British Waterways by National Opinion Polls (NOP), there is use by occasional anglers and by the under 12s, and so the Board estimates that as many as a third of the country's three million anglers probably use its fisheries each year. The Board manages directly the fisheries on 320 kilometres of canals and eight reservoirs. Most fishing, however, takes place through agreements with angling clubs and associations, most of which offer angling to the general public by means of day permits or season tickets. Canal fisheries are popular with match anglers for their ease of access and the competition fairness afforded by their relative uniformity of flow. In order to improve facilities for anglers, the Board is seeking to provide more car parks and better towpaths, and to improve restocking systems. The Board also undertakes periodic surveys of the fish population, and the culling of predators, such as zander.

Powered pleasure boating is another popular use, comprising three main forms. The main usage is by privately owned pleasure boats (approximately 20,000). In addition, approximately 1,400 commercially run hire boats and 100 commercially run trip and restaurant boats use the network. All categories of boat need a British Waterways licence or, for use of rivers, a registration certificate. The Board itself manages 2,500 moorings, and many others are leased to private clubs. Generally the Board encourages the provision of off-channel moorings, including associated facilities such as housing, pubs and boat building.

British Waterways operates its own hire fleet from Nantwich, Cheshire, and, with the Association of Pleasure Craft Operators, runs UK Waterway Holidays Ltd to market hire boat holidays overseas. In addition, it operates the National Waterways Museum in Gloucester, which opened in 1988 and attracted 112,000 visitors in its first year, and the Visitor Centre and Waterways Museum at Stoke Bruerne, Northamptonshire, which attracted over 76,000 visitors in 1988–89 (British Waterways 1990).

Unpowered boating—canoeing, sailing and rowing—takes place on many waterways and several reservoirs. It is prohibited in certain canal tunnels, and limited on some commercial waterways. Each craft must be licensed individually, except that British Canoe Union (BCU) members obtain a British Waterways canoe licence as part of their BCU membership. The canal system, with its slow-moving, shallow and narrow waterways, is particularly safe and popular for canoe training, and attractive to young people. Some canals, notably the Kennet and Avon and the Leeds–Liverpool are used for canoe marathon events.

Part of the value of the waterways system lies in its rich repository of wildlife, and its considerable collection of buildings of historic and architectural interest. The Board's properties include over 1,800 listed buildings and ancient monuments, and 50 Sites of Special Scientific Interest.

Further recreational use is based on the towing path network, which is used extensively for walking, picnicking, bird watching, and photography. Approximately one-third of towing paths are public rights of way. In general the Board has difficulty in financing the maintenance of the entire towing path system, and it is keen to encourage local authorities to enter into towing path agreements, whereby maintenance and public liability are transferred, and the local authority may make such provisions as car parking, picnic sites and circular walks.

Since 1984 the Board has appointed Project Officers and Rangers to promote towpath recreation in particular areas, sometimes jointly with the Countryside Commission or Sports Council. Work undertaken by Project Officers includes small scale environmental improvements, the provision of information and interpretive services, and publicity of the waterways system. They liaise particularly with schools and youth groups and with their local communities more generally.

In 1988–89 British Waterways income derived from government grant in aid (£44.6 million) and from external revenues (£20.8 million). Of the latter, £5.4 million (26 per cent) was income from the leisure uses of the waterways. Overall, British Waterways has moved progressively further towards commercial objectives and used recreation as a major means of achieving them:

> 1988 was a year of tremendous change for British Waterways with the move to a business oriented organisation nearer to the customer . . . . . British Waterways are determined to develop the waterways into one of the most important environmental assets across the United Kingdom, one that is enjoyed by more people, particularly for leisure, but also for living and working . . . . . The future opportunities for leisure and tourism on the waterways are remarkable, particularly for the one or two-day attractions. *(British Waterways 1990, pp. 2–3)*.

The Sports Council

The Sports Council was set up in 1965, initially as an advisory body to the government on the development of amateur sport and physical recreation. In 1972 it became an executive body, its independence established by Royal Charter. In some matters its remit extends to the UK as a whole, but there are separate Sports Councils for Wales, Scotland and Northern Ireland. The Council comprises 15 members, appointed by the Secretary of State for the Environment, and employs approximately 600 staff, 100 at its London headquarters, the remainder in ten regional offices and five national sports centres. Its government grant for 1988–89 was £39 million.

The Council's responsibilities are to promote mass participation and excellence. From the outset, the development of sports policy and the work of the Sports Council, have been more closely bound up with general social policy and welfare concerns than have the activities of other agencies. *Coalter et al (1986)* chart the reasons for this, and its ramifications. The effect is a strong concern with inequity, and a prominent policy goal to extend sports opportunities to all sectors of society. From this derives a continuing concern with the barriers to participation faced by certain social groups, and the development of policies and provisions to alleviate recreational disadvantage:

> There are . . . . . major inequities in participation. To use an analogy, the sports franchise has been greatly extended, but the suffrage is far from universal: most women, many middle-aged and older men, and most of the poor, handicapped and ethnic minorities take no part, often because of barriers to access, cost and lack of information . . . . . the social challenges are enormous. Not to tackle the needs of these groups would put the Council in breach of its Charter. *(Sports Council 1982, p.7)*.

The Sports Council works to a ten-year strategy, produced initially in 1982 and reviewed in 1988 *(Sports Council 1982, 1988)*. The strategy sets out targets for participation levels and facility provision, giving particular emphasis to opportunities for young people and women. The Council's endeavours to increase participation in sport and physical recreation have been developed under the banner 'Sport for All', with special campaigns from time to time aimed at particular sectors of the community, eg, women, disabled people, young people, and the over 50s. To promote participation the Council also offers Regional Participation Grants to assist local sports organizations, and funds the appointment of development staff to help the governing bodies and to be more proactive in attracting new participants. The Council also operates a number of special programmes of sports leadership notably Action Sport, established mainly in urban areas, and a series of participation demonstration projects which seek to promote sport in partnership with other organizations, including the Women's Institute, a Health Authority, library services, employers, and a brewery.

Another major sphere of activity, and one that dominated the work of the executive Council in its first decade, is grant-aid for facility provision. In 1972 there were only 24 sports centres and just over 400 swimming pools in England *(Sports Council 1972)*; by 1981 there were 461 sports centres and 964 pools *(McIntosh and Charlton 1985)*. By 1987 a further 350 sports halls had been built *(Sports Council undated)*. In addition to grant-aiding new facility provision, the Council encourages the better use of existing ones, the community use of school-based facilities, and the conversion of redundant buildings to sport and recreational use.

While much of the Council's work is urban based and facility oriented, it has an important influence too on countryside recreation provision. Several sports — such as mountaineering, climbing, caving and canoeing — specifically require countryside resources. Others, such as golf and horse riding, tend to be pushed out to the urban edge for lack of space.

Like the Countryside Commission, the Sports Council has been swift to seize upon the potential benefits for recreation of agricultural change. Its strategy *(1988, p.24)* notes, for example, the opportunities which could arise for providing sports facilities for rural residents, by converting land into playing pitches or buildings into indoor sports space. Studies are in progress with MAFF to examine the economics of sports enterprises on farms.

Sports participation generally has increased over the years, and nowhere more so than in outdoor and countryside pursuits. Its first strategy document stated that the Council would give priority to encouraging provision for active sports in the countryside, and would seek to work jointly with other agencies and organizations to improve access for recreation, especially in urban fringes. In its strategy review *(Sports Council 1988, p.65)* the Council noted that 'the area dedicated to recreation as a prime use has continued to increase with the development of new country and water parks. However, demand continues to grow for all countryside and water pursuits, especially those with an adventurous element'. The Council had therefore established a specialist Countryside and Water Recreation Policy Group, and appointed staff to deal with countryside matters. Growing pressure on countryside sites, and widespread resistance to certain sports, have prompted the Council to consider ways of protecting outdoor areas of special importance to sport, and research is currently under way. Obtaining sites for the practice of motorized sports is a particularly acute problem. Following the commissioning of several studies on water, land and air sports *(Elson et al 1986a, b, 1989a, 1989b)* the Council proposes to establish demonstration projects and to work with other agencies such as the Countryside Commission to secure and expand opportunities for these sports without adversely affecting farming and conservation interests.

The Regional Councils for Sport and Recreation

Regional Councils for Sport and Recreation were established by the Minister for Sport in 1976 as independent, unfunded bodies to co-ordinate the planning and provision of all forms of sport and outdoor recreation, and to advise on priorities for grant aid. The Sports Council provided secretarial and administrative support to the Councils, and those who chair the Regional Councils are members of the Sports Council itself. The Regional Councils provide a forum for discussion between local authorities and a wide range of user groups and affected interests, including voluntary organizations and the regional branches of the governing bodies of sport. Each Region was charged with the responsibility of producing and implementing a Regional Recreation Strategy to guide the development and provision of sport and recreation, and to provide a framework for the policies to be formulated within statutory structure plans and local plans. The earliest of the strategies, produced by the North West and South West regions, are now being reviewed and updated.

Reality has strayed from intention in a number of respects. Sport, rather than recreation more broadly, has always been a dominant concern of the Councils, and reinforced by the close links with Sports Council regional offices acting as secretariat. The regional strategies, while providing a valuable framework for policy within each region, have to date been much less consistent in scope, approach and timescale than was originally intended. The Sports Council is endeavouring to co-ordinate approaches and to ensure that the revised strategies form a genuine bridge between policies at national and local level.

The Nature Conservancy Council

The Nature Conservancy Council (NCC) came into being by Royal Charter in 1948 as the Nature Conservancy, its present title deriving from the *1973 Nature Conservancy Council Act*. It presently covers the whole of Great Britain, but changes are in prospect under the *1989 Environmental Protection Bill* which will combine it in Scotland and Wales with their respective Countryside Commissions.

The present Nature Conservancy Council employs 800 staff, deployed in headquarters offices and 15 regions. Its main responsibilities are to establish and manage National Nature Reserves, advise the government on nature conservation, provide advice and information to landowners and the general public, support relevant research, notify Sites of Special Scientific Interest and take steps to protect them, and advise ministers on the issue of licences affecting particular species. These responsibilities were extended under the *1981 Wildlife and Countryside Act*, particularly with regard to farming and forestry operations affecting SSSIs, an increase in the number of protected species, and new powers to designate Marine Nature Reserves.

The NCC is funded by the Department of the Environment. In 1988–89 its total income was £38.6 million. Nineteen per cent of its spending was allocated to management agreements, 13 per cent to scientific support, six per cent to grant aid, and four per cent to maintaining National Nature Reserves.

The purpose of nature conservation is 'to ensure that the national heritage of wild flora and fauna, geological and physical features remains as large, diverse and well distributed as possible for the use and enjoyment of society' *(Nature Conservancy Council 1989, p.105)*. The Council has the power to negotiate agreements with landowners to establish nature reserves, it can purchase land compulsorily, and it can make bylaws to protect nature reserves.

The process of notifying new Sites of Special Scientific Interest and renotifying existing ones has come to dominate the Council's workload since the mid 1980s. By the end of the 1980s, 5,184 SSSIs had been notified, covering 1.64 million hectares, and there were 234 National Nature Reserves in England, Scotland and Wales covering 166,000 hectares *(Nature Conservancy Council 1989)*. Following notification, landowners are required to consult the Council on any 'potentially damaging operations' of pre-defined types. The Council readily recognizes that purely site-based protection is unsuitable for species with large territories or ranges, and measures to conserve the countryside generally include collaborating with farmers and landowners to develop appropriate codes of practice. The Council relies heavily upon working with the voluntary conservation movement, and in 1988–89 four-fifths of all grants given went to local and national voluntary bodies. Approximately 2,000 voluntary wardens assist in the running of the National Nature Reserves.

The NCC advises and comments upon the conservation implications of planning proposals, including, from time to time, proposed recreation developments. In 1988–89, for example, the Council advised on the proposed development of skiing facilities at Aonach Mor, near Fort William. Part of the proposed project lies within the Ben Nevis SSSI, defined as such for its mountain plateau vegetation community. The NCC therefore wished to ensure that ways of preventing or overcoming environmental damage would be incorporated into the scheme: 'The £10 million development . . . . . is likely to have an impact on the mountain environment but with commitment from all parties to sound management, and the closing of the top chairlift in the summer months, the long-term viability of both nature conservation and recreation can be achieved' *(Nature Conservancy Council 1982, p.21)*.

The Council works with various recreation interests in trying to secure environmental protection. It liaises with the various angling bodies regarding restrictions on the use of lead weights, controlling bait digging in wetlands used by wildfowl and waders, the proposed designation of Marine Nature Reserves, and water quality. It works with the British Association for Shooting and Conservation regarding wildfowling on SSSIs, to ensure that the activity is properly conducted and that shooting and disturbance are kept clear of reserve areas.

The NCC's apprehension about specific activities extends to recreation much more broadly, and there are signs of growing resistance: 'the introduction or expansion of recreational activities on reservoirs which are SSSIs should require the NCC's agreement' *(Nature*

Conservancy Council 1987, p.32). The renotification of SSSIs has caused concern to many recreation interests. In the West Midlands in 1984–86, for example, 71 renotifications of existing SSSIs were received and 56 new notifications. Fifteen of the former and twelve of the latter were regarded by the Sports Council as having significance for sport *(Sidaway 1988)*.

The likely effects of the transfer of responsibilities to the new Countryside Councils in Wales and Scotland are unclear. As *Sidaway (1990)* points out, however, the draft bill failed to encompass the full range of functions presently served by the Countryside Commissions and the Nature Conservancy Council. In particular, it took the *1949 National Parks and Access to the Countryside Act* as the enabling legislation for the Countryside Commission, not the *1968 Countryside Act*. If unamended, therefore, the new Countryside Council for Wales would not have the full powers of the present Countryside Commission; it would only have those stemming from the *1949 Act,* namely in relation to National Parks and Areas of Outstanding Natural Beauty. Furthermore, the *1968 Act*, unless repealed, still allows the Countryside Commission in England to appoint a Committee for Wales. There are threats too to the existing balance of attention to different countryside functions in a combined agency. As Sidaway notes, the regulatory function of the Nature Conservancy Council to notify Sites of Special Scientific Interest will be a continuing commitment.

The Tourist Authorities
Holidays in Britain are promoted overseas by the British Tourist Authority, and domestically for their respective territories by the English Tourist Board, Wales Tourist Board, Scottish Tourist Board, and Northern Ireland Tourist Board. Since their establishment, under the *1969 Development of Tourism Act,* all five have been concerned with developing and marketing the tourism 'product'. Increasingly since the early 1980s, tourism has become a tool of economic recovery, for its potential in terms of both job creation and income generation.

The beauty of the countryside is a major tourist pull: 'England's small market towns, attractive villages and the variety of the English countryside have great appeal to both domestic and overseas visitors' *(English Tourist Board 1987, p.21)*. In turn, of course, tourism can bring employment opportunities and revenue to rural areas, and help to support local facilities such as village shops, pubs and public transport. In 1988, the English Tourist Board launched a strategy for rural tourism, with three main aims: to strengthen the rural economy; to conserve the countryside as a tourism resource; and to provide for visitors' enjoyment of countryside attractions. Outcomes of the strategy include special promotional campaigns to develop tourism in the Marches, the Norfolk Broads, Borders and the Peak District, and a competition for rural tourism projects promoted jointly with the Rural Development Commission. A series of Local Area Initiatives has also been implemented, in areas such as Shropshire, Cornwall, the Forest of Dean and the Isle of Wight.

As conservation has become an increasingly prominent public concern, so too has it come to the fore of tourism policies. In 1989, for example, the English Tourist Board and the Countryside Commission jointly published an agreed list of *Principles for Tourism in the countryside*, which stressed the importance of respecting the natural environment, and of reaping social and economic benefits for local residents from tourism. The first principle stated that 'The promotion of tourist enjoyment of the countryside should be primarily aimed at those activities which draw on the character of the countryside itself, its beauty, culture, history and wildlife' *(English Tourist Board and Countryside Commission 1989)*. Others concerned the potential of tourist developments to bring new uses to historic buildings, generate income for farms, and reclaim derelict land. A further principle urged the wider geographical spread of tourism investment, both to prevent the over-use of popular places, and to spread the financial benefits. A joint conference with the Countryside Commission and the Rural Development Commission in 1990 entitled 'Shades of Green' promoted these principles further, examining ways of developing tourist opportunities which are compatible with the well-being of rural residents and the countryside. A Green Tourism Award has also been added to the categories of award in the English Tourist Board's 'England for Excellence' scheme, which aims to raise standards throughout the tourism industry and to reward providers who set standards for others to emulate.

The voluntary sector

The National Trust
The National Trust for Places of Historic Interest and Natural Beauty was founded in 1895, 'as part of a general movement which sprang from upper-class horror at the impact of industrial and urban expansion' *(Lowe and Goyder 1983, p.138)* The Trust was formally constituted under the *1907 National Trust Act*. Its inception and evolution are well documented *(Fedden 1968, 1974)*. Its founding trinity were Robert Hunter (honorary solicitor to the Commons Preservation Society), Octavia Hill (a pioneer in housing reform) and Canon Hardwicke Rawnsley, steadfast defender of the Lake District. Hunter in particular had learned that only by the actual acquisition of property could its effective preservation be assured. The Trust is an independent organization with charitable status, funded primarily from members' subscriptions (25 per cent of total income) and donations from supporters. It aims premanently to preserve for the benefit of the nation land and buildings of beauty or historic interest. It obtains its properties by purchase, donation or leasehold. It has the power to declare its properties inalienable. That is to say, the Trust cannot divest itself of them, nor can they be acquired compulsorily wihout recourse to parlia-

ment. Inalienability was intended to prevent the Trust from disposing of properties it ceased to value, and to instil faith in its supporters that preservation would indeed be permanent. The Trust can also create bylaws to regulate and protect its properties. Further protection came with the *1946 Acquisition of Land Act* which gave the Trust the right to appeal to a joint committee of the two houses of parliament in the event of a public authority proposing to acquire its land by use of compulsory powers.

The Trust has headquarters offices in London and Wiltshire, and sixteen regional offices. Its policy is determined by a Council of 52 members, half elected by the membership and half nominated by prominent national institutions (eg the British Museum). Most of its work is delegated to an Executive Committee of 28 members, and to 14 regional committees. The Trust employs approximately 1,400 staff. Policy making is highly centralized. It echoes the roots of the Trust: 'although preserving land for the people, the trust was never meant to be of the people. The founders, in keeping with the contemporary spirit of patrician reform, intended the trust to be controlled by responsible people committed to aesthetic ideals. This deliberate elitism now sits incongruously with the mass membership acquired over the past 30 years' *(Lowe and Goyder 1983, p.140)*. In 1945 the Trust had fewer than 8,000 members. Concerted efforts to broaden its appeal and to seek the support of the nation at large succeeded modestly in reducing its early exclusivity. In 1989 there were 1,865,000 members of the Trust, and over 10 million visitors to Trust properties *(National Trust 1990)*.

Mass leisure, then, is something of a mixed blessing for the Trust. While mass membership may be welcomed for the subscription income it generates, there has long been apprehension that it might begin to divert and dictate the direction of Trust policy: 'The Trust did great things with less than a thousand members, and set high standards. Any lowering of these standards, and compromise in deference to a vast membership and the irrelevant pressures that such a membership might exert, would in the long run undermine its authority and hazard its future' *(Fedden 1968)*.

The Trust owns 224,000 hectares of land in England, Wales and Northern Ireland, including fine landscapes, one-sixth of the coast and one-tenth of the Sites of Special Scientific Interest *(National Trust 1990)*. Many of its land holdings are in the National Parks, where its holdings are far greater than those of the National Park Authorities themselves: it owns 24 per cent of the Lake District, ten per cent of the Peak District, and nine per cent of Snowdonia. Coastal properties have been acquired mainly under the 'Enterprise Neptune' campaign, first launched in 1965, which exceeded its 8,000th kilometre of coastline in 1989. In 1962–63 the Trust had undertaken a survey of the coastline of England, Wales and Northern Ireland. It concluded that one-third of the coastline was already 'ruined beyond redemption', one-third was 'of no significant recreational or scenic importance', and the final one-third was 'of outstanding natural beauty and worthy of permanent preservation': Enterprise Neptune was to be the campaign for achieving that preservation. Overall, the properties of the Trust comprise lowland farmland (23 per cent of total area), commons (20 per cent), hill farmland (19 per cent), coast (17 per cent), woodland (six per cent), and parks and gardens (three per cent); other categories of properties make up 12 per cent.

The Trust presents its houses in varied ways: 'in general the aim is to show them to the public as they might have been had their owners just left the rooms for the day — dining-table laid, flowers in the drawing-room, newspapers in the library' *(National Trust 1990, p.4)*. An increasing problem for the Trust is the revenue cost of maintaining its properties: a 'balance that constantly has to be struck is that between a readiness to take an important but threatened area under the Trust's protective wing and making sure that resources are not spread too thin to provide proper care for the properties already in its ownership' *(National Trust 1990, p.3)*.

Council for National Parks

The Council for National Parks began in 1936 as the Standing Committee on National Parks, to campaign for the creation of National Parks. The 1949 Act which brought them into being changed the emphasis of the Standing Committee's work towards strengthening their provisions for conservation and recreation *(Council for National Parks 1986b)*. While the Standing Committee clearly welcomed the legislation, it lamented the lack of adequate safeguards to sustain the fundamental purpose of the parks, most notably a lack of effective planning controls over farming and forestry, the paucity of government funding allocated to the parks, and the limited powers of the National Parks Commission and the individual park authorities. It therefore campaigned to defend the Parks against inappropriate development and usage, successfully opposing, for example, the proposed Gautries limestone quarry in the Peak District, and the proposed Swincombe Reservoir on Dartmoor. In the 1970s, after the Sandford Committee enquiry into National Park policies, and in recognising the growing public interest in the Parks, the Standing Committee reviewed its role and decided to become an independent voluntary organization. From 1977 it was renamed the Council for National Parks, with the following objective: 'to promote the purposes for which National Parks were designated: the conservation and enhancement of natural beauty and the promotion of the areas designated as National Parks by the public' *(Council for National Parks 1986a, p.26)*. Thirty nine national and local amenity, recreation and wildlife bodies are members of the Council, including the British Trust for Conservation Volunteers, the Byways and Bridleways Trust, the Council for the Protection of Rural England, the Council for the Protection of Rural Wales, the Geographical Association, the National Trust, the Ramblers' Association, the Royal Society for the Protection of Birds, the Youth Hostels Association, and the national governing bodies of mountaineering, camping and caravanning, cycling, and caving. It acts as an authoritative and independent voice on the National Parks, making representations on specific Parks issues and drafting policy papers. Increasingly it is also involved in promoting education and public awareness, for example, through the Friends of the National Parks membership scheme, and the *Know Your National Parks* (1984) education pack. After the Countryside Commission's 1984 National Survey of Countryside Recreation revealed that only half of the population could name a National Park unprompted, the Council also joined with the Commission and the National Park Authorities to launch a public awareness campaign, *Watch over the National Parks.*

Other voluntary amenity bodies

The widespread appeal and long term growth of interest in the countryside may be gauged from trends in the membership of environmental groups, amenity associations and countryside sports bodies. *Lowe and Goyder (1983, p.1)* estimated that one adult in ten belonged to an environmental group:

> With an estimated two-and-a-half to three million supporters, the environmental movement is now larger than any political party or trade union; its present strength is roughly double that in 1970, which in turn was probably double that of 10 years earlier. . . . . There are nearly a hundred national environmental groups and several thousand local ones.

The total annual income of the national bodies in the early 1980s was £26 million, a sum equal to the combined annual expenditure at that time of the Countryside Commission, the Nature Conservancy Council and the Historic Buildings Councils.

Figure 3.2   Dates of formation of national environmental groups

	No. of groups
pre-1875	2
1876–1885	3
1886–1895	2
1896–1905	6
1906–1915	3
1916–1925	3
1926–1935	9
1936–1945	5
1946–1955	6
1956–1965	11
1966–1975	23
1976–1980	9

Source: Data from Lowe and Goyder (1983) Fig.2.1

The growth of environmental concern in the past quarter century is evident in the formation of new national associations. The very first group, the Commons, Open Spaces and Footpaths Preservation Society dates from 1865. A hundred years later there were fifty national environmental groups, a third of them established since the second world war. Then, in a single decade (1966–75) 23 more were created, with another 9 by 1980 (Fig. 3.2). Expansion is echoed at local level, with a virtual ten-fold increase in the number of local amenity societies since 1950. In that year, 137 local groups existed. There were 300 by 1960, over 700 in 1970, and 1250 in 1975. *Lowe and Goyder (1983)* trace the value chages wrought by post-war economic growth, and the rate of environmental change which have fuelled this upsurge of interest.

Overview

Countryside recreation provision is both fragmented and fluid, as the various organizations, particularly in the public sector arena, converge and then realign on different issues. At national level the Chairmen's Policy Group, comprising the chairmen and directors of the national agencies, provides a forum for discussion if not a mechanism for complete harmonization of effort, and their research programmes are co-ordinated through the Countryside Recreation Research Advisory Group (CRRAG). These mechanisms, however useful, do not so much prevent areas of overlap, conflict or neglect as recognize them, and from time to time act upon them. Organizational change, most notably in the water industry and the nature conservation field at the time of writing, brings further policy discontinuities and possible changes of direction. At regional and local levels, mainly through the Regional Councils for Sport and Recreation and the local authorities, the field is much less fragmented, but developing integrated policies for informal recreation, sport, conservation and land use is a difficult task when at national level they remain splintered and separate.

4 Special measures for special places

Though recreational interest extends to the whole of the countryside, policies, provisions and providers' intentions are most clearly articulated for certain special categories of resources. This chapter examines special measures taken to protect or promote those resources, and the place of recreation within them.

National Parks

The designation of National Parks in England and Wales followed soon after the enabling legislation of 1949. First to be confirmed was the Peak District, in April 1951. Second, and largest of the Parks, was the Lake District, a month later. Snowdonia and Dartmoor followed the same year, with the remainder of the ten being designated between 1952 and 1957. A further two, the Norfolk Broads and the Cornish Coast, came close to designation in the mind of the National Parks Commission, but proposals were dropped due to strong resistance from local councils in these areas. In total the ten parks occupy 13,600 sq. kilometres, nine per cent of the land area of England and Wales, predominantly in the uplands (Table 4.1, Figure 4.1).

The title is confusing, for the designated areas are neither national nor parks. Indeed, they do not satisfy internationally agreed criteria for national parks. The two principal conditions defined by the International Union for the Conservation of Nature and Natural Resources (IUCN) are that national parks should be essentially wilderness areas not substantially affected by human exploitation or occupation, and that they should be owned or managed by the government. In England and Wales, most National Park land is privately owned, and little is used solely for pleasure:

> Our national parks are different from those in other countries where they are usually nationally owned and have no industrial uses. Our parks are a partnership — a national designation, under local stewardship, with national objectives of conservation and public enjoyment bound up with regard for

the social and economic interests of those who live in the parks. *(Countryside Commission 1987e, p.2)*

Table 4.1   National Parks

	Date of confirmation	Area (sq.km)
Peak District	1951	1,404
Lake District	1951	2,243
Snowdonia	1951	2,171
Dartmoor	1951	945
Pembrokeshire Coast	1952	1,432
North York Moors	1952	583
Yorkshire Dales	1954	1,760
Exmoor	1954	686
Northumberland	1956	1,031
Brecon Beacons	1957	1,344

*Source: Countryside Commission **Annual Report 1988–89***

They are not fossilized landscapes. Over a quarter of a million people live in the parks. Overall, just 17 per cent of the park area is in public ownership, including 7.5 per cent owned by the Forestry Commission and 5.8 per cent owned by the National Trust. Furthermore, not all of the public owners hold public amenity to the fore; just over three per cent of the park area, for example, is owned by the Ministry of Defence. The National Park Authorities, the bodies charged with administering the parks, own a mere 0.6 per cent; another 0.08 per cent is leased to and managed by them.

The extent of public ownership, and the dominant landholders, vary between the parks. As much as 46 per cent of Dartmoor and 44 per cent of the Northumberland National Park are in public ownership, compared with only 12 per cent of the Pembrokeshire Coast and a mere two per cent of the Yorkshire Dales (Figure 4.2). In Dartmoor the dominant public landowner is the Duchy of Cornwall; there are also significant Ministry of Defence holdings, together with substantial areas of Duchy of Cornwall land leased to the MOD. In Northumberland National Park the Ministry owns over half the publicly owned area. Substantial tracts of Snowdonia are owned by the Forestry Commission and the Central Electricity Generating Board. Ironically, at the very time when government and public opinion are increasingly sympathetic to 'green' issues, the government is privatizing utilities which presently own substantial National Park resources, notably the water industry and electricity; as yet the consequences for conservation and public access are unclear, but the likelihood must be that in some instances land will be sold off or turned to more profitable uses than amenity.

Figure 4.1   National Parks and Heritage Coasts in England and Wales

State ownership of the land in the National Parks was never a realistic possibility; hence the reliance on planning designation rather than direct ownership. However, as *Shoard (1987)* pointed out, the inherent weakness from the start was that two of the major forces for change in the countryside — farming and forestry — are substantially exempt from planning control. As the *Lake District National Park Authority (1990, p.3)* put it:

Figure 4.2 Land ownership in National Parks

	Public land as % of park area
Dartmoor	46
Northumberland	44
Lake District	40
Peak District	26
Brecon Beacons	24
Snowdonia	23
North York Moors	22
Exmoor	20
Pembrokeshire Coast	12
Yorkshire Dales	2

Source: Data from MacEwen and MacEwen 1987, Fig. 15, pp 106-7

The Parks contain the country's best and most distinctive land-scapes . . . . . which are both sensitive to change and vulnerable to society's activities. Yet society has not provided National Park Authorities with the powers and resources adequately to protect the Parks. Specific powers and resources have been made available to defend other lands, such as SSSIs and NNRs . . . . . while National Parks are left to be managed with broadly the same powers and controls available to any local planning authority in the remaining 90 per cent of England and Wales.

From the outset the Lake District and the Peak District were given their own independent planning boards. Thereafter, however, the government acceded to pressure from the county councils, and set up National Park Authorities which were committees of the constituent counties covered by the park areas. Inevitably, local control of this kind meant that local needs took precedence over the national interest. Furthermore, little finance was available for running the parks, as costs had to be borne entirely by the local rates.

With the reorganization of local government in 1974 the administration of National Parks was changed. Each park was given a National Park Authority, a specially constituted executive committee or board with greater planning powers, together with an executive staff headed by a National Park Officer. Eight parks are administered by committees of the county councils. Four of them straddle country boundaries. In three of these, one of the constituent county councils acts as the 'lead' authority, with the others represented as members; in the fourth, the Brecon Beacons, there is a joint committee of the four constituent counties. The other two parks have the Peak Park Joint Planning Board and the Lake District Special Planning Board, which are independent authorities in their own right. They can settle their own budgets, and levy a rate by precepting their constituent local authorities, appoint their own staff, use or decline the services of local authority officers, buy land, and enter into management agreements of their choosing. The committees have much less autonomy than the boards: planning policies are defined by the county council(s), and the counties choose whether or not to delegate to the park authorities functions such as preparing local plans, conserving areas of historic interest, rights of way reviews, footpath maintenance, and the making of management agreements. The committees, like the boards, do exercise development control.

Two-thirds of the members of the Authorities are appointed by the constituent local authorities, and one-third by the Secretary of State for the Environment (Secretary of State for Wales for the Welsh parks). Three-quarters of the administrative costs of the parks, together with funding for specific projects, are borne nationally; the remaining 25 per cent is met from local authority sources. Even so, resources must be viewed in perspective: in 1987–88 the ten National Parks received a combined government grant of £9.8 million; in the same year a single facility, the Royal Opera House, Covent Garden, received £13.4 million. The Council for the Protection of Rural England (1990) has called for a quintupling of resources for the Parks by the mid 1990s.

Each National Park Authority was required to produce a National Park Plan by 1977 to provide a framework for land management and the organization and provision of services and facilities. The early plans have since been reviewed, and some revisions have been published (eg Lake District National Park Authority 1986) or drafts for consultation (eg Peak Park Joint Planning Board 1988) have been issued.

The plans strive to foster integrated land management for multiple use. Detailed approaches and concerns vary from park to park, but all reiterate the twin statutory purposes of recreation and conservation, and all have regard to the needs of agriculture and forestry, and to the economic and social interests of rural areas. As the *Countryside Commission (1987e, p.5)* stressed:

> The co-operation of local people and landowners is vital to protect the parks. It is their work and craftsmanship, from generation to generation, which has created and preserved much of the character of the national parks. It is essential to preserve viable local communities so that they can continue this stewardship.

In integrating national and local needs, and in combining environmental, social and economic concerns, the National Park Plans form a model for rural development generally, as *Greenprints for the countryside (MacEwen and MacEwen 1987)*.

Each National Park Authority is responsible for development control in its area, and for dealing with planning applications, minerals applications, and proposals to alter listed buildings. Since 1986 they must also be consulted on any plans for farm buildings and farm or forest roads. Development control is intended to be stricter in the National Parks than in the undesignated countryside. The park authorities can offer grants to farmers and landowners to achieve conservation aims, and can negotiate voluntary management agreements to conserve moorland, hay meadows and other threatened habitats. Several offer an

Upland Management Service to carry out work such as tree planting, woodland management, and projects to improve access for visitors. They also advise on restoring historic buildings and field monuments, and can help to fund restoration. Most have responsibility for the public paths network within their areas, and many have entered into access agreements with landowners to allow public access, subject to certain conditions and to supervision by the park ranger service. National Park Authorities have powers to provide wardens, rangers, recreation provisions such as car park and picnic sites, information services and visitor centres, and several run residential study centres. In addition, some provide camping sites, youth hostels, cycle hire schemes, and public transport services to facilitate public access. To cover this range of work most park authorities include a planning section, an estate management or upland management service, a ranger or warden service, an information section to provide interpretative services and youth and schools liaison work, and an administrative division.

Financial resources vary greatly from park to park, partly for reason of historical accident, and partly depending on the degree of autonomy of the park authority in bidding for money and spending it. The Peak District and Lake District enjoy much greater resources (but endure much greater pressures) than the other parks. Spending priorities also vary (Figure 4.3). Conservation, recreation and administration each consume around a quarter of the spending, with interpretation and information taking a further sixth. Conservation, though, gains around a third in the Peak District, Exmoor and Dartmoor but less than a fifth in the Brecon Beacons, Pembrokeshire Coast and Snowdonia. Recreation fares best, in proportional terms, in the Pembrokeshire Coast, Snowdonia and Yorkshire Dales, and worst in Exmoor and the Brecon Beacons. Support to the local community is a minor item in all ten parks, accounting for just two per cent of spending overall, and at most just under four per cent, in Dartmoor.

When the role of the parks was first defined, conservation and recreation were seen as equally important and mutually compatible. As the range and volume of recreational uses burgeoned, however, stresses between the two purposes became evident. The National Park Policies Review Committee (Sandford Committee) set up in 1971, therefore advised that where there was direct and irreconcilable conflict between landscape conservation and recreation provision, the former should take priority and recreation should take second place.

Recreation, however, is far from being the only threat to National Park landscapes. They have been far from sacrosanct in terms of other development, and indeed the state itself has proved not to be the staunchest guardian of amenity. *MacEwen and MacEwen (1982)* concluded that in almost every case where pressures for major change had been brought to bear, the National Park purpose had been over-ridden. A few examples suffice. Ministry of Defence use of Dartmoor and Northumberland has already been mentioned. Of course, military use long predates the designation of the Parks, but demands for additional

Figure 4.3 Total net expenditure in National Parks 1987-8

% of total

	All	Brecon Beacons	Dartmoor	Exmoor	Lake District	Northum-berland	North York Moors	Peak District	Pembs. Coast	Snowdonia	Yorks. Dales
Conservation	25.4	19.8	30.4	32.6	22.7	21.3	29.7	35.7	13.4	16.8	26.2
Town and country planning	8.1	7.4	4.2	6.2	17.5	1.4	6.2	7.6	8.5	7.8	7.8
Interpretation and information	16.9	25.6	12.0	19.3	19.3	28.2	17.3	13.1	15.3	17.3	20.2
Recreation	23.5	15.8	23.4	19.9	21.9	21.8	23.5	23.9	33.1	28.3	27.3
Support to local community	1.9	2.4	3.9	2.5	2.4	-	0.6	3.0	1.1	0.8	0.9
Management and administration	24.1	29.0	26.2	19.4	19.7	27.3	31.0	17.4	28.6	29.0	33.8

Source: Data from Countryside Commission 1987e p.18.

training areas continue, as do complaints about damage to habitats and ancient monuments, unsightly structures, noise, low-flying aircraft and access restrictions. The Pembrokeshire Coast has its oil port and massive refineries at Milford Haven. Road improvements pose another threat: in 1983–84, after lengthy consideration of various alternatives, the Okehampton by-pass on the A30 trunk road in Devon was routed through the Dartmoor National Park. Quarrying and mining have also gained ground as many of the National Parks contain rich deposits of limestone, tungsten, china clay, gold, copper, coal and other minerals. Notable developments include the extraction of limestone in the Peak District and Yorkshire Dales, and potash in the North York Moors.

The North York Moors also contain one of the more notorious National Park oddities, the ballistic missile early warning station at Fylingdales, high on the open moor. This particular structure is shortly due for a change of shape: the giant triple white 'golf balls' of the present station are to be replaced with a single pyramidal structure. Alternative sites have not been seriously considered. Controversy also raged over the decision taken in 1959 to site the Trawsfynydd Nuclear Power Station and its associated jungle of pylons and transmission lines in Snowdonia. Ironically, the very quality of remoteness of the area which was instrumental in the decision to designate the park in the first place was used as an argument confirming its suitability as a location for the power station. The existing lake supplies the 35 million gallons of cooling water needed every hour. Such an industrial intrusion is all the more paradoxical in view of the exclusion from the Park of the town which lies at its geographical centre. The slate mining town of Blaenau Ffestiniog, whose slate caverns at Llechwedd and Gloddfa Ganol are now a significant recreational attraction, was explicitly omitted from the Park as it was deemed too unattractive to include. Overall, then, *MacEwen and MacEwen (1982, p.28)* concluded that 'Development control was far more successful in stopping the small man doing a small thing than in controlling the big private or statutory developers'. Furthermore, according to the findings of *Blacksell and Gilg (1981)*, development control has not been significantly more successful in the National Parks than outside them.

At national level responsibility for supporting and promoting the work of the National Parks lies with the Countryside Commission. It has the power to designate further parks, and review the boundaries of existing ones, subject to confirmation by the Secretary of State for the Environment or for Wales. It advises on the appointment of members to the National Park Authorities, and acts as broker between the authorities and the government, advising the first on the level of grant support that they should seek and the second on the level they should give. The Commission advises individual park authorities on the National Park plans and on controversial development proposals. Its commitment to National Parks was renewed in 1987 with the publication of a ten point manifesto for the next five years *(Countryside Commission 1987f)*, with the following goals:

1 To seek full recognition for National Parks in public policy for farming, forestry and planning, and special treatment for the Parks in policies for defence, roads, energy, water and minerals.

2 To press for adequate resources for National Parks, both through direct funding and through other policy avenues, including farming.

3 To increase public awareness of, and involvement with, the National Parks.

4 To seek a status equivalent to National Parks for the New Forest and the Broads. The former has since been given a non-statutory Heritage Area Committee. The latter formally achieved status equivalent to a National Park in 1989.

5 To develop international links, promoting recognition of the parks as protected landscapes.

6 To improve arrangements for conservation work, including partnerships between the National Park Authorities, the Nature Conservancy Council and other agencies.

7 To create partnerships with local communities, recognizing that 'the local community, and especially farmers and landowners who may not benefit directly . . . . . manage the great majority of the land in the parks and the nation at large must ensure that they are supported in their vital work of stewardship of these traditional landscapes' *(Countryside Commission 1987f, p.3)*. Proposals included experiments to integrate conservation, recreation and rural development, and to foster enterprise among the community at large.

8 To encourage voluntary action to support National Parks, involving national voluntary organizations and creating a base of local support from people living in and near the parks.

9 To strengthen the links *between* the National Parks to encourage them to share experience, identify common needs (eg for training) and present a unified view.

10 To defend the integrity of the parks, opposing inappropriate developments and anticipating and resisting other threats such as water pollution.

At a conference to mark the fortieth anniversary of the 1949 Act, the Countryside Commission launched a major review of the means by which National Park purposes are pursued. The consultation document for the review defines the key issue as:

Whether the current way in which the national parks system works, including the powers and resources available to the National Park Authorities and the priority these are given by decision makers at all levels, adequately reflects the growing value that the community at large attaches to the national parks — especially to their conservation importance. *(Countryside Commission 1989d, p.1)*.

With regard to recreation, the consultation document notes the potential for conflict with the conservation function, and the vastly increased pressure on the parks brought about by mass car ownership, better road access and improved living standards. The parks play host to nearly a hundred million visits per year. Usage of individual parks ranges from around a million visitor-days per year in Northumberland and Exmoor to 16–20 million each in the Peak District and Lake District *(MacEwen and MacEwen 1987)*. These variations clearly reflect catchment populations, with the Peak having nearly 17 million people within an hour's drive.

MacEwen and MacEwen identify two trends in recent National Park policy for recreation, which echo the increasing polarization of society into rich and poor. The first is to work with the tourist boards in seeking to offer up-market holidays. The second, less obvious, trend is to encourage the provision of low-cost accommodation for hikers and campers, in the form of field barn conversions ('bunkhouse barns'), farm tourism and bed and breakfast. By their nature, these latter schemes are low key and widely scattered. The former are more evident, none more so than the Langdale centre in the Lake District, a prestigious time-share development with a hotel, pub, restaurant and leisure centre, as well as access to lake and countryside. As *MacEwen and MacEwen (1987, pp.85–86)* asked:

> Is it really in the spirit of the national park to be offering 'a holiday in the Caribbean, a tropical dream come true' where you can 'sip your drinks under the palm trees?' And what about the 'private lake frontage with four acres of land on the shores of nearby Coniston Water' in a park where the public has very limited access to the lake sides, and it is the policy of the park authority to try to increase it?

The National Parks Review Panel raised the same issue, and went on to suggest that the tourist industry might justifiably be expected to help pay the way for maintaining the environmental and scenic quality on which it depends:

> National parks are . . . . . under great pressure to admit large-scale tourist and related developments (eg time share schemes, holiday villages, conference centres, marinas and ski slopes). These bring jobs and make use of the scenic appeal of the area, but it is questionable whether they represent the kind of 'green' tourism for which the national parks as well suited. Further, the parks lack the means to 'capture' some of the income that tourism brings to help them protect and manage the landscape resources upon which the tourist industry depends. It would cost, for example, some £2 million annually to keep the Lake District footpaths in good shape, and there is a case that the tourist industry should help to meet that sum. *(Countryside Commission 1989d, p.3)*.

The *Council for National Parks (1990, p.5)* is in no doubt that many forms of recreation should be forced to find a home outside the National Parks: the parks 'are in danger of trying to accommodate too much development and too many types of activity, for example motor sports and tourism attractions . . . . . Park Authorities should encourage only the distinctive types of recreation which draw inspiration from the special environmental qualities of the Parks'. It went on to state *(p.7)* that 'the enjoyment duty should refer more specifically to quiet, non-motorised, open-air recreation' and that *(p.26)* 'All enjoyment promoted by National Parks should have at its root the spiritual fulfilment people experience in wilder countryside. The Parks are places for contemplative withdrawal, in which people can draw inspiration from and explore their relationship with nature and regain a sense of perspective'. Other forms of recreation should be rejected *(p.28)*: 'Off-road, air-borne and water-based motorised recreational activities are inappropriate in National Parks and should not be allowed . . . . . the range and volume of motorised recreational pursuits, from jet-skis to four-wheel drive caravanning will continue to increase. Decisive exclusion from National Parks is essential'.

Many might agree, but there is little justification for blanket policies or bland refusal. While respecting the overriding park purpose and the need to resist inappropriate intrusions, a more positive approach would consider the significance and suitability of specific sites for specific activities, and the availability of alternative sites outside the National Parks.

The Broads

In 1989 The Broads were given the status, though not the name, of National Park. Indeed, the Broads Authority, established under the *1988 Norfolk and Suffolk Broads Act,* has been granted some additional powers that the National Park Authorities do not share. The Countryside Commission first proposed the designation of a National Park in 1976, by which time the Broads had suffered considerable ecological deterioration due mainly to water pollution in the form of phosphate enrichment from domestic sewage and farm effluent, and from unmanaged recreational use. A National Park, however, was neither the appropriate mechanism, nor welcomed by local interests. It would have had little control over such vital matters as water purity, water management, land drainage, and farming. Furthermore, the district councils (then) would have had no statutory right of membership of the authority; understandably they resisted. Faced with public pressure to respond to the environmental crisis, however, they proposed the creation of a Broads Authority as a joint planning committee of the local authorities, with the Countryside Commission and the navigation and water authorities also represented.

The Authority came into being in 1978, funded by the local authorities and the Countryside Commission. Its planning powers were confined to those delegated to it by the local authorities. The experiment worked, generating a successful programme of research, management and public relations. The most significant achievement was the resolution of the Halvergate Marshes crisis referred to in Chapter 1. The case for a more autonomous authority was clear. The Countryside Commission concluded that a national park was not the appropriate designation, but that legislation be prepared to create a permanent authority with the requisite remit and resources.

The *Norfolk and Suffolk Broads Act* was duly passed. The statutory Broads Authority which came into being in 1989 has the same autonomy as a National Park Board in matters of finance, policy and administration, and receives the standard 75 per cent grant from central government. It has no special powers, however, to control damaging farm or land drainage operations. The Authority's membership is substantially larger and more widely representative than the National Park Authorities: there are 35 members, comprising a majority from the local authorities, two each from the water and navigation authorities, and approximately one-third appointed variously by the Secretary of State for the Environment and the Countryside Commission. Boating, angling, tourism and voluntary conservation bodies are all represented.

The Broads, as designated, comprise 28,000 hectares whose open country is mainly water, and whose shape is not so much an area as a succession of interconnecting linear parks. Its main recreational activities are boating, angling and nature study. It contains the largest hire-boat fleet in Europe. The Broads Authority's most pressing priority is not, therefore to develop recreation, but to improve and conserve the environment, and provide interpretative services to foster public awareness of, and support for, environmental issues. Compared with the National Parks, therefore, the Broads Authority has to date apportioned a far greater share of its expenditure to conservation, including the restoration of water quality and repairing eroded river banks and bankside vegetation.

Areas of Outstanding Natural Beauty

The provisions of the *1949 National Parks and Access to the Countryside Act* were not restricted to a single form of designation. Outside the National Parks, Section 87 of the Act provided that the National Parks Commission (and now the Countryside Commission) may designate Areas of Outstanding Natural Beauty (AsONB) in smaller areas whose scenic quality was worthy of equivalent protection. The origins of the provision pre-dated the Act. In proposing areas for national park status in 1945, John Dower added 34 'Other Amenity Areas' which he felt needed special treatment to safeguard their landscape beauty, farming use and wildlife, and to increase their facilities for open air recreation. Two years later, the Hobhouse Committee adopted this proposal and recommended the designation of 52 Conservation Areas, to be administered by local authorities, with advice and finance from the National Parks Commission. The Act adopted instead the title Areas of Outstanding Natural Beauty, and made somewhat paradoxical provision for recreation: while the promotion of public enjoyment was specifically excluded from the role of AsONB, the need to secure adequate public access for open air recreation was given special emphasis. Further provisions of the Act allowed local authorities to make bylaws, subject to consultation with the Commission, to prevent damage and ensure good behaviour in AsONB, and to appoint wardens for such areas. The *Countryside Commission (1989e)* recently reaffirmed the more modest recreational role of the AsONB — and acknowledged their limited penetration of the public consciousness:

In contrast . . . . . (to National Parks) . . . . . AONBs have a much lower profile. Of course, many of their areas are popular with visitors. But, because of their fragile natural beauty or the vulnerability of traditional farming, conservation is the primary aim of AONBs, rather than their active promotion for public enjoyment. In fact, some people don't even know they live in one!

Definition and delimitation are inevitably difficult:

> There has to be compromise and pragmatism in drawing a boundary.....
> Another.....problem is that of the 'buffer zone'; this may be visual or
> practical..... A panoramic view from a ridge or summit warrants some
> form of protection, and there may be a case for protecting the view from the
> plain to the hill, but it would be unrealistic to designate as far as the eye can
> see from every designated eminence. *(Himsworth 1980, p.19)*

Attracting national status to local landscapes appealed to local pride and helped to generate a continuing local authority response. The 38th and largest AONB was designated in 1988 in the North Pennines, bringing the total AONB area to 19,287 sq. kilometres, just under 13 per cent of the land area of England and Wales *(Countryside Commission 1989f)*. Table 4.2 shows the continuing creation of AsONB since the mid 1950s.

The designated areas vary in size, shape and character. The largest include the North Wessex Downs (1,738 sq. kilometres), the smallest Dedham Vale in the Constable country of Suffolk (57 sq. kilometres, later extended to 72 sq. kilometres). Some are coastal (eg Gower, Solway Coast, and South Hampshire), some are wild moorland (eg Forest of Bowland), some are richly farmed, (eg Cotswolds). Not all derive their attractiveness wholly from natural beauty: towns and villages are a vital part of the character of the Cotswolds, castles an important element of the Northumberland coast, and derelict tin mines, the desecration of an earlier age, an essential symbol of the Cornish Coast. Many are enhanced by legend and literature, such as Hardy's Wessex, Housman's Shropshire Hills, and the Cornwall of Arthurian legend.

Demand for recreational use varies with location. Many AsONB, such as the North and South Downs and Cannock Chase, are much closer than the National Parks to large centres of population, and therefore subject to greater pressures. Some are in popular holiday areas, such as South Devon and the Wye Valley.

Responsibility for managing AsONB rests with local authorities and the normal planning system. Local approaches vary considerably, and are complicated by the fact that most AsONB extend beyond the boundaries of a single authority. In order to promote consistent policies and integrated management, the Countryside Commission encourages the formation of Joint Advisory Committees including representatives of the constituent local authorities, farmers, residents and conservation bodies. It also recommends appointing AONB officers to co-ordinate practice, and the preparation of Statements of Intent as planning strategies.

Table 4.2   Areas of Outstanding Natural Beauty

	Date of Confirmation	Area (sq. km)
Gower	1956	189
Quantock Hills	1957	99
Lleyn	1957	155
Northumberland Coast	1958	129
Surrey Hills	1958	414
Cannock Chase	1958	68
Shropshire Hills	1959	777
Dorset	1959	1,036
Malvern Hills	1959	104
Cornwall	1959	932
— extension	1983	25
North Devon	1960	171
South Devon	1960	332
East Hampshire	1962	391
East Devon	1963	267
Isle of Wight	1963	189
Chichester Harbour	1964	75
Forest of Bowland	1964	803
Solway Coast	1964	107
Chilterns	1965	800
Sussex Downs	1966	981
Cotswolds	1966	1,507
Anglesey	1967	215
South Hampshire Coast	1967	78
Norfolk Coast	1968	450
Kent Downs	1968	845
Suffolk Coasts and Heaths	1970	391
Dedham Vale	1970	57
— extension	1978	15
Wye Valley	1971	325
North Wessex Downs	1972	1,738
Mendip Hills	1972	202
Arnside and Silverdale	1972	75
Lincolnshire Wolds	1973	560
Isles of Scilly	1976	16
High Weald	1983	1,450
Cranborne Chase and West Wiltshire Downs	1983	960
Clwydian Range	1985	156
Howardian Hills	1987	205
North Pennines	1988	1,998

*Source: Countryside Commission **Annual Report 1988–89***

A review of the effectiveness of AONB designation a decade ago concluded that there had been significant achievements and widespread satisfaction with AsONB among the various interest groups *(Himsworth 1980)*. There was room for improvement too, including with regard to recreation, which should be 'accepted as a proper function . . . . . of AONBs' *(Himsworth 1980, p.4)*. Specific reference was made to the need for local authorities to properly define, signpost and maintain public paths, and consider whether there was a case for increased public access to open country within AsONB. They were encouraged to elicit the support of landowners for permissive access, without the necessity of formal agreements. Where AsONB offered physical conditions suited to more specialized forms of recreation, the importance of reconciling use with the needs of farming and conservation was stressed, and it was recommended that such recreation be encouraged within the same limits as the Sandford principle for National Parks. Regarding tourism, the review welcomed existing levels of promotion of AsONB by the tourist authorities, and urged that the provisions of the 1949 Act regarding interpretative services in National Parks be extended also to the AsONB.

Heritage Coasts

For long the recreational impact on the coast was confined to the resort towns reached by the railways. Mass mobility, though, in the post-war years, brought an upsurge in use, and a wider spatial impact extending to the remoter, undeveloped coastline. In 1963 the Ministry of Housing and Local Government asked local authorities to undertake special studies of their coastal areas, to identify areas for protection and development. Efforts varied from place to place, but the National Parks Commission injected new impetus with the holding of nine regional Coastal Conferences in 1966 and 1967. The ensuing reports *(National Parks Commission 1967a – d, 1968a–e)* brought together new and important data on coastal resources and usage, and allowed a national view to be taken. The *National Parks Commission (1969a, 1969b)* published two further topic studies, one on recreation and holidays, the other on conservation. The newly formed Countryside Commission translated diagnosis into planning and management principles for the coast in two further reports *(1970a, 1970b)*.

As with the countryside, however, direct action is impeded by lack of ownership. The acquisition policy of the National Trust, in the form of Enterprise Neptune, has already been referred to. By contrast, public sector authorities have had to rely largely on arm's length influence, persuading and encouraging coastal landowners to co-operate in plans to secure environmental protection and public enjoyment. Much of the coast was already designated as National Nature Reserve, National Park or Area of Outstanding Natural Beauty. As a direct outcome of the conferences of the 1960s, a new form of special status specific to the coast was defined. Local authorities were invited to put forward proposals for stretches of coastline to be designated by the Countryside Commission as Heritage Coast *(Countryside Commission 1970a, 1970b)*. The latter report identified 34 potential areas for designation, amounting to 1,175 kilometres of coastline. To be considered for designation an area of coastline had to be of exceptional scenic quality, over a mile long, substantially undeveloped, and contain features of special significance, whether natural or man-made. Policies for such areas were set out later in the Department of the Environment Circular *The planning of the undeveloped coast (DOE 1972)*. The Secretary of State supported the idea of designation, but declined to make it a national statutory function; instead the concept was to be adopted and implemented by local authorities. Stated objectives for Heritage Coasts were to conserve natural coastal scenery and to facilitate and enhance its enjoyment by the public. The Circular stressed that local authorities should not devise policies which were purely protective and restrictive. Positive management was essential in order to direct activities to appropriate areas, and authorities should prepare management plans in consultation with the Countryside Commission.

To provide practical experience and guidance in Heritage Coast management and to generate enthusiasm for the concept, the Countryside Commission funded three pilot projects in Glamorgan, Suffolk and Dorset (Purbeck). Each area appointed a Heritage Coast Officer, employed by the relevant county council but funded largely (90 per cent) by the Commission. Wardens were also appointed. The Heritage Coast Officers had a crucial co-ordinating role, in working with the constituent local authorities within their area, and with landowners and local user groups. They also had the autonomy and a modest budget to carry out practical land management tasks. Each area convened a Heritage Coast Committee, including representatives of county and district councils, parish councils, naturalists, ramblers, local history groups, residents, and other interest groups. After periods of public consultation management plans were published, and considerable success was achieved in implementing them. *Williams and Howden (1979)*, writing of the Glamorgan experiment, attributed this to the ability to 'incorporate ground level management into the planning process, so that residents and visitors alike can see tangible benefits to the area'. These included the removal of eyesores, clearing footpaths, repairing stiles, dry stone walls and fences, controlling soil and sand erosion, small scale planting, improved protection for coastal flora and nesting sea birds, litter control, traffic management, new picnic sites, signposting, and providing information and interpretative services. Considerable success was achieved also in harnessing the energies of local voluntary organizations to undertake conservation tasks. All three experimental programmes were continued beyond the pilot phase by their respective local authorities.

The Countryside Commission's role in relation to Heritage Coasts is to work with local authorities to identify and define suitable areas of coast, advise them on effective planning approaches and management plans; and give grants towards staff and schemes to promote conservation or public enjoyment.

Forty one Heritage Coasts amounting to 1,396 kilometres have now been defined, including the original 34. Individual Heritage Coasts range from a mere 4 kilometres (Trevose Head) to over 90 kilometres

Table 4.3   Heritage Coasts

	Date defined	Length (kms)
Completely defined		
Sussex	1973	13
Isles of Scilly	1974	64
North Norfolk	1975	63
Suffolk	1979	56
North Yorkshire and Cleveland	1981	55
Purbeck	1981	52
West Dorset	1984	40
East Devon	1984	28
Hartland, Cornwall	1986	11
Pentire – Point – Widemouth	1986	54
Trevose Head	1986	4
St. Agnes	1986	11
Godrevy – Portreath	1986	10
Penwith	1986	55
The Lizard	1986	28
The Roseland	1986	54
Gribbin Head – Polperro	1986	24
Rame Head	1986	8
South Devon	1986	74
Spurn	1988	18
Tennyson	1988	35
Hamstead	1988	11
Laterally defined		
North Northumberland	1973	93
Gower	1973	55
Glamorgan	1973	22
North Anglesey	1973	29
Holyhead Mountain	1973	13
Aberffraw Bay	1973	8
Great Orme	1974	7
Lleyn	1974	88
South Pembrokeshire	1974	66
Marloes and Dale	1974	43
St. Brides Bay	1974	8
St. David's Peninsula	1974	82
Dinas Head	1974	18
St. Dogmael's and Moylgrove	1974	23
South Foreland	1975	7
Dover – Folkestone	1975	7
Flamborough Head	1979	19
Ceredigion Coast	1982	34
St. Bees Head	1989	6

*Source: Countryside Commission **Annual Report 1988–89***

(North Northumberland). Details are shown in Table 4.3 and in Figure 4.1. Heritage Coasts which are 'laterally defined' are defined in linear terms only; those described as 'completely defined' have a landward boundary too. The former are expected to work towards complete definition as their management plans evolve. Over a decade into the programme, however, three-fifths of the Heritage Coasts then in existence had no management planning under way and few local authorities were adopting the proactive management stance enjoined upon them in the 1972 Circular: 'Many local authorities see Heritage Coasts as another development control tool rather than an opportunity to provide local leadership and land management' *(Cullen 1982, p.viii)*.

The rights of way system

Legal rights of way and their complex origins were traced briefly in Chapter 1, but the nature of the resource warrants fuller treatment. At the pinnacle of the network are the National Trails, until the late 1980s more prosaically labelled Long Distance Footpaths and provided for under the *1949 National Parks and Access to the Countryside Act*. The aim was to provide a national system of long distance routes that would take the user through the finest upland and coastal scenery of England and Wales. The paths were not completely new routes opening up previously inaccessible areas, but formed primarily by linking existing rights of way. Hence 85 per cent of the South West Peninsula Coast Path is made up of pre-existing rights of way, as are three-quarters of the North Downs Way and over 90 per cent of the Ridgeway *(Shoard 1987)*. Funding was to be provided nationally, and the National Parks Commission was charged with designating the routes. Implementation and management were to be local responsibilities. The current network, amounting to 2,800 kilometres, is shown in Figure 4.3 and detailed in Table 4.4.

The span of years between confirmation and completion is significant, for this was to be a field in which intent was far simpler than implementation. The complication lay in the extent of consultation necessary to achieve acceptance of the concept, and acceptable routes on the ground, over such long distances. Establishing the Offa's Dyke route, for example, entailed negotiations with as many as 36 local authorities, and countless individual landowners. The extent of local resistance sometimes led to defeat. The proposed Cambrian Way route across the mountains of central Wales met with such overwhelming opposition from landowners, farmers and local authorities that, after a ten year struggle to establish it, plans were finally dropped in 1982.

The 1949 Act did not restrict its footpath provisions to the pinnacle of the system. It required county councils, as highway authorities, to survey their areas and prepare definitive maps of public rights of way, encompassing footpaths, bridleways and 'roads used as public paths'. Many authorities were ill-resourced, and some were ill-disposed to do this. Thirty years later the *Ramblers' Association (1980, p.4)* could claim that 'many definitive maps are incomplete and out-of-date. There are still many rights of way in existence that are not recorded on the maps'. However, the appearance of 'public paths' on Ordnance Survey maps marks significant progress.

Table 4.4 National Trails

	Report approved	Officially opened	Length (kms)
Existing			
Pennine Way	1951	1965	402
Cleveland Way	1965	1969	150
Pembrokeshire Coast Path	1953	1970	299
Offa's Dyke Path	1963	1971	270
South Downs Way	1963	1972	129
extension	1988		42
South West Coast Path:			
Cornwall – North	1952	1973	431
Cornwall – South	1954	1973	
South Devon	1959	1974	155
Somerset and North Devon	1961	1978	168
Dorset	1963	1974	116
Ridgeway	1972	1973	137
North Downs Way	1969	1978	227
Wolds Way	1977	1982	127
Peddars Way and Norfolk Coast Path	1982	1986	150
			2,803
Proposed			
Thames Path			262
Hadrian's Wall Path			117
Pennine Bridleway			402
Shortlisted for consideration			
Coast to Coast walk			306
Viking Way			225
Mercian Way			209
Ribble Way			68
Dales Way			129
Glyndwr's Way			193
Pembrokeshire Coast Path extension			97
Cotswold Way			161
Ridgeway extension			161

Source: Countryside Commission leaflets

The total network is considerable — 193,000 kilometres in England and Wales. Existence alone, though, is no guarantee of ease of use. The *1968 Countryside Act* required that highway authorities signpost public paths where they leave metalled roads. *Shoard (1987)* cites many examples of defaulting authorities. In Gloucestershire in 1981, for example, as many as 90 per cent of paths lacked signposts at the points where they left the roads, and two of the eleven signposts that had been provided pointed in the wrong direction!

While local authorities bear the main responsibility of defining and maintaining the paths network, the Countryside Commission can assist and cajole. The *1974 Local Government Act* gave the Commission powers to grant-aid footpath work generally, not just the long distance routes, and the Commission has responded vigorously. Schemes include the grant-aiding of footpath officers to develop programmes of signposting, waymarking, path restoration and guided walks.

Definition is one thing; supporting a viable system is quite another. Having come into being for other reasons, many public rights of way are neither attractive not convenient for the recreational user, and no amount of effort and expenditure would change that. Others are plainly inconvenient to present day farmers and landowners. New rights of way can be created by means of negotiation or compulsory purchase, and existing ones may be re-routed, or extinguished if not needed for public use. Approximately 1,500 proposals each year are made to alter the network — more, it must be said, for closure or diversion than for creation of new paths. The outcome is 'far from being an ideal pattern of recreation routes. It is the result of historical accident modified by the muscle of landowners' *(Shoard 1987, p.341)*.

While evidence of neglect abounds, there are also instances of care and creativity. In 1980 South Yorkshire Metropolitan County Council (abolished along with the other metropolitan counties in 1986) pioneered a scheme entitled Adopt-A-Path. Leaflets distributed to local people invited them to adopt one local path, walk it at least every few weeks, and report any problems or obstructions to the Council. Each participant was given a round route of about five or six kilometres as 'his' or 'her' path, and was issued with a copy of the definitive map for the county. Within three years 500 people or groups had joined the scheme, and three-quarters of the county's paths had been adopted. Importantly, the Council was conscientious in keeping its side of the bargain: reported difficulties were acted upon by serving notice to landowners to put right the problems caused and, as a last resort, by prosecuting them for wilful obstruction.

In line with its growing concern for access to the wider countryside, the Countryside Commission put forward proposals for consultation in 1988 for planning and developing the rights of way system in future. A policy statement produced a year later *(Countryside Commission 1989g)* defined four categories of paths, each with a distinctive role to play:

1 *Parish paths and community paths*
These must be signposted from the road and kept open, but should not be actively promoted; rather their role is to provide for people seeking the quiet beauty of the countryside and wanting to find their own way. They were also seen as providing a reservoir of paths to meet new uses in the future. Emphasis is placed on local management, and parish councils and community councils are encouraged to set up adopt-a-path schemes to inspect them regularly.

2 *Local walks and rides*
These are envisaged as catering for the largest sector of demand, for easily accessible walking, riding and cycling. They should be signposted and waymarked, and promoted for local use among residents and visitors, offering opportunities for a day out. They should be easy to reach and recognize, with appropriate car parking and public transport links. They should offer a circular route and preferably a network of routes, to give local people a choice of distance and destinations. They should be easy to use by all users, including those with little experience of the countryside, the elderly and the disabled. They should be promoted by means of leaflets and guides, both to local people and through tourist information centres. Management is essentially a local authority responsibility, ideally involving landowners, farmers and local user groups, but the Countryside Commission will give particular support to paths close to major centres of demand, and to those which link with country parks, other recreation areas, and National Trails.

3 *Regional routes*
These are to be longer, named routes offering the possibility of journeying for more than a day. They might follow a particular theme, and offer tourism potential. They should be linked to other Local Paths or National Trails, and should be planned with accommodation needs in mind.

4 *National Trails*
These were defined as 'Paths that have the character and quality to be truly national: allowing an extensive journey on foot, horseback or bicycle and capable of attracting tourist use from home and abroad' *(Countryside Commission 1989g, p. 7)*. Three-quarters of the maintenance costs are met by the Countryside Commission. Trails might be established in lowland or upland areas. They must offer an adequate length of route, generally avoiding roads; great scenic attraction which will encourage people to undertake long distance journeys; evidence of potential demand; sufficient existing rights of way; tourism potential; and local authority support. Existing Long Distance Paths are now subsumed under the new title. However, in creating new National Trails, the Countryside Commission only intends to use the formal legal procedure for designation if necessary. Additional trails planned are listed in Table 4.4 and located in Fig. 4.4.

As a sequel to its policy document, the Countryside Commission published a statement on the condition of rights of way, and a related management agenda. A rights of way survey took place in 1988, with 1,000 volunteers walking, riding or cycling all rights of way in 131 randomly selected five by five kilometres grid squares throughout England and Wales. Detailed information was recorded for each path 'link', defined as a stretch of path between junctions with another right of way or road. In total 10,000 links (4,700 kilometres) were surveyed. Indeed, the extent of rights of way in the sample areas led to a revised estimate of the total for the country as a whole, now put at 255,000 kilometres.

Figure 4.4   National Trails

In the Commission's survey, under a third of the paths were signposted where they left the road. Of the remainder, half were easy to find, and half difficult; the shortfall amounts to 280,000 signposts! Fewer than half of the path links (average length 470 metres) could be followed easily without a map. Eleven per cent, making up 17 per cent of the footpath network, were difficult or impossible to follow even with a map. Bridleways were much easier to follow. The condition of most paths was satisfactory, but 21 per cent of the footpath length and eight per cent of the bridleways were unusable — a total of over 35,000 kilometres. As *Countryside Commission News (No 39, Sept/Oct 1989, p.1)* put it: 'Rights of way in England and Wales are so unpredictable that people on a two-mile walk, planned with a map, stand a two in three chance of not being able to complete it because of obstacles'. The prime barriers to use were ploughing and cropping. Others were impenetrable natural vegetation, and fences, hedges or walls crossing the paths without gates or stiles.

Effort is reflected in expenditure. Countryside Commission data for 1986–87 *(Countryside Commission 1989g)* showed that total expenditure on rights of way in England and Wales was less than £14 million, ie. £100 per year for each mile of the network, and the equivalent of three pence for each of the 400 million walking trips made in the countryside each year. The Commission urged highway authorities to earmark greater funding for this work, and be more vigilant of the network, and more stringent with landowners who shirk their responsibilities. It recommended local authorities to establish advisory groups to bring together relevant interest groups, develop overall policies, and devise codes of practice for authorities, landowners and users. Renewed efforts are also needed to ensure that farmers understand and comply with the *Ploughing Code*, first issued by the Commission jointly with MAFF in *1986*.

Surveys of public rights of way in National Parks corroborate the wider view. A recent appraisal in the Lake District found 3,917 items requiring attention in the 2,900 kilometres of footpaths in the park. The Peak District found 3,840 items needing attention on its 4,800 kilometres network, including the installation of 2,200 missing roadside signs *(Dower 1989)*. The highway authorities in the Peak Park spend approximately £80,000 per year on maintaining rights of way; over five years the National Park Authority spent £72,000 on just eight kilometres of heavily used path in Dovedale. Dower estimates that, on the 'bog-trotting' section of Kinder Scout and Bleaklow, where the Pennine Way can be up to 100 metres wide, the cost of repair is £20 *per metre*; this compares with £10 *per mile* spent on paths each year by the highway authorities.

Common land

The label 'common land' conveys a simplicity that reality belies. Such land is common not in ownership but in the existence of certain shared rights. It is private land over which other people have rights in common with the owner to do certain things, such as graze stock and collect wood. Commons embrace a huge variety of landscapes — the wild heather moors of Dartmoor, Lake District crags, ancient woodlands in the New Forest and Epping Forest, alluvial meadows, stretches of coast, and suburban commons such as Wimbledon and Clapham. Many have engendered a deep sense of attachment and historic association:

> They were fashioned by ordinary people over the centuries exercising odd-sounding rights . . . . . Their names speak evocatively of old uses and of local characters long gone: Goose Marsh, Cow Mere, Pollard Moor, Jack's Dell, Pleasant View, Horse Fen, Maypole Field, Poor's Wood, Free Heath, Gibbet Hill, God's Blessing Green, Sam Bell's Common. *(Countryside Commission 1989h, p.1)*

For some the bucolic image infuses the title of their keepers, such as Beverley Westwood's Pasture Masters.

Rights of common generally run with property. Commoners' rights may include grazing, pannage (grazing pigs on fallen acorns), estovers (collecting wood for fuel or repair, and bracken for animal bedding), turbary (cutting peat for fuel), piscary (fishing), and common in the soil (taking sand, gravel, stone or minerals). A further important use of commons, though not generally an ancient right, is recreational use. Yet the public has a legal right of access to only one-fifth of our common land.

Common rights are thought to derive from much older rights which predate the private ownership of land. The growth of private estates, and progressive enclosure over the past 700 years, have led to a continuing diminution of common land. Urban expansion in the nineteenth century brought a further threat, in recognition of which the Commons Preservation Society (now the Open Spaces Society) was founded in 1865. The society led the campaign to protect and manage commons, and raised funds to purchase threatened commons and pass them over to the National Trust.

Successful campaigning brought about the *1876 Commons Act*, under which several large commons, including Darwen Moor in Lancashire and the Clent Hills in Hereford and Worcester, became regulated by Boards of Conservators. The Boards may make bylaws to prevent encroachments and allocate areas for playing games. A further *Commons Act* in *1899* permitted local authorities to manage and regulate commons where recreation is the prime use, as at Burbage Common, Leicestershire. Significant further progress regarding public access came with the *1925 Law of Property Act:* henceforth the public had a right of access to all urban commons, and landowners of rural commons could grant a deed of access if they so wished.

Owing to the open character of most common land, fencing and other works must generally be approved by the Secretaries of State for the Environment or for Wales, who take particular account of 'the benefit of the neighbourhood'. Car parks, sports pavilions, playgrounds and other such facilities have generally been allowed. Encroachment, however, is rarely reproached; there is no duty of enforcement against unauthorized works.

Efforts to take stock of the nation's commons stemmed from a Royal Commission convened in 1955. The Commission made three recommendations: commons should be registered, open to public access as of right, and properly managed. The first was implemented — or at least instigated — under the *1965 Commons Registration Act*. Within three years all commons, their owners, and associated common rights were to be recorded on county council registers. Two further years were allowed for objections to be lodged. However, loopholes in the Act, and the brevity of the registration period, conspired against a perfect result. According to *The Open Spaces Society (undated. pp.9–10)*

> Much land which ought to have been registered was not, and lost its status and protection for all time. Conversely, some land was wrongly registered; . . . . . mistakes were rarely spotted because, absurdly, no one was required to inform the owner that his land (sometimes even his house) had been registered as a common.

The Royal Commission's aspirations for access and management remain largely unattained. Only one-fifth of commons are open for public access. These are metropolitan and urban commons, National Trust commons, and those under deeds granting access, or under local Acts of Parliament, such as the *Malvern Hills Act*. Very few commons have management associations or boards of conservators, and in most instances no single authority has taken a lead, either for lack of interest or because of the multiplicity of interests potentially involved. Over 4,000 hectares have no registered owner; under the *1965 Act* these have passed into the care of local authorities, but with no associated power of management.

In 1984 the Countryside Commission set up the Common Land Forum. Its members comprised farming, landowning, recreation, conservation and local authority interests. It reached impressive strength and breadth of consensus *(Countryside Commission 1986)*, proposing a new common land act, essentially untangling the complications stemming from the 1965 Act. Deregistration of commons would only be allowed if the owner could give conclusive proof that it was wrongly registered in the first place. All commons should be open for public access on foot for quiet enjoyment after five years. The five years were intended to allow owners, commoners and local authorities to establish management associations and develop suitable management schemes to balance the needs of agricultural common rights, public access, nature conservation, the landscape, and other interests. Departures from this general management approach would only be allowed in special circumstances, and on the approval of the Secretary of State for the Environment or Wales. Where no management scheme was developed within five years the general model would apply automatically. Land without an owner would be vested in the local authority or National Park Authority, along with suitable powers of management. Specific, and generally temporary, restrictions on public access would be permissible if necessary for public safety, protecting scientific or historic sites, protecting young trees and lambing ewes, or recovering vegetation. Access to village greens is also to be clarified, with a general right for local residents to use them for purposes of sport and recreation. The *Common Land Bill* is a government manifesto commitment, and preparation of the proposed legislation will not be straightforward; it has yet to appear.

The total resource is not insignificant. There are 8,675 commons in England and Wales, covering over 550,000 hectares, an area equivalent to Surrey, Berkshire and Oxfordshire combined *(Countryside Commission 1989h)*. They vary enomously in size: 34 per cent are under half a hectare; at the other extreme, 15 per cent are over 40 hectares.

Country parks

Burgeoning pressure on a finite resource sharpened concerns in the 1960s about the ability of the countryside — and especially the National parks — to sustain the load. The proposed solution lay largely in the creation of positive counter-attractions. As the White Paper, *Leisure and the Countryside*, recognized *(para. 17)* (Minister of Land and Natural Resources 1966), 'other areas might do just as well and be easier to reach. But at present there is no positive reason for going there, and there may be drawbacks; there is nowhere off the road to park the car, nowhere to picnic or ramble and nowhere for the children to paddle and play games'. The *1968 Countryside Act,* and *1967 Countryside (Scotland) Act* therefore empowered local authorities to purchase land for the provision of country parks, to lay out, plant and improve sites, erect buildings and works, and provide facilities for recreation. Private landowners could also seek to establish country parks. Countryside Commission grant-aid was payable for up to 75 per cent of the costs for private landowners, and up to 50 per cent for local authorities. In country parks, recreation is always the prime use, and often the only use.

In deciding to establish country parks, the Commission takes into account four criteria. Firstly, they must be easily accessible to large numbers of people. Secondly, they must have the capacity to absorb large numbers. Thirdly, they must be able to offer a variety of recreational activities. Fourthly, they must enable town dwellers to enjoy open air recreation without travelling long distances and without congesting the roads.

In essence, country parks were conceived as interceptors, diverting use from more remote, solitary and vulnerable places. The Countryside Commission promoted them as 'real countryside virtually on your doorstep'. Of some that label is patently untrue; their emphasis is on entertainment rather than a direct experience of the countryside, and the countryside setting can seem almost incidental. Others facilitate access to the real thing, such as Moel Famau in Clwyd, and Beacon Fell in Lancashire.

The pace of growth was rapid. By 1974, 111 country parks had been created. The tally is now 233. Country parks were encouraged especially in areas with acknowledged deficiencies in countryside provision, on sites already used for recreation but with scope for improvement, and in areas with derelict or underused land. The Commission advises that management plans should be drawn up for all country parks, and early guidelines were issued for doing so *(Countryside Commission 1974a)*. Country park plans should contain a background statement on the physical character of the park and the reasons for it becoming a country park, a statement of aims for the park, and proposed means of implementing the park's objectives. Preparation of a trial management plan for Cannock Chase was funded by the Commission *(Rodgers et al 1982)*, as was a five year programme for implementing it *(Countryside Commission 1985c)*. The lessons learned have been used as a basis for management advice to other country parks.

Country parks are far from being standard packages. All have car parks and toilets, and many offer refreshment facilities, picnic sites and information centres; beyond that basic range they vary greatly. First to be approved was the Wirral Way in Cheshire, the conversion of a disused railway line into a new right of way for walking and riding, with car parks, information centres and picnic areas along the route, mainly using the sites of former stations. Running alongside the Dee estuary for much of its length, it offers pleasant scenery, easy access from the Merseyside conurbation, and the restoration of a derelict area. Some, such as the Battle of Bosworth Field in Leicestershire, exploit historic associations; others, such as Sherwood Forest, have been developed around legend or literary links.

Less than half the country parks represent a net addition to the nation's stock of countryside attractions. Many reflect rather the opportunity to improve existing facilities with a new form of grant aid. Some have been used to lend a new slant to existing opportunities, such as Cheshire's Tatton Park and Liverpool's Croxteth Park; some have helped to supplement the range of attractions or activities at existing sites, such as safari park to stately home. Others have revived aspects of the industrial heritage, such as the slate quarrying museum at Padarn Country Park, site of the former Dinorwic Quarry. Yet others represent desirable restorations of formerly derelict land, where mineral operators' motives may have had less to do with providing for public enjoyment than with the ability to attract favourable rates of grant aid for a country park.

The development of country parks has been more opportunistic than early aspirations hoped for. The plan was for a systematic spread, and much of the promise lay in 'the ultimate creation of a carefully conceived pattern of recreational opportunity rather than a sporadic and haphazard response to demand' *(Patmore 1972, p.241)*. A decade later the same writer described country parks as 'perhaps the most innovative yet frustrating outcome of the legislation embodied in the 1968 Countryside Act' *(Patmore 1983, p.197)*. Others who have urged greater effort into the fight for a general right of access to the countryside, have been harsher:

> The setting up of country parks and picnic sites in the countryside as minia-ture Red-Indian reservations for the urban underclass marked a moment when the hegemony of the landowner was as complete as it had ever been . . . . . the idea of invading townspeople being decoyed into country parks and picnic sites before they got as far as the real countryside suited landowners very well . . . . . planners have sought to cage visitors in carefully confined locations. *(Shoard 1987, pp.390–391)*.

Quite apart from the motives for containment, however, the effective-ness of the parks in decanting use from far away places was never well-founded; logically it was equally likely that the parks would act as a stepping stone to the wider countryside, not satisfying people's needs but rather stimulating them, giving them the interest and confidence to explore farther afield. That reversal of purpose is now recognized even by the Countryside Commission. With the fears of the 1960s now unfounded, and evidence of widespread public ignorance of countryside opportunities and attractions, the Commission can take the opposite of its original view and state that 'We shall press for existing parks to be developed and managed as gateways to the countryside' *(Countryside Commission 1987d, p.12)*.

Green belts and urban fringes

Green belts today serve a vital recreational purpose but this was not at the forefront of their early rationale. For good reason, London was first by far in creating its band of open space, in the early 1930s, and the prime purpose was to shape the expansion of the city, and regulate further growth. Adoption of green belts elsewhere awaited ministerial encouragement in the 1950s, when the *Ministry of Housing and Local Government (1955)* recognized the wider need to check urban sprawl, prevent neighbouring towns from coalescing, and preserve the character of individual towns. Recreational benefits represented not a reason for green belts, but a welcome spin-off.

Most large cities now have green belts (or green wedges). They have no statutory basis, except that they may be included in Structure Plans. Their area amounts to 11 per cent of England. The contribution which they will make to recreational opportunities for urban residents has been emphasised in establishing virtually every one. However, the existence of a green belt does not give the public any rights of access they would not otherwise have.

Not all urban fringe land, of course, has been earmarked as green belt. Even so, its recreational value can scarcely be overstated. Its proximity to large centres of population, its easy accessibility, and in many areas the opportunities presented by derelict land, exhausted mineral workings, and low grade farmland, make the fringe a crucial opportunity area. Realization of opportunity must be a continuing process, but recognition at least came clearly to the fore in the 1970s: 'the recreation potential of the fringe locale, the opportunity it offers for blending urban and rural environments and leisure pursuits in a unique way, have not been exploited *(Davidson 1976)*. Opportunities are not necessarily easily won, or with ideal neighbours, for the urban fringe frequently houses those essential features such as abbatoirs, sewage works, cemeteries and refuse disposal tips, that are unacceptable in an urban area or in a countryside area *(Davidson 1974)*. Nor is the urban fringe easy to plan for; almost invariably it straddles the territories of several local authorities, and attracts a bewildering variety of interest groups whose claims frequently clash. Not without reason is the most scholarly work on the green belt subtitled *Conflict mediation in the urban fringe (Elson 1986)*.

Existing opportunities for access are not inconsiderable. In the late 1970s *Ferguson and Munton (1978,1979)* found that at least nine per cent of all land in the metropolitan green belt comprised informal recreation sites — a total of 390 sites and over 26,000 hectares. On many other sites recreation was a secondary use. Quantity alone, of course, cannot make for equality of access; virtually half the sites were in the single county of Surrey. More access, however, does not necessarily require more sites: Harrison (1980–81) concluded that the carrying capacity of many green belt sites could be significantly enhanced through better management. The urban fringe is important not just for informal recreation, but also for more organized pursuits. Indeed, an appraisal of recreational use of the London green belt in the 1970s showed that organized pastimes, such as individual and team sports, water sports, horse riding and golf generated over half the trips to the green belt for recreational purposes *(Greater London Council 1975)*.

The accessibility and attractiveness of urban fringe countryside can easily be overplayed. Use is predominantly local. The Hertfordshire–Barnet study, for example, found that very few visitors came from central London, and under five per cent had travelled by public transport. Half had walked *(Countryside Commission 1981)*. Similar patterns are evident elsewhere *(Greater London Council 1975, Fitton 1976)*. *Harrison (1981a,b)* found that few sites attracted even five per cent of their visitors from the inner city. London clearly poses the biggest problems of travel cost, time, distance and inconvenience, and there is evidence of rather greater urban use of the fringes of Greater Manchester, Tyneside and Merseyside *(Elson 1986)*. Overall, though, as *Elson (1979, p.14)* earlier concluded. 'Users and use patterns of the general countryside of the immediate urban fringe appear more similar in profile to those of large urban parks than sites in the deeper countryside'. The urban fringe at the very least lacks identity, and it may lack attractiveness and accessibility too. Reaching the metropolitan green belt is hard enough for the car-owning Londoner, let alone the non-car owner.

Many have urged a more co-ordinated approach to urban fringe recreation provision, including the development of regional parks, as in the Colne and Lee Valleys. These remain, however, the isolated examples, for their models have not been adopted more widely. Leisure parks, akin to the hierarchy of parks developed in the Ruhr, West Germany, by the Ruhrkohlenbezirk, the Ruhr Coal Area Reclamation Board, have also been advocated, for example, by *Travis (1976)*. *Davidson (1974)* saw them as:

> Developments (which) . . . . . could link together a variety of covered and open air facilities . . . . . many of which are not easily available in urban or rural areas in this country . . . . . facilities might include open air theatres, places for dancing and concerts, zoos and children's farms, outdoor as well as indoor equipment for chess and table tennis, boating lakes and adventure playgrounds.

Most planning authorities, however, keen to placate local residents, seek to minimize change, and use green belt status for purposes of control rather than creativity. *The House of Lords Select Committee on Sport and Leisure* sought to change all that:

> Recreational facilities are a proper use of an existing green belt and can help to preserve it against other demands . . . . . a positive approach in recreational terms, making the green belt into a lung for the town, rather than the negative approach which sometimes threatens to convert the green belt into a demilitarized zone, should secure that the urban fringe is properly exploited *(1973, 193–1)*.

Local authorities, however, preferred not to hear the message, and the subsequent slackening of the pace of growth of recreational demand provided an excuse. Only in some of the former metropolitan counties was a more positive, and urban, view taken. In the metropolitan green belt the *Standing Conference for London and South East Regional Planning (1979, p.4)*, for example, stated that 'in certain areas and in certain circumstances recreation should have priority over other interests', and that recreational use should be promoted positively. The more usual approach is a low level of investment by public authorities, and a planning climate unconducive to private sector projects. *Munton (1983, p.90)* therefore concluded that, for the metropolitan green belt, 'Only faltering steps in favour of a more positive approach to recreation and landscape improvements are being made at present'. *Elson (1986, p.xxx)* portrayed the wider applicability of that conclusion to the national canvas: 'the "recreation interest" appears weak in the absence of improved powers over access to private land. Many of the sports and recreations with the greatest potential for growth appear to infringe a strict application of the criteria for green belt development control'.

What constitutes appropriate recreational use of the green belt has never been clear. The *Ministry of Housing and Local Government (1962)*, confirming that no further building would be allowed except where there were positive reasons for permitting it, went on to state that 'buildings for sport and recreation may be allowed . . . . . In such cases the decision is likely to turn on the need for the proposal as against any damage it will do to the rural appearance of the land'. Fifteen years later, the *Countryside Review Committee (1977, para.76)* appeared to be taking the opposite view: 'Recreation in the general sense has always been associated with Green Belts. But not highly organised sports which need extensive ancillary buildings, generate heavy traffic, and in particular give rise to large spectator followings'. The *Standing Conference on London and South East Regional Planning (SCLSERP 1979)* has developed an acceptability matrix for recreational uses. They conclude that low intensity activities are acceptable almost everywhere, except on managed farmland, floodplains, water meadows and marshlands. High intensity uses are generally unacceptable, except on existing sports fields, disused airfields and golf courses, or with the most stringent siting, design and management considerations.

Several agencies have sought to inspire positive provision, including the Countryside Commission and the Regional Councils for Sport and Recreation. Their arguments in favour of increasing recreational opportunities in the green belt include the continuing future growth of demand for leisure activities, the close proximity to principal sources of demand, the need to rectify deficiencies in open space in urban areas, the opportunity to re-create derelict or damaged landscapes, and to capitalize upon existing resources such as the rights of way network, and the opportunity to use recreational developments to create a positive identity for green belt areas. Green belts are also promoted as prime locations for environmental education and interpretative programmes. It is also argued that a mixture of specific recreation provisions along with an integrated approach to countryside management can reduce the level of conflict between farming, conservation, recreation and other interests.

County policies for green belts mostly approach strategic land use issues through zoning. With regard to recreation, such policies generally seek to minimize conflict with primary users, allow a wider range of recreational uses in the most accessible parts of the green belt, develop access in defined green wedges, and identify areas for landscape renewal with potential for recreational after-use. The Rother Valley Regional Park near Sheffield and the Pennington Flash Country Park near Wigan were both developed on National Coal Board land. In Hertfordshire, for example, open land is classified into Agricultural Priority Areas and Amenity Corridors. Recreational use of the former is confined to low intensity, quiet activity, using the rights of way system and a network of scenic drives. In the latter, essentially the transport links between the main towns, priority is given to leisure development and landscape improvement *(Hertfordshire County Council 1986)*. Landowners generally seek to be included in the Amenity Corridors, thus enhancing the value of their property for possible alternative uses. Residents seek to be in the Agricultural Priority Areas, thus distancing themselves from likely leisure developments. More recently, planning

authorities have sought to obtain recreation 'gains' from urban development projects, such as the provision of a community sports hall by a
property developer as part of a new residential estate.

The Countryside Commission and Forestry Commission are now
promoting the concept of Community Forests for the urban fringe,
combining opportunities for leisure with the enhancement of
landscape, protection of nature, and job creation. The vision is set out
as follows:

> Imagine a magnificent forest with an exciting range of leisure facilities at the
> edge of the city — as well-wooded landscape right on the doorstep for tens
> of thousands of people. Woven into the forest is a rich variety of other
> landscapes, including farmland, heathlands, flower-filled meadows, and
> lakes. Set among the trees, offering a unique experience, there are opportu-
> nities to enjoy a multitude of sports activities. The forest also provides space
> for the arts, with open-air concerts, exhibitions and festivals. And amid all
> the activity there are still secluded corners where people can relax and enjoy
> the peace of the forest.
>
> This is a living forest, supporting a rich variety of wildlife. It is also a
> working forest, providing employment for hundreds of people — in forestry,
> farming and leisure. But above all, this is a Community Forest, shaped by
> local people for themselves and their children to cherish for generations to
> come. *(Countryside Commission and Forestry Commission 1989, p.4)*.

Overview

The place of recreation in specially designated areas varies between and
within the various categories of resource. In National Parks it must
often take second place to conservation interests, and there is a
widespread presumption against forms of recreation other than the
informal, quiet, and contemplative. Even so, the vigour with which
National Park Authorities have been able to provide for public access
and enjoyment varies with the financial resources at their disposal, their
degree of autonomy, and the nature of the more pressing concerns of
park protection. In AsONB the amenity role is intended but largely
undefined, and, except in a few enthusiastic local authorities, largely
unprovided for in any real sense.

The Heritage Coast concept has become well established, but used
more as a defensive mechanism than a positive planning device; consequently, achievements for public access, though considerable, are
piecemeal, even within the confines of a single Heritage Coast. Country
parks provide a valuable resource and some imaginative sites, but their
full promise remains unfulfilled. There is scope to develop regional or
county-wide strategic plans, to encourage further country parks to meet
existing deficiencies, and design different types of parks to act respectively as 'interceptor' and 'introductory' sites.

For the longer term, one of the most positive achievements of the
1980s was the untangling of the status of common land, and the
positive proposals for management and public access, though at the
time of writing the all-important *Common Land Act* is still awaited. For

the urban fringe, the concept of Community Forests opens up exciting possibilities for unusual mixtures of recreational activity, ranging from quiet contemplation to water sports centres and outdoor concerts. For the wider countryside, the Countryside Commission's policy for rights of way will be hard to achieve in its entirety, but it brings welcome rationalization to a complex system, and priorities for management. It also allows the Commission to concentrate on the more strategic parts of the network, while fostering community pride and involvement in maintaining the resource locally.

5 Contemporary demand and usage

Measuring demand

Defining the countryside is difficult enough; determining how many people go there for purposes of recreation is harder still. Unlike a built facility, such as a sports centre, there is no single point of entry, no opening and closing times, and no turnstile or cash till; any of these makes monitoring easily controllable, if not entirely uncomplicated. At certain countryside sites, of course, some of these simple aids to monitoring are available. For most countryside recreation, however, there is not such starting point. Most is informal, spontaneous, unmanaged, and unconfined in time or space.

Nor is demand a straightforward measure. The complications are well documented (for example by *Clawson and Knetsch 1963, Miles and Seabrook 1977, Patmore 1983, Pigram 1983*). Used without clarity, the term demand can refer to either behaviour or intent, ie to what people actually do, or what they desire to do. The more common usage, and the more important for analysing existing patterns of recreational activity, is that of expressed or effective demand, referring to current levels or patterns of demand as witnessed in present participation. Pattern of participation, however, are rarely unconstrained; people's leisure activities are conditioned by a complex mix of opportunities and constraints. More time, more facilities, more money, better access or more friends might enable us to take up activities which we are presently unable to do, or to engage in existing activities more often. As *Mercer (1980)* showed, demand can be created or diverted by the introduction of new provision. In other words, expressed demand is merely that share of demand which has been satisfied. Equally important to the recreation planner is that share which has not. This is referred to as latent or frustrated demand.

The complications of measuring expressed demand will become apparent in the course of this chapter. Attempting to measure frustrated demand is more hazardous still, for the obvious reason that latent demand is invisible. The true measure would require studies of participation before and after the removal of a particular constraint, to find how many additional participants had been generated. Such studies are rare, partly for reasons of cost and complexity, but also because they are impossible to design effectively, other than for usage of built facilities or enclosed sites. The more usual approach to measuring latent demand is to ask people about their recreational aspirations, but this creates problems of a different kind. Firstly, aspirations are constrained by the range of opportunities presently available, or by the range which people can conceive of or think possible. Secondly, aspirations are notoriously ambitious: witness the bold survey respondents who say they would like to go hang gliding, parachuting, water - skiing and the like! In other words, aspirations overstate likely activity. They are best studied alongside existing participation patterns. A survey undertaken by National Opinion Polls in 1986, for example, found many more people who had 'seriously considered' taking part in outdoor leisure activities than were actually taking part, in some cases by a factor of eight, and in one case by a factor of over 60 (Table 5.1)!

Table 5.1 Leisure and tourism activities on the inland waterways, 1986

	No. of adults	No. of user days (millions)	Market potential* (millions of adults)
Walking/informal recreation	4,830,000	96.1	1.29
Angling	770,000	16.2	1.14
Trip boats	500,000	1.0	4.20
Private boating	400,000	1.8	3.13
Unpowered boating	400,000	2.8	1.53
Hire boating	140,000	1.2	9.26

* number who had not undertaken the activity but had seriously considered it

Source: National Opinion Polls data, quoted in British Waterways 1989

In the recreation field expressed demand poses problems enough. The first is the sheer diversity of activities to be covered, and how to delimit and categorize them. Although the sum total of recreational activity is enormous, individually most pursuits attract only a minority of the population. To draw valid conclusions for minority activities therefore requires potentially huge population samples. The second problem is seasonality, which for many activities renders annual averages meaningless. The third is social profile. Demand for most recreational activities is socially selective, and any attempt to identify contrasts and comparisons between different age groups or social classes again requires large samples. The fourth is fad and fashion. For established forms of countryside recreation, such as going for drives and picnicking, this may pose little problem. For others, especially the more adventurous and glamorous pursuits such as windsurfing, water skiing and microlight flying, it may mean rapid shifts in demand. A one-off survey covering demand at a single point in time could portray a highly inaccurate picture a year later. Even traditional activities such as walking and cycling are expanding with increased commitment to healthy lifestyles. The fifth problem is to define participation. The deceptively simple question 'Do you visit the countryside?' permits of no usable answer. It must first relate to a defined time period, such as the past week, month or year. The shorter the period, the less likely is it that the answers will be representative of a person's normal behaviour, because a single week might be highly atypical. The longer the period, the less accurate will be the respondents' powers of recall. Furthermore, for planners and managers, the mere fact of participation or non participation is rarely a sufficient basis for action or investment; it must be supplemented by some measure of frequency. What matters is not only the number of participants, but the volume of participation in a given period.

Approaches to demand measurement in countryside recreation take two main forms. The first is home based, the second site based. Each has merits and shortcomings. Both provide information on participants, but only the first can explore the characteristics and aspirations of non participants, or yield information on leisure and lifestyles which is representative of the population at large. The site based approach can only be representative of existing users. If information is required for purposes of site marketing, management or maintenance, however, the site based approach is generally sufficient, enabling the detailed examination of current user characteristics, catchment areas, activity patterns and attitudes.

Present participation

For reasons of expense and analytical complexity, general demand surveys in the recreation field are few and far between. Two surveys undertaken in the 1960s were the first, and to date only, specialist recreation demand studies carried out in Britain *(British Travel Association/ University of Keele 1967, Sillitoe 1969)*. A spate of regional surveys of similar compass followed swiftly *(North Regional Planning Committee 1969, Rodgers and Patmore 1972, Greater London Council 1975, Countryside Commission 1977)*, but none has been carried out since 1973. From that year, however, questions on leisure activities have been included from time to time in the Government's annual omnibus, the *General Household Survey (GHS)*. The evolving series, with leisure data for 1973, 1977, 1980, 1983, 1986 and 1987, is beginning to generate useful trend data as well as periodic cross sections. Several forms of countryside recreation are included in the GHS.

Apart from the GHS, comparisons between other surveys are confounded by contrasts of scope, categorization of activities, categorization of respondents (eg different surveys using different age bands), and different timespans referred to. Indeed, not even the GHS is straightforward in these respects, for there have been changes between 1973 and the other years in the precise form of questioning, and some changes of definition and reference periods between 1986 and 1987. Differences of definition account for much of the apparent discrepancy between surveys; such differences, for example, enabled the GHS to conclude that in a four week period in summer 29 per cent of the population took part in 'open-air' outings, while the Countryside Commission's National Survey of Countryside Recreation for the same year could claim 54 per cent taking part in 'countryside activities' *(Patmore 1983)*. In any single year the overall scale of countryside usage in impossible to gauge, however, because it is unclear how much of the participation in activities such as walking, swimming, cycling, horse riding, and canoeing takes place in the countryside.

The GHS comprises a Great Britain sample of approximately 20,000 adults aged 16 and over. Covering leisure more generally, it helps to place countryside recreation in broader context. The pursuits with mass appeal are home-based and social (Table 5.2). In percentage terms others are small by comparison. Countryside activities are not treated as a discrete category. The 'visits to the countryside', which attract a participation rate of only three per cent, are only part of the picture. What the GHS lists as other categories of visiting will have included trips to and through the countryside, as will many of the activities classed as 'sightseeing'. Several sports, and a substantial share of walking, will also have taken place in the countryside.

The GHS shows that sport is markedly socially stratified. Except in a few activities, men take part more than women, young people more than old, the professional and managerial classes more than unskilled manual workers, and car owners more than non car owners. For countryside recreation and informal pursuits, some of these contrasts remain, but in softer relief. Walking, for example, attracts virtually equal proportions of men and women (24 per cent and 22 per cent respectively), as do outdoor swimming (seven and six per cent), camping and caravanning (two and two per cent), and sailing (one and one per cent). Cycling, fishing, field sports and motor sports remain more of a male domain. Walking and open air outings are among the few pursuits where involvement increases with age (Table 5.3). They conform, though, to conventional class contrasts. Only half as many semi-skilled manual workers as professional people take part in walking. Visiting the countryside slides from five per cent participation at the top of the social scale to one per cent at the bottom. Cycling and fishing show a more mixed class profile (Table 5.4).

Table 5.2   Adult participation in recreational activities, Great Britain 1986

	% taking part in past 4 weeks
Outdoor activities:	
Walking (2 miles+)	19
Outdoor swimming	2
Cycling	2
Fishing	2
Camping/caravaning	1
Horse riding	1
Motor sports	1
Snow sports	1
Sailing	1
Field sports	+
Climbing/potholing	+
Rowing/canoeing/punting	+
Air sports	+
Open air outings:	
Visits to seaside	7
Visits to parks	4
Outings by car, boat, motorcycle	4
Visits to countryside	3
Sightseeing:	
Historical buildings, sites, towns	9
Museums, galleries	4
Exhibitions, shows	3
Zoos	1
Safari, wildlife parks	1
Prompted activities:	
Watching television	98
Visiting/entertaining friends/relatives	94
Listening to radio	86
Listening to records, tapes	67
Reading books	59
Going out for drink	55
Going out for meal	47
Gardening	43
DIY	39
Dressmaking, needlework, knitting	27
+ Less than 0.5 per cent	

Source: General Household Survey 1986

Table 5.3 Outdoor activities and age
% taking part in past 4 weeks

	16–19	20–24	25–29	30–44	45–59	60–69	70+	Median age of participants
Walking (2 miles+)	14	18	21	22	22	21	11	43
Outdoor swimming	4	4	3	3	2	2	–	37
Cycling	5	3	2	2	1	1	–	33
Fishing	3	2	3	2	2	1	–	36
Visits to seaside	6	7	8	10	6	6	3	40
Visits to parks	3	3	6	6	2	2	1	36
Visits to countryside	1	3	3	3	2	3	2	42
Outings by car, boat. motorcycle	3	4	4	4	4	5	4	46

Source: *General Household Survey 1986*

Table 5.4   Outdoor activities and social class
% taking part in past 4 weeks

	Professional	Managerial	Other non manual	Skilled manual	Semi skilled manual	Unskilled manual
Walking (2 miles+)	30	24	22	17	15	12
Outdoor swimming	5	4	3	2	1	-
Cycling	3	2	2	1	1	2
Fishing	2	2	1	3	1	1
Visits to seaside	10	8	9	6	6	4
Visits to parks	5	4	5	3	3	2
Visits to countryside	5	3	4	2	2	1
Outings by car, boat, motorcycle	4	5	5	4	3	3

Source: General Household Survey 1986

Additional questions on forest recreation were included in the 1987 General Household Survey. Over half the population claimed to visit forests or woodland for pleasure or recreation, slightly more men than women, many more non manual workers than manual, and nearly twice as many car owners as non car owners (Table 5.5).

Table 5.5   Visiting forests or woodland for recreation

	% ever visiting
All	54
Men	57
Women	52
Car owners	64
Non car owners	30
Non manual	65
Manual	45

Source: General Household Survey 1987

However, the survey almost certainly will have overstated true participation levels, as visiting was not related to a specific reference period; respondents were simply asked 'do you ever visit forests or woodland nowadays?'. Equally, the question on facilities desired (Table 5.6) will have amplified real needs, as people were presented with a list of facilities and asked whether they would like to have them. Nonetheless, the responses to the various items are indicative in a relative sense, and give some guidance for provision.

Table 5.6 Facilities visitors would like in forests

	% of visitors
Toilets	86
Nature trails	83
Car parks	83
Picnic areas	83
Seats	81
Visitor information centre	74
Plant/tree labels	71
Cafe	48
Exhibitions	45
Wood sales	29

Source: General Household Survey 1987

Table 5.7 Countryside activities

* Visited the sea coast or cliff tops (but not seaside resort).
* Visited historic buildings, stately homes, museums, gardens or parks in the countryside (excluding country parks).
* Visited country parks.
* Visited zoos, safari or wildlife parks in the countryside.
* Visited nature reserves in the countryside.
* Been on drives, outings, picnics etc. in the countryside (including visits to attractive villages).
* Been on long walks, hikes or rambles of at least two miles (round trip) in the countryside, either from car or home.
* Been birdwatching/nature study in the countryside.
* Been fishing in the countryside.
* Been horseriding or ponytrekking in the countryside.
* Been shooting in the countryside.
* Been hunting in the countryside.
* Taken active part in other organised sports (eg football, cricket, cycling, golf, sailing, running, climbing, motor sport etc) in the countryside.
* Taken active part in other informal sport (eg jogging, kicking a ball about, beach games, throwing frisbees etc) in the countryside.
* Watched any organised sport in the countryside (in person, not on TV).
* Visited friends or relatives in the countryside.
* Carried out any organised conservation or recreation work in the countryside (eg tree planting, clearing of footpaths etc.)
* 'Picked your own' (fruit, vegetables etc) in the countryside.

Source: Countryside Commission 1985a

To obtain fuller coverage of countryside pursuits, and to elicit more detailed information on activities, attitudes and destinations visited, the Countryside Commission has undertaken its own periodic *National Surveys of Countryside Recreation*, in *1977, 1980 and 1984*. These cover England and Wales only. The 1984 survey comprised six waves of fieldwork spread throughout the year, producing a total sample of 6,302 people aged between 12 and 75 years. Countryside trips were defined broadly, to cover the eighteen activities listed in Table 5.7 (*Countryside Commission 1985a*).

As expected, there were seasonal variations in use. In winter, just over half the sample had visited the countryside at least once in the past four weeks. In spring this rose to 60 per cent, and in summer to 70 per cent. Frequent visitors, defined as people making five or more trips in a four week period, rose from 20 per cent of the sample in winter to 28 per cent in spring and 38 per cent in summer.

Though the scale of activity is impressive, its distribution is inequitable. As many as 68 per cent of all trips were made by a mere 17 per cent of the population. Forty per cent made no trips at all in a typical four week period. In absolute terms six to seven million people were frequent countryside users, while 15–16 million visited rarely or never.

Participation varies with personal, social and geographical circumstances. Ownership of a car is an obvious facilitator (Table 5.8a). People having personal use of a car comprise under half the population (46 per cent) but make nearly two-thirds (63 per cent) of all countryside trips. Conversely, people in households without a car make up over a third (34 per cent) of the population, but make only 18 per cent of countryside visits. Acquisition of a car transforms mobility and swiftly generates additional visits in the first year or two of ownership. Thereafter, activity stabilizes. Recent reductions in the rate of car acquisition have dampened the effect further, with signs that car ownership is edging toward its ceiling.

Table 5.8 Countryside visiting, car ownership and social class

	%	
	Proportion of people	*Proportion of trips*
(a) Car ownership		
No car in household	34	18
Car in household	20	19
Use of own car	46	63
(b) Social class		
A	2	2
B	13	20
C1	23	28
C2	27	27
D	16	12
E	12	7
Unemployed	7	4

Source: Countryside Commission 1985a

Social class, too, is a powerful influence (Table 5.8b), with people in managerial occupations almost three times as likely to visit the country-side as those who are unemployed or on minimum incomes.

Car ownership and class, of course, are related, and they intercorre-late too with other factors such as income and ethnic origin. Their composite effect may be summarized in multivariate classifications of social areas. The classification most widely used in the leisure field is ACORN, acronym for A Classification of Residential Neighbourhoods. ACORN classes Census Enumeration Districts into eleven types, based on 40 variables. Their link with countryside visiting is shown in Table 5.9. Compared to their proportion in the population, people living in affluent suburban areas and in modern family housing make a dispro-portionately high number of countryside trips; by contrast, those living in poor council estates, multi-racial areas and other areas of poor quality housing are underrepresented in countryside visiting.

Table 5.9   Countryside visiting and neighbourhood type

	% Proportion of people	Proportion of trips
Agricultural areas	2	3
Affluent suburban housing	16	21
Better-off retirement areas	4	5
Modern family housing (higher incomes)	15	18
Older housing (intermediate status)	24	26
Better-off council estates	11	10
Less well-off council estates	9	8
Higher status non-family areas	4	3
Poor quality older terraced housing	5	3
Multi-racial areas	4	2
Poorest council estates	6	2

Source: Countryside Commission 1985a

Although car ownership and class exert a strong influence on who participates and who does not, their effects among participants are far more muted. In other words, the non car owners and members of the manual classes who *do* participate in countryside recreation, do so with virtually the same frequency as their more mobile and affluent counter-parts.

The vast majority of visitors pursue their countryside recreation entirely informally, and not through membership of formal clubs and societies. The *1984 National Survey,* however, found that one in five people belonged to at least one countryside-related organization, such as the National Trust, Royal Society for the Protection of Birds, or local amenity or recreation societies. Interestingly, membership was not concentrated among people living in or close to the countryside; it clearly reflected people's concern for, rather than accessibility to, the countryside. Nonetheless, the one in five people who belonged to such clubs made a third of all visits, demonstrating not only their motivation to enjoy the countryside, but also their means to do so.

Destinations visited

The essential informality of most countryside visiting is expressed in activities and destinations. Most popular are drives, outings, picnics, long walks (two miles or more), visiting friends and relatives, and informal sport (Table 5.10). Managed sites, such as country parks and historic buildings, are by no means the prime destinations; indeed, the wider, unmanaged countryside absorbs three times as many visits.

Table 5.10   Participation in countryside recreation activities

	% of trips
Drives, outings, picnics	19
Long walks	18
Visiting friends, relatives	14
Sea coast	8
Informal sport	12
Organized sport	7
Pick your own	4
Historic buildings	4
Country parks	4
Watching sport	3
Other	7

Source: Countryside Commission, 1985a

People who had visited the countryside in the past three months were asked for details of their most recent trip. The majority of use was not long-range but local (Table 5.11). Half of all trips involved a round-trip distance of twenty miles or less, and more than a third were of no more than ten miles. Short range trips were undertaken especially by unemployed people, car-less families with young children and, more surprisingly, young people under the age of twenty. Long-range trips were made especially by the most frequent and infrequent countryside users, reflecting the mobility of the first group, and the location of the second. Many of the most infrequent users were people living in multi-racial areas, generally in inner urban locations, for whom any country-side trip — even just to the urban fringe — is, of necessity, a long trip. Overall, the average time spent away from home on the last trip was five and a half hours.

The social importance of countryside recreation is evident in the companions people go with. Ninety per cent of trips are taken in the company of others. The solitary ten per cent are taken mainly by people living in or close to the countryside, taking part in walking, organized sport or fishing. Nearly half of all trips were taken with spouses, 41 per cent with other adults, and 35 per cent in the company of children.

Table 5.11 Distance and travel mode of most recent countryside trip

	% of trips
Round trip distance (miles)	
0–10	35
11–20	14
21–40	17
41–60	11
61–80	7
81–100	4
over 100	12
Mode	
Car	72
Foot	13
Public transport	5
Hired coach, etc.	5
Bicycle, motorbike	3

Source: Countryside Commission, 1985a

Almost three-quarters of trips are car-borne (Table 5.11). Clearly we can expect those who own cars to use them. More surprising is the number of non car owners who travel to the countryside by car, usually with car owning friends and relatives. The second most common mode of travel is on foot. Public transport plays a very small part indeed in providing effective access to the countryside.

For the car owner in particular, distance is not necessarily disutility. For many, the journey is not merely the means to a recreational experience, but the very focus of it. As many as one in five people did not make a single stop of fifteen minutes or more on their most recent trip. Even among the four-fifths who did stop, for many at least part of the pleasure of the visit will have rested in the freedom to set their own pace and follow byways more than highways. This was borne out by *Jackson (1982)* in a study of Dovedale. Twenty eight per cent of visitors had not taken the shortest journey to the site, but had followed a more scenic or quieter route; they sought to maximize recreational benefit rather than minimize travel time.

In the National Countryside Recreation Survey, those who did stop demonstrated again the recreational importance of the wider, unmanaged countryside; sites specifically managed for recreation accounted for only one in four of all stops. Only one in five of those who stopped paid an admission or parking charge. On average, three different things were done at each stop, predominantly strolling around, sightseeing, relaxing, and buying and consuming food. Time spent at main stops ranged from 15 minutes to over six hours, but with an average of three and a half hours.

As the most popular activity, walking was examined in greater detail. Those who had walked at least two miles had used a variety of terrain (Table 5.12), and walked on average for just under five miles. Most had walked on paths, through woodlands, fields or farmland, and a third had walked to, or near, water. Many did not venture away from metalled roads, although nearly one in six walked across land with no paths.

Table 5.12   Terrain used for long walks

	% of walks
On paths	38
Fields, farmland	32
Woodland	32
On roads	22
Across land with no paths	15
Heathland, moors	14
By rivers, canals	13
Along beaches, sea cliffs	12
By lakes, reservoirs	10

Percentages sum to over 100 due to walks encompassing several terrains

Source: Countryside Commission, 1985a

Choice of destination is more habitual than adventurous. Asked how they had found out about the places visited most recently, as many as 40 per cent of people had been before, and another 19 per cent had always known about them. A further seven per cent went on the recommendation of others. Formal publicity channels appeared to play very little part in influencing people's choices. Only one per cent each had chosen their stops from guide books or tourist information centres.

There were signs of latent demand as yet unmet. When asked whether they were happy with their present frequency of visiting, nearly half the sample said they would like to go to the countryside more often. Twenty-eight per cent presently went a little and would like to go more often. Six per cent presently went a lot, but would like to go more frequently still.

Trends over time

Without continuing and comparable surveys, trends over time cannot be charted with true accuracy. A few pointers must suffice. The real explosion of demand occurred over two decades from the mid 1950s. Admission figures for 45 National Trust properties from 1955 to 1978 showed a seven per cent growth per year *(CRRAG 1980)*. A slackening came with the oil crisis of 1973–74 but the effect was short-lived. Expansion resumed, and the Countryside Commission could conclude by the end of the decade that 'recreation travel has proved very resilient to significant increases in the price of petrol' *(Stoakes 1979)*.

The 1980s witnessed continuing growth but at lessening pace. For countryside visiting overall, the National Surveys of Countryside Recreation bear witness to this. In 1977 53 per cent of adults had visited the countryside in the previous month. A dip in demand came in 1980 when only 42 per cent did so, then by 1984 participation had risen to 68 per cent. Frequent users of the countryside, visiting five times or more in a four week period, comprised 15 per cent of the population in 1977, 13 per cent in 1980, and 26 per cent in 1984. Informal recreation showed modest growth, but faster expansion occurred in formal and informal sport in the countryside. Though trips rose in number, however, they shrank somewhat in range. In 1977, 39 per cent of trips covered distances of 20 miles or less, and in 1980 40 per cent did so; by 1984, however, these had increased to 46 per cent.

Site based studies

Site surveys are the mainstay of management information. In scope and approach recent studies vary little from the pioneer surveys of the 1960s and early 1970s, concentrating on visitor characteristics, catchment areas, modes of travel and frequency of visiting. This basic, site-specific data is crucial for management and marketing. Its abundance was evident more than a decade ago. Evaluating the methods and results of site-based questionnaire surveys of visitors, *Elson (1977)* identified 37 different surveys undertaken between 1966 and 1976, covering some 280 specific sites.

Confining attention to self-contained sites does not dispel methodological difficulty. There are many decisions to be made. The crucial starting point is to have clearly defined aims. Is the intention to survey peak use, typical use, or both? How many days or weeks of sampling will be necessary to obtain an adequate and random sample of visitors? Which days of the week should be covered? At what times should the survey day start and finish? The British Waterways Board national count of waterways users in 1988, for example, was undertaken on ten days by observers walking five to ten kilometres stretches commencing at 8.00 am *(British Waterways 1988)*. The early start was designed to record the maximum number of anglers using the waterways system, but in so doing, other users such as towpath walkers, will have been grossly undercounted. From the counts undertaken, average daily usage appeared to be 4,307 walkers, 723 canoeists, and 5,229 anglers.

There are further decisions on approach. Is the intention simply to observe and record behaviour, or is it necessary to obtain information directly from visitors, whether by interviewing them or asking them to complete forms? When should visitors be contacted: on arrival, during their stay, or on departure? How should they be contacted at open access sites with no defined entry and exit points, and on sites where there is free range to wander at will and do any number of activities?

Information sought in site surveys falls into three main types. The first is profile data on visitor characteristics, such as age, sex, social class, employment status, place of residence, car ownership, and visitor group composition. The second relates to the trip, such as distance travelled and travel mode, travel time, frequency of visiting the site, other activities undertaken during the trip, length of stay, spending, reason for visiting the site, and how visitors came to know about it. The third concerns visitors' attitudes and opinions, such as their attitudes to the site, their likes and dislikes about it, their attitudes to other users, and suggestions for improvements.

Elson (1977) distilled a range of general conclusions from the disparate studies reviewed. As we have seen, the decade since has seen a near stabilizing of demand, attributable largely to the general economic downturn. More recent surveys, though, indicate that Elson's broad conclusions are as true today. Most sites had a large core of regular visitors; approximately 30 per cent of visitors were newcomers. Most people decided where to go before setting out from home, and 90 per cent of trips to inland sites were made directly from home. Half involved at least two stops, whether at other countryside sites, or to visit pubs, restaurants, shops or friends. Over 90 per cent of trips were made by car or motorcycle. Most people setting out in the morning tended to leave home at around 11.30am, and those in the afternoon at 3.30pm. On site, arrivals peaked at 4.00pm, and departures at 6.30pm.

Much can be gained from a mixture of methods, as opposed to investment in a single approach. *Locke's (1985)* study of Sherwood and Rufford Country Parks, Nottinghamshire, is a case in point, combining an extensive visitor self-completion survey, and a more detailed personal interview survey. The self-completion survey, scheduled over twelve months, provided basic descriptive data for visitors throughout the year, such as the starting point of their journey, where they had heard about the park, what they proposed to do during their stay, and characteristics of members of their visitor party. A total of 10,916 questionnaires was distributed, yielding 6,800 usable returns, a response rate of 62 per cent. The personal interview survey sought to obtain fuller detail on these subjects, together with further information about visitors' use of the parks and their attitudes towards them. This was administered at the visitor centres in the parks on three weekends in November, July and August, yielding 624 completed interviews, 67 per cent of the contacts made.

The concerns of the surveys may be summarized in five basic questions crucial to assessing the effectiveness of a site in meeting its management objectives and to shaping its future management strategy. Who are the visitors? Where do they come from? Why do they choose to go to Sherwood or Rufford? What do they do there? What do they think about the sites?

Table 5.13 Sherwood and Rufford Country Parks: visitor characteristics

Age of adult visitors	%	Employment status	HOH %	All adults %
16–24	16	Full time employed	78	62
25–44	47	Unemployed	2	5
45+	38	Retired	16	14
		Housewife	2	16
		Other	2	3

Total size of party		Social class	
1 person	5	Professional	9
2 people	32	Managerial	20
3 people	19	Other non manual	33
4 people	25	Skilled manual	28
5 people	11	Semi skilled manual	5
6+	8	Unskilled manual	1
		Other	3

Children in party		Frequency of taking countryside trips	
Yes	48	More than once a week	11
No	52	Once a week	32
		2–3 times a month	20
		Once a month	20
		Several times a year	14
		Once a year or less	2

First timers or old hands?	
First visit to park	26
Repeat visit	74

Source: Countryside Commission 1985

Present users were predominantly in the age range 25–44, in full time employment, and in white collar occupations (Table 5.13). The sites appealed almost equally to groups with and without children, and all but five per cent of users visited with other people; over three-quarters visited in groups of two to four. Most users were repeat visitors to the sites, and frequent visitors to the countryside more generally. Seventy four per cent had been to Rufford or Sherwood previously, and 43 per cent visited the countryside at least once a week. Use was predominantly local (Table 5.14), with virtually half the visitors living within ten miles of the site visited, and 64 per cent residing in the county of Nottinghamshire. All but 13 per cent of visitors travelled to the sites directly from their own homes, or from the homes of friends and relatives. Most decisions to visit were made on the day, either before setting out (37 per cent), or during the course of the journey (19 per cent). A further one-fifth were made the day before. Only nine per cent of visitors planned their trip more than a week previously (Table 5.15). Reasons for visiting the sites were varied. However, much of the flavour of that variety was lost in the coding, for although the personal interview survey asked open questions about people's reasons for visiting, and allowed the recording of full and spontaneous responses, analytical parsimony forced the answers into a few rather vague categories. Of these, going for a walk or outing predominated, followed by showing the site to friends or relatives, and just passing through.

Table 5.14   Sherwood and Rufford Country Parks: Visitor origins

County	%	District	%
Nottinghamshire	64	Mansfield	15
South Yorkshire	9	Newark	15
Derbyshire	9	Nottingham	10
Lincolnshire	2	Bassetlaw	8
Leicestershire	1	Sheffield	5
Rest of UK	13	Ashfield	5
Outside UK	2	Gedling	5
		Elsewhere	37
Distance travelled		*Place set out from*	
10 miles or less	48	Own home	72
11–20 miles	24	Friends'/relative's home	15
21–30 miles	17	Hotel etc	10
31+ miles	10	Other	3

Source: Countryside Commission 1985

What visitors did was addressed mainly in terms of how long they stayed on site and how much they spent. Most (69 per cent) stayed for one to three hours, and the same proportion made use of the visitor centres on site. Over a third (36 per cent) spent nothing in the centres. Newcomers to the sites spent considerably more than repeat visitors, and holiday makers more than local residents.

Table 5.15 Sherwood and Rufford Country Parks: decisions to visit

	%	%
(a) When decision was made		
15+ days ago	6	
8–14 days ago	3	
4–7 days ago	6	
2–3 days ago	7	
Previous day	22	
On the day, before setting out	37	
On the day, after setting out	19	

(b) Main reason for visit	Sherwood	Rufford
Walk or outing	29	36
Show relatives/friends	14	15
Passing through	10	10
Bring children	8	5
Robin Hood legend	18	–
Visit craft centre	–	9
Other	19	22

(c) How first heard about the parks		
Always knew	37	
Word of mouth	30	
Saw sign when driving past	13	
Tourism information	4	
Guidebook	3	
Advertisement	3	
Other	10	

(d) Where heard about parks in past 6 months*		
From friends/relatives	33	
Newspaper advertisements	18	
Newspaper articles	14	
Libraries	11	
Tourist Information Centres	10	
Guidebooks	7	
TV and radio	8	
Other	5	
None of these	33	

(e) Repeat visitors: influenced by publicity?		
Yes	22	
No	78	

* % sum to over 100 due to multiple responses

Source: Countryside Commission 1985

Table 5.16 Sherwood and Rufford Country Parks: What visitors think

(a) *Reactions to Visitor Centres*		% liking 'a lot'
Sherwood:	Robin Hood Exhibition	85
	Shop	65
	Cafe	49
	Studio	70
Rufford:	Craft shop	79
	Souvenir shop	60
	Buttery cafe	88
	Gallery	75

(b) *Expectations and experiences*	%	
	Sherwood	*Rufford*
Much as expected	43	60
Better than expected	51	38
Worse than expected	2	–
No answer	3	2
Differences from expectations:		
More organized/developed	30	12
More commercial	8	6
Bigger	–	8
Other	38	54

Source: Countryside Commission 1985

Attitudes towards the facilities provided were generally favourable (Table 5.16). At Rufford each facility asked about was liked 'a lot' by at least 60 per cent of visitors, and the various craft and catering centres by at least three-quarters. At Sherwood the cafe received rather less acclaim, but all other facilities were liked by a substantial majority. All but a tiny minority felt that the sited matched up to or exceeded their expectations. Many, especially at Sherwood, found the sites more organized or commercialized than they had anticipated, but this apparently did not detract from their experience; indeed, the inference from the figures is that it enhanced their day out.

A more modest but innovative study of use employing a mixture of research methods was undertaken by *Nichols (1986)* on the Tissington Trail in the Peak District. Nichols used a combination of car park counts, moving observer counts, user interviews and participant observation to establish usage levels and on-site behaviour patterns. The Tissington Trail follows the line of the disused Buxton to Ashbourne railway line for 21 kilometres from Ashbourne to Parsley Hay. It was opened in 1971 as a footpath, cycle track and bridleway, with car parks located on the sites of former railway stations, and cycle hire points at two of them. Car park counts gave an indication of the total number of users present. Moving observer counts to obtain an approximate 'point in time' portrait of total usage, involved the observer cycling along stretches of the route and mapping the users encountered, differentiating between walkers and cyclists. Much of the effectiveness of the method depended on the fitness of the researcher: as Nichols recorded (p.37), 'the quicker the observer..... could cover the trail, the more accurate were the observations'!

Despite their ubiquity, the full potential of site surveys remains unrealized. While each is useful in its own right, most have been designed as one-off studies, with no thought of comparison with other sites or other years. Even comparisons between studies which have sought the same basic information are thwarted by a lack of standardization in questions asked, definitions used, samples selected and categories coded. Guidance on survey design and standardization is readily available *(Davidson 1970a, 1970b, Countryside Commission 1974b, Tourism and Recreation Research Unit 1983b)* but not so readily heeded. Though their value to site management is unquestionable, it could be greatly enhanced. Surveys replicated at different times for the same site would permit the monitoring of trends in use, and the effect of any design, management or facility changes. Comparable surveys for neighbouring sites would demonstrate the overlap or independence of their catchments, in both geographical and social terms.

Visitor behaviour

More is known of visitor profiles than of visitor pastimes, yet for management purposes the way in which demand is expressed is at least as important as knowing the simple volume of demand. Few surveys examine visitor behaviour on site, and how this relates to landscape features, the siting of facilities or the presence of other users. *Locke (1985)* included a number of behavioural questions in his user surveys of country parks in Nottinghamshire, asking people about their use of visitor centres, their spending on site, and their likes and dislikes. Locke's study also did more than most in translating survey message into management action. For example, it was found that as many as one in five visitors had not decided where to go on setting out from home, but decided to visit the country parks on seeing signposts as they drove along. As a result, the County Council now pays greater attention to the provision of local roadside information as a way of influencing visitors' decisions.

Greater detail on patterns of site use was obtained by *Burton (1974)* and *Glyptis (1981a, 1981b),* using a combination of observational and questionnaire methods. Studies such as those in North Humberside highlight management solutions as well as problems *(Glyptis 1981a, 1981b).* Visitor numbers and spatial distributions at Spurn Peninsula and the Westwood common, Beverley, were recorded on several occasions on several weekdays and Sundays at each site. Many similarities of behaviour were found, despite considerable contrasts in the character of the sites.

Spurn Peninsula is a sand and shingle spit protruding 5.6 kilometres across the mouth of the River Humber, with Hull the nearest major centre of population, 42 kilometres to the west. Spurn Nature Reserve, managed by the Yorkshire Naturalists' Trust comprises 113 hectares of land above high water mark, and nearly 200 hectares of foreshore. Spurn has extensive sandy beaches on its seaward side, and smaller beaches facing the estuary. Outside the coastguard area at the head of the peninsula, visitors may wander at will throughout the site, apart from occasional temporary restrictions to protect certain species at critical times of year. Access along the peninsula is by single track road. Visitor facilities are limited to a modest information centre near the entrance to the site. Beverley Westwood is an undulating site comprising 242 hectares of common pasture land on the north western edge of the town of Beverley, 13 kilometres from Hull. The site contains scattered clumps of woodland, Beverley racecourse, a disused windmill, and several viewpoints overlooking Beverley town and Minster. The public has freedom of access to the entire site for recreation on foot, and car parking is permitted within defined margins of the four roads which cross the site. There are no specific recreation provisions on site apart from seats at several vantage points, and ice cream vans at key locations at weekends.

Recreational use at both sites is dominated by sitting, sunbathing, walking, picnicking, playing informal games, and sitting in the car. On busy summer Sundays, Spurn attracts approximately 1000 visitors, and Westwood 2000. At neither site does use adhere to an even spread in time or space. At both, usage is concentrated into peak times and favoured places, in a pattern which repeats with remarkable consistency. At both sites, the greatest visitor pressure starts in early afternoon, regardless of the absolute numbers involved. At Spurn, peak use occurs between 2.30pm and 3.30pm, with numbers typically doubling between 12.30pm and 2.30pm. Peak use at Westwood occurs slightly later, reflecting its appeal primarily as a destination for half-day rather than whole-day trips.

On site, one would expect to find the greatest dispersion of visitors at the time when the greatest numbers were present. However, temporal influx is not wholly evident in spatial spread. Fig 5.1 demonstrates this for a busy summer Sunday at Westwood. The distribution observed in the first count of the day reflects many features reinforced later on. Visitors show a clumped distribution pattern, underpinned by a mixture of preference and site characteristics. Most evident of all is a desire by the majority to stay close to the car. A second influence is enclosure; several people were attracted into the relatively enclosed, wooded area at the eastern end of the site. A third factor is the 'edge' effect: several visitors locate themselves at the edge of either the eastern wooded area, or Burton Bushes at the western end of the site. Indeed, far from the final count of the day showing the greatest spread of people across the site, it actually revealed some contraction. At the time shown, 70 per cent of the 1,094 people on site were located along the roadsides, and 500 of them along a single road!

Figure 5.1 Visitor distribution: Westwood Common, Beverley.

Figure 5.2   Model of visitor dispersion

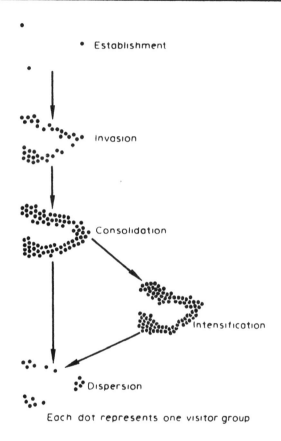

Each dot represents one visitor group

Source: JA Patmore 1983 Recreation and resources. Blackwell

Both pattern and process are similar on other days, and at Spurn peninsula, a very different site in landscape terms. The dynamics of visitor dispersion may therefore be expressed in a simple descriptive model, adapted from theories of the diffusion of innovations (Fig. 5.2). Those who arrive first at a site establish themselves in a few favoured places, mainly linked to parking areas, focal landmarks or sheltered locations. Visitor inflows thereafter, especially in an early afternoon 'invasion' phase, extend these initial clusters. As the pace of arrivals slackens, further infilling and 'consolidation' take place. Later, as people leave, 'dispersion' occurs, with the distribution reverting once more to an irregular scatter. Before this takes place, however, there may be a phase of 'intensification' with new arrivals continuing late into the after-noon, and clustering even more tightly into the most favoured locations. Thus, although, as numbers increase, sites clearly experience an increase in visitor density, visitor dispersion in a spatial sense remains fairly constant, even with space to spare and no restrictions on public access.

The propensity to cluster can be measured mathematically. The distance between each visitor (or visitor group) and the nearest other visitor can be measured from observation maps (or, with less subtlety, on the ground!). The average of the 'nearest neighbour' distances then summarizes the degree of visitor clustering at a given point in time. That average, of course, decreases as numbers increase through the phases of invasion, consolidation and intensification. However, results from observations for several days at Westwood and Spurn reveal some less obvious findings. Firstly, actual distances between visitors are quite similar for the two sites, which suggests there may be a level of proximity which people prefer (or, at least, find comfortable or tolerable), irrespective of the nature of the surroundings. Secondly, nearest neighbour distances are remarkably low given the overall areas of the sites.

Knowing the area of a site and the number of visitors (or visitor groups) present, it is possible to calculate the nearest neighbour distance that would pertain if people sought to locate themselves to maximize their personal space. The amount of space available per group is clearly the site area divided by the number of visitor groups present. Assuming (rather inappropriately) that the distribution of visitors is unaffected by site characteristics, a group wishing to maximize its space will locate itself at the centre of a hexagon of that size, and the linear distance to its nearest neighbour may be derived by simple geometry. Actual nearest neighbour distances may then be compared with the resulting theoretical neighbour distances. Expressed in percentage terms, the comparison is a measure of the visitors' propensity to cluster: as Table 5.17 shows, visitors occupied only 14 per cent to 31 per cent of the space actually available to them. Furthermore, as levels of use increase on a given day, the percentage occupancy of space actually decreases: visitors only ever use about a fifth of the space available to them, and at times of heaviest use they choose to occupy even less! In other words, site carrying capacity changes continually, and at these particular sites capacity appears to increase faster than the rate of visitor arrivals. In certain areas, the capacity to absorb visitors is both high and cumulative, with existing nodes of activity attracting further use at an accelerating rate. Activities and impact are highly localized, at predictable times, in predictable places.

Use of a single site cannot be explained wholly in isolation, for its appeal depends not only on its own intrinsic attractiveness and accessibility, but also on the availability of alternatives. Each site is but part of a system, its use affected by public awareness of, and attitudes towards, other opportunities. This is recognized by some consortia of managers, mainly in the commercial sector, in the collective marketing of sites, such as 'Devon's Top Ten Attractions'. It is rarely the subject of research, yet its planning and management messages are crucial.

Table 5.17 Visitor dispersion

| | | Spurn Peninsula | | | | | | Westwood. Beverley | | | |
| | | | Nearest neighbour distance (metres) | | | | | | Nearest neighbour distance (metres) | | |
Day	Count	No. of groups visitor	Actual	Theoretical	Actual ÷ theoretical %	Day	Count	No. of groups visitor	Actual	Theoretical	Actual ÷ theoretical %
Sunday I	1	139	25.0	143.1	17.5	Sunday I	1	148	35.2	164.6	21.4
	2	212	17.9	115.8	15.5		2	302	19.9	115.2	17.3
	3	243	18.2	108.2	16.8		3	305	16.8	99.5	16.9
	4	237	17.2	109.6	15.7		4	397	15.7	100.5	15.6
	5	114	28.4	158.0	18.0						
Sunday II	1	113	43.6	158.6	21.8	Sunday II	1	106	54.9	194.5	28.2
	2	150	24.1	137.7	17.5		2	103	36.6	197.3	18.6
	3	138	27.8	143.6	19.4		3	285	25.5	118.6	21.5
	4	114	35.9	158.0	22.7		4	387	18.6	101.8	18.3
	5	99	34.6	169.5	20.4						
Weekday I	1	35	62.6	285.1	21.9	Weekday I	1	76	49.0	231.2	21.2
	2	33	84.9	293.6	28.9		2	182	27.6	148.4	18.6
	3	39	75.4	270.1	27.9		3	228	21.1	132.6	15.9
	4	55	54.4	227.4	23.9		4	159	26.5	158.8	16.7
	5	57	68.8	223.4	30.8						
Weekday II	1	53	51.8	231.7	22.3	Weekday II	1	37	88.9	329.1	27.0
	2	108	30.6	162.3	18.6		2	80	56.6	223.8	25.3
	3	167	23.3	130.5	17.8		3	101	39.1	199.2	19.6
	4	193	17.9	121.4	14.7		4	63	52.9	252.5	21.0
	5	110	24.4	160.8	15.2						
Overall mean					20.4						20.2

Cooper's study of tourist behaviour in Jersey provides a model approach, and provides insights into visitor behaviour which are worthy of wider testing. The more familiar visitors became with their surroundings, the farther they ventured away from their base. Exploration, though, was fairly cautious, with visitors seeking sites that would offer low risk of disappointment. *Jackson (1982)* reached similar conclusions in Dovedale, and also examined awareness. Eighty nine per cent of visitors to Dovedale claimed to have heard of Chatsworth House, 70 per cent knew of Milldale (8 kilometres away), and 66 per cent of Monsal Dale (14 kilometres). Only 42 per cent had heard of Froggatt Edge, over 20 kilometres from Dovedale. Actual levels of awareness are likely to have been lower than those stated: 12 per cent claimed to have heard of Bittledale, a fictitious site included in the survey to test the accuracy of the responses!

Motivations and satisfactions

Standardized survey tools can portray profiles and patterns, but do little to explain them. The bluntness of the tool belies the subtleties of purpose and of meaning which motivate behaviour and condition response. The superficiality of the survey approach in this context is evident in the National Survey of Countryside Recreation. The 1984 survey asked respondents who had been to the countryside recently 'what prompted you to make this trip?' Answers were coded into five predefined categories, and composite 'others'. The vagueness of the results (Table 5.18) serves neither to explain behaviour nor enlighten management.

Table 5.18 Motivation for most recent trip to the countryside

	%
Wanted to go to that particular place	29
Just wanted to go somewhere in the countryside	28
Wanted to take part in that particular activity	19
To be with the family	10
Because something there at the time	2
Other reasons	12

Source: National Countryside Recreation Survey 1984

Sometimes, of course, there may be little to explain. Much behaviour is spontaneous, the whim of the moment with no deeper rationale. For many, though, the countryside holds more profound meaning, borne of intensely personal experience or a common cultural heritage. Far more revealing at this level are qualitative approaches, such as the small group discussion technique derived from group-analytic psychotherapy by *Harrison et al (1989)*. This was used to explore what the countryside means to people and how these feelings are formed. The study investigated four sample groups from different neighbourhoods in the London Borough of Greenwich — two white working class groups, one middle class, and a group of Asian women. Each group met weekly for six weeks. The values they held encapsulated three broad themes.

The first concerned the pleasures of nature and the countryside:

> Group members described a kaleidoscope of sounds, smells, sights and tactile experiences of nature. These intangible, intrinsic properties of the countryside are a source of great delight: the sensory experiences of being exposed to the weather and different seasons and in different environments, surprise encounters with wildlife that are always possible, the opportunities for adventures and natural settings were feelings and values shared by individuals from very different social and cultural backgrounds. *(Harrison et al 1989, pp.47–8)*

Beneath these shared values were certain social contrasts. The Asian and working class groups enjoyed the countryside in the company of others, and valued the variety of opportunities to walk, visit historic sites and farms, and stop at pubs, villages and shops. The middle class group preferred solitude — or, rather, the company of 'sympathetic others' — and absence of facilities, enjoying 'a more self-conscious encounter with nature and landscape'.

The second theme concerned definitions of countryside. Most saw it as farmed and settled countryside, only a minority as wild and open country. The latter was essentially a middle class view held by those who viewed as contrived the working countryside of farms and villages cherished by the other groups. For the vast majority, though, including many of the middle class, 'the countryside . . . . . encompasses villages and pubs, farms and woods, walks through fields, commuter settlements and village greens . . . . . admiring the view is mentioned as well as admiring people's houses . . . . . feeling relaxed and actively engaging in the pleasures of walking, visiting farms, village shops or cafes are pleasures mentioned by people in all the neighbourhoods' *(ibid., p.54)*. Enjoying the countryside goes far beyond the solitary and reflective stance of the popular policy stereotype.

The third theme was the social meaning of countryside, most notably its evocation as a better world, embodying the positive qualities — social as well as environmental — lost in an urbanized age. In the urban image, 'country people are part of a community which cares for all its members . . . . . doors can be left open; there is no crime or vandalism; no local authority; no tower block; and children can play in safety' *(ibid., p.49)*. Adulation, though, stopped short of wanting to live in the countryside, for lack of company, convenience and creature comforts.

Attachment to the countryside stemmed from both individual and social experience, especially in childhood. Importantly, it was felt not only by frequent visitors to the countryside, but also by those who rarely

Table 5.19 Trends in club membership

	1950	1960	1970	1980	1985
Camping & Caravanning club	13,800	52,000	110,000	187,200	182,000
Ramblers Association	8,778	11,300	22,178	35,731	57,936
National Federation of Anglers	+	+	354,401	478,000	332,934
British Canoe Union	1,231	3,523	5,348	10,800	11,400
Royal Yachting Association	1,387	10,543	31,089	65,180	73,520 •
British Surfing Association	+	+	+	1,000	1,325 •
British Sub Aqua Club	2,097	4,469	13,721	27,075	33,988 •
British Water Ski Federation**	10	30	100	155	159
British Cave Research Association	+	+	450	657	800
British Cycling Federation	66,528	20,918	10,594	14,461	14,350 •
Cyclists´ Touring Club	53,574	25,786	18,894	39,245	35,229
British Field Sports Society	27,269	20,250	20,965	+	69,000 •
British Association for Shooting and Conservation***	+	+	21,255	47,500	75,000
Clay Pigeon Shooting Association	371	455	1,659	9,776	13,000
British Ski Federation	+	+	53,991	51,000	71,000
British Horse Society	+	+	17,000	32,000	35,500 •
Pony Club	4,000	6,000	13,300	53,958	39,001 •
British Gliding Association****	20,000	30,000	8,000	10,600	9,999
British Hang Gliding Association	+	+	+	5,300	5,800 •
British Orienteering Federation	+	+	+	22,000	50,700

+ Figures not available   *** Formerly WAGBI — Wildfowlers Association of Great Britain and Ireland
• 1984 figure   **** Flying members
** Number of clubs

Source: Countryside Recreation Research Advisory Group 1976, 1980; Sports Council 1986

or never went there: 'People may not want to live in the country, may not want to visit regularly or even infrequently, but they need to know that the possibility exists' *(ibid., p.50)*.

Overview

Demand is neither generated nor expressed in an unconstrained way. It arises from personal preference, shaped by means, mobility and fashion, and facilitated or constrained by the real and perceived availability of opportunities. To measure or monitor demand is by no means straightforward, but a multiplicity of studies show that demand is buoyant, widely spread across the social spectrum, and static in some activities but growing rapidly in others. There is scope for growth in both volume and variety. Despite its breadth of social spread compared with many other leisure activities, the majority of countryside recreation is undertaken by a minority of the population, with evidence of considerable latent demand among non-users and infrequent users. Growth derives not merely from removal of constraint but also from creation of opportunity, not least in the form of newly developed activities resulting from technological advance and the quest for adventure. The essential informality of mass demand remains, however, and with surprisingly predictable expression. Evidence shows that people focus their countryside recreation on the local and familiar, and that patterns of site (and area) use are remarkably consistent in both a spatial and temporal sense. While demand ranges over a wide geographical area and through all seasons of the year, the real impact is experienced not in any blanket spread of use, but at predictable times and popular locations. Visitor management techniques can easily reinforce or redistribute the load, and these are considered in Chapter 6. Their true effectiveness, however, should be measured not merely in terms of visitor behaviour, but also in terms of visitor expectations and satisfactions, and these are relatively under-researched. More positive approaches are emerging, but with recreation having been so readily perceived as a threat, rather more management attention has been given to customer control than customer care in the countryside.

6 Providing a service: planning and management issues and approaches

Demand and supply in countryside recreation have no simple interface. Demand is large, growing, varied and diversifying. Some is specific to site and season, but much is unconfined in space or time. Some brings benefits to countryside areas, some brings threats. Supply is not simple or static. Multiple ownership and multiple use make provision fragmented and policy powers limited. However, while the resource is finite — and in places fragile — its recreational capacity is not, in any real sense, fixed. Making positive provision for recreation while protecting the resource itself is the core objective of countryside recreation management. This chapter examines planning approaches, management techniques and services which attempt to strike that balance.

Management by objectives

As Chapter 2 showed, throughout most of the 20th century countryside legislation, planning and management have evolved more for the solving of problems than the setting of positive strategies. The 1980s, though, brought a climate of change. Specific influences are hard to discern, but the swing from reactive to proactive approaches drew impetus from a number of sources. Firstly, recession and restraint caused policy makers and providers to review the effectiveness of their spending and account for the deployment of resources. Secondly, the scale of social, economic and technological changes in progress and in prospect caused agencies to reassess community needs. Thirdly, the main public sector agencies charged with a responsibility for recreation had been in existence long enough to evaluate the effects of earlier approaches. Fourthly, in the environmental field, the growing awareness of the fragility and finite supply of natural resources fostered public concern for conservation and a growing conscience on the part of providers and politicians. Fifthly, the change to independent status in 1982 of the main countryside agency, the Countryside Commission, gave that particular organization greater freedom than hitherto to define the purpose and direction of its work. Increasingly, at both strategic planning and tactical management levels, countryside recreation management has become 'management by objectives'.

Strategic planning

A strategic planning approach is by no means the sole preserve of the Countryside Commission. Indeed, in the recreation field, the first strategic plans were, arguably, the Regional Strategies produced by the Regional Councils for Sport and Recreation from 1976 onwards. At national agency level, collective acknowledgement of the challenges that lay ahead came with the publication of the discussion document *Leisure Policy for the Future (Chairmen's Policy Group 1983)*. The translation of acknowledgement into action rested with individual agencies. In strategy formulation, and in the painstaking review of social and economic trends and past policy measures, the Sports Council was the pioneer *(Sports Council 1982, 1988)*. Others followed *(Countryside Commission 1983b, 1987a; English Tourist Board 1987)*, with rather less presentation of research evidence, but equally articulate statements of intent.

More recently, in the light of further research evidence and new challenges, the Countryside Commission published further policy documents on specific issues, notably the rights of way network, common land, and access to the wider countryside. Its recreation policies have become more people-oriented, drawing in particular from the *1984 National Countryside Recreation Survey* and from associated qualitative research on attitudes to open space and motivations for visiting the countryside. The public's deep sense of attachment to the countryside, coupled with evidence of lack of access, lack of awareness of opportunities, or lack of confidence in using the opportunities, prompted the Commission's policies for delivering countryside information, developing better public transport links, and the management of the countryside as an integrated system, rather than a series of discrete sites. *Phillips and Ashcroft (1987, p.323)* signify the lessons drawn from the Commission's research: 'A central conclusion which can be drawn from these results is that the providers of recreation should try to understand the needs of people, rather than simply be technically expert at providing facilities. Opportunities to enjoy the countryside are of little value unless people are aware of them, value them and are able to enjoy them'.

Area management

Management by objectives is no less important at area level and for individual sites and facilities. This has long been recognized by the Countryside Commission in experimental management schemes for upland areas, urban fringe sites, Heritage Coasts, and country parks. Area management for recreation is the exception rather than the rule in the UK, but the exceptions are worthy of address for the lessons they offer. They have arisen where concerted action has been needed to protect threatened landscapes, ensure positive after-use of exhausted mineral land, or resolve acute conflicts. No standard mechanism has been adopted. This section refers to illustrative examples.

One is the standing conference, such as that which manages the Colne Valley Park, an area of 100 sq. kilometres in the inner green belt west of Greater London. The Standing Conference has no separate Act of Parliament but operates simply as a loose-knit consortium of authorities dedicated to achieving the park plan. The area is crossed by three motorways (M3, M4, M40), and subject to severe development pressures. Its southern end contains extensive sand and gravel extraction. Much land is owned by local authorities and statutory bodies, some is covenanted under the *1938 Green Belt Act,* and substantial tracts are owned by gravel companies. In the late 1960s the Greater London Council and neighbouring local authorities produced an appraisal of the recreational potential of the area, and set out policies for achieving it *(Greater London Council 1972).*

The main aim of the Park is to preserve its rural character. Subject to that overriding objective, it also seeks to provide accessible recreation opportunities for the large urban population living close by. Informal recreation is concentrated into 'activity centres', focused around facilities such as stately homes and water sports centres. Low intensity activities, such as walking, horse riding and cycling, are permitted elsewhere. Other areas are in productive farming use, or protected for purposes of conservation.

The Standing Conference comprises representatives of the county and district councils of the Park area, with varying attitudes to open land. The former Greater London Council was keen that the area should serve as a recreational lung for West London. The shire counties were keen to see the park absorb urban recreation pressures that might otherwise range further out into the green belt and the Chilterns. The loose-knit mechanism of a Standing Conference enabled them to work together to produce practical improvements to serve these differing ends.

Policy formulation has worked well. Policy implementation has been much slower. However, modest results have been achieved. There are two country parks and a farm centre, and the recreational after-use of wet gravel pits has been agreed. The landscape of the area, though, has deteriorated considerably, prompting the Countryside Commission to fund a Colne Valley Countryside Management Project from 1978. The project comprises three officers who work with landowners and volunteers to undertake landscape and access improvements, such as tree planting and footpath clearance.

A revised strategy for the park was published in 1983 *(Colne Valley Standing Conference 1983).* Several major recreation and conservation projects were identified, and lead agencies appointed to develop proposals more fully. The Greater London Council had already urged more vigorous action, including a major educational and interpretative centre, a projects fund for environmental improvements, and a Trust to generate funding from the private and voluntary sectors. These proposals met little support, however, from the authorities of the outer green belt, and with development and recreational pressures increasing there are signs that the 'inner' and 'outer' authorities may find it increasingly difficult to agree on concerted action. Without additional powers and resources, many of the aspirations of the Standing Conference will remain unmet.

A different approach has been adopted in the Greater Manchester area, where county and district authorities decided to work together in a more formal and regular partnership. The arrangements stemmed from concerns in the mid 1970s about the lack of public open space and large scale dereliction from past industrial activity. A county-district agreement on strategic environmental improvement was reached in 1975, and six Green Belt River Valley management schemes have been created *(Webster 1976, Maund 1982)*.

Each project has a programme of reclamation schemes to bring land into recreational use. Farm tenancies and grazing licences are used as mechanisms for low cost land management. Each valley has an information and interpretative centre, and conservation issues are dealt with through a Wildlife Working Group including representatives of local nature conservation trusts, the Nature Conservancy Council and the Royal Society for the Protection of Birds. 'Identity areas' defined in statutory local plans on the basis of differing landscape character, form the basis for recreation planning, and proposals include the need for both 'urban' recreation in the form of children's play opportunities, playing fields and allotments, and 'countryside' recreation, including walking, picnicking, visiting information centres, places of historic interest, and nature trails.

Management decisions are made for each project by a Joint Management Committee comprising representatives of the constitutent local authorities and the water industry. Members may also be co-opted from other agencies, such as the Countryside Commission. Each local authority makes land within its ownership available to the Joint Management Committee. The Joint Committees now manage over 800 hectares of land. Thirty-eight reclamation schemes have been implemented, and thirty-five tips restored.

The success of the scheme has many ingredients. The first is the agreement between the partner local authorities on the severity of environmental blight and the need for positive action. The second was a pre-existing commitment to derelict land reclamation. The third was the will to work together and pool resources. The fourth was the commitment of the former Greater Manchester Council to inject the bulk of the necessary finance. Success, however, brings its penalties, most notably the increasing revenue burden of sustaining the successful schemes.

Upon the demise of the former Greater Manchester County Council the work of the project transferred to the Greater Manchester

Countryside Unit, attached to Tameside Metropolitan Borough and supported financially by the ten Districts Councils of Greater Manchester and the Countryside Commission. Its budget for 1989–90 was £407,000, of which two-thirds was contributed by the district councils and one third by the Countryside Commission. The Unit has 17 permanent staff, together with volunteers and additional project officers engaged in specific schemes. These include a Countryside Commission sponsored project officer undertaking a pilot programme to promote countryside information in urban areas *(Greater Manchester Countryside Unit 1989)*.

Only the Lee Valley has a purpose designed authority. The Park comprises 4,000 hectares, stretching for 37 kilometres from the east end of London, near the Thames at Limehouse Basin, to Ware, Hertfordshire. Its northern half falls within the green belt. Main uses in the southern part include gravel extraction, sewage works, water supply reservoirs, and derelict industrial sites, and the need to remove dereliction clean up the river, and provide opportunities for recreation were the prime impetus for creating the Park. The voluntary amenity body, the Civic Trust, suggested establishing sixteen distinctive parks, 'linked' north–south by the canal and river *(Civic Trust 1964)*.

To expedite the plans, and to circumvent the complications of joint working between so many different local authorities and agencies, the Government agreed to establish a special authority, created under the *1966 Lee Valley Regional Park Act*. The duty of the Authority is 'to develop, improve, preserve and manage..... the park as a place for the occupation of leisure, recreation, sport, games or amusements or any similar activity, for the provision of nature reserves and for the provision and enjoyment of entertainments of any kind' *(Lee Valley Regional Park Authority 1986, pp.9–10)*. The Regional Park Authority was given powers to acquire land, and to provide and manage facilities. It has no power of development control, though it has the right to be consulted on development proposals. The Park is run by a Committee comprising representatives of the 12 local authorities over whose area the Park extends, and the Authority employs approximately 250 staff. It is funded through a precept on the community charge of the local authorities. Its aims and approaches were first defined in a Plan published in 1969, and revised seventeen years later *(Lee Valley Regional Park Authority 1969, 1986)*.

The Authority has acquired 880 hectares of land, and has pursued a vigorous policy of recreation provision at the southern end, including sports centres, leisure centres, horse riding facilities, a cycle racing track and a caravan park. In the northern, green belt, area priority is given to low-key forms of recreation. Land is acquired opportunistically rather than compulsorily, and the Authority's landscaping and management work have been confined to the land it actually controls; there is no overall landscape strategy, although greater emphasis has been placed on Park-wide improvements in recent years. Increased attention has also been paid to small scale environmental improvements, especially within the green belt, where possible harnessing the resources of local voluntary effort.

Despite its evident achievements, the mechanism of the ad hoc authority has not met with strong acclaim. Surrounding local authorities tend to be wary of its autonomy and resentful of its power to precept funds in a period of retrenchment. Its lack of accountability extends also to user and interest groups, who are not strongly represented in its decision making.

Upland management experiments

Seeking to ensure that farming was encouraged, and at the same time recreation opportunities were created and the landscape protected, the Countryside Commission, soon after its formation, began to experiment with positive forms of area management. The approach involved bringing together different interest groups, harnessing voluntary labour and goodwill, and co-ordinating the use of public and private funds *(Countryside Commission 1981)*. It was used first in the uplands. The Upland Management Experiments (UMEX) were initiated by the Countryside Commission in 1969 in the Lake District and Snowdonia *(Countryside Commission 1974c, 1976, 1979a)*. Aimed at reconciling the conflicting claims of recreation and farming, the schemes focused on small scale practical assistance of farmers to undertake landscape conservation works. Central to the success to each scheme was the appointment of a project officer with the autonomy to identify the work needed, and a modest budget to get it done. Activities included rebuilding dry stone walls, constructing stiles, and waymarking. The success achieved, both in tangible improvements for recreation, and in heightened goodwill between farmers and visitors, ensured the continuation of the schemes beyond their experimental phase, and the adoption of similar approaches in other National Parks.

Urban fringe experiments

The Countryside Commission recognized the potential of the area management approach in urban fringe areas too. Here the emphasis was on encouraging positive use of urban fringe land, to eliminate dereliction and make fuller provision for recreation. The intention also was to focus the attention of the many different interest groups on the problems to be rectified, and to foster co-operation between them; typically urban fringes tend to be located towards the edge of administrative areas, where policies for town and country often conflict. The first pilot scheme began in 1972 in the Bollin Valley in the southern urban fringe of Manchester. Success there persuaded the Commission that the experiment should be taken to a more complex urban fringe situation with stronger development pressures and greater intensity of use. The areas chosen were parts of the metropolitan green belt in Hertfordshire/Barnet and Havering, where projects began in 1975 and 1976 respectively. The areas had high proportions of derelict and disused land, a number of farm holdings owned by the local authorities, and examples of other rural land uses, such as horse grazing. They also had sympathetic local authorities committed to improving the local environment. The Hertfordshire/Barnet project covered 130 sq. kilometres, the Havering scheme 19 sq. kilometres. There was no pre-defined plan of action. The projects developed simply by the project officers getting to know their areas and local communities, and identifying specific instances of conflict or degradation which could be speedily resolved. The tangible results won the confidence of landowners and local councillors. Tasks undertaken were similar to those in the uplands, together with farm visits and tree planting undertaken by school children. Major schemes, such as clearance of large-scale dereliction, were referred for possible funding to the local authorities or other relevant agencies.

In terms of recreation and access, the projects sought to increase facilities for informal recreation and deal with problems of illegal access onto private land. Work to increase provision focused on creating bridleways, re-using derelict land, developing circular walks, and providing small scale facilities for informal recreation, especially near the urban edge. At the end of the Hertfordshire-Barnet experiment in 1979, the Countryside Commission funded a further experiment to examine the problems of managing publicly owned land. A five-year plan was also produced, to address the longer term future of countryside management *(Cairns 1983)*, and greater emphasis was placed on working with the local community, and involving local voluntary groups.

Though differing in emphasis, the projects shared the same broad aims. All were concerned with conserving and enhancing the landscape character and wildlife of the urban fringe, and all sought to improve public access. All sought to protect farming and forestry from urban development and other pressures. All set out to increase public understanding of the countryside and encourage voluntary action within the community to enhance the environment. Three broad techniques were employed in pursuit of these aims. The first was the practical resolution of small-scale conflicts. The second was the production of management plans by the project officer and project steering groups, to ensure that specific actions were guided by a framework of broader policy objectives. The third was the implementation of site-specific agreements, whether on an informal or legal basis.

As in the Upland Management Experiments, the key figure was the project officer, negotiating mutual respect and practical compromises between private landowners and the wider public interest. To be effective, project officers had to be seen as helpful and approachable, open-minded, and not tied to the perceived slowness of normal public sector bureaucracy. They had to win the confidence of landowners, secure the support of local people, inspire and organize voluntary effort, and be able to identify and respond rapidly to achievable improvement tasks. The success of the early pilot projects resulted in a proliferation of further schemes. *Elson (1986)* reported that 25 such schemes existed in the green belt by the mid 1980s.

Based on their evaluation of the Hertfordshire/Barnet and Havering experiments, the *Countryside Commission (1981)* identified the essential features of a successful countryside management service as follows:

1 The support of county and district authorities in providing the planning context and giving political commitment;

2 Forging strong co-operative links with the farming community as principal users of land and managers of the landscape;

3 An enthusiastic, knowledgeable and tactful project officer, who knows the area's people, problems and opportunities;

4 Delegated financial and administrative responsibility, allowing the project officer to respond quickly and effectively, and apparently independently from any single authority;

5 Positive response to suggestions from the local community;

6 Capacity to carry out a wide range of small scale practical work to alleviate farming problems, improve recreation facilities or conserve the landscape;

7 Ability to recognize opportunities and relay information to local authorities to help them respond more effectively and sympathetically to local needs.

The schemes were felt to bring benefits to the local authorities, farmers and landowners, local residents and visitors. For local planning authorities they provided a means of translating broad planning goals into practice, clarified countryside issues for local planning purposes, highlighted areas in need of action, fostered closer links with farmers and land owners, and engendered a multi-disciplicary approach to countryside issues. For farmers, the schemes helped to reduce problems caused by visitors, assisted with wardening and conservation work, and provided a source of advice and help. For local residents, they helped to reduce the adverse impact of visitors, improved the local landscape, provided attractive facilities for informal recreation free of conflict with other uses, and made people aware of opportunities to become involved in conservation projects and the work of local organizations. Visitors also benefitted, from better managed recreation facilities.

Success was not absolute, for in some areas ambition was tempered by reality. Strategic land use and land management problems in some areas, such as unclear policies on dealing with large scale dereliction, and a climate of uncertainty and speculation limited what could be achieved. Indeed, in some localities the countryside management · approach could be counter-productive, making small scale cosmetic improvements but obscuring the underlying cause of the problems. As the *Countryside Commission (1981, p.42)* emphasized, 'Countryside management was never meant to be a substitute for adequate policies for planning and strategic land management'; to maximize its potential it must be underpinned by a strong and adequately resourced planning framework.

Environmental trusts

Modest approaches achieve modest results and some areas need bolder treatment. This became evident in the Havering London Green Belt Experiment, where as much as one-fifth of the project area had been subject to gravel extraction in the previous fifteen years. In this particular case, efforts to bring together the major public, private and voluntary sector interests in the area failed, and there was no commitment to a joint programme to tackle the problems of the area. Elsewhere, the mechanism of the environmental trust has been used to achieve this purpose. It entails establishing a limited company, and securing charitable status and appointing trustees from various public and private sector interests in the area. The trusts serve as a focus to bring together the different agencies, gain their commitment, and harness their financial and human resources. Their slogan is 'Partnership for Action'. Trusts typically employ a project director, landscape designers, countryside managers and conservation managers.

The first such project was Operation Groundwork, established in 1981 in the urban fringe of St Helens, Merseyside. Two years later the programme was adopted more widely in the north west region, with the establishment of five more schemes, under the banner Groundwork North West, in Macclesfield, Rochdale-Oldham, Rossendale, Salford-Trafford and Wigan. The projects seek to involve local people and organizations more fully than traditional management approaches, and this is encouraged through a patrons' group, the Friends of Operation Groundwork, comprising local companies, organizations and individuals willing to sponsor improvement works or help the trust as volunteers. Activities of the Trusts comprise community projects, and those which are carried out on a commercial basis. The former typically include project officers working with young people and community groups, ranger services, and seconded teachers to work with children on environmental education projects. The latter include selling design services, and carrying out consultancy work in landscaping and land management.

The projects were given a large public sector boost, principally in the form of central and local government grants for clearing derelict land. The Countryside Commission also received additional grant aid to assist in getting the trusts established, and has funded them on a tapering basis in successive years. The trusts were expected to raise 15 per cent of their funds from outside sources in their first year, 30 per cent in the second, and be independent of Countryside Commission support in five years (Stansfield 1982).

Co-operation with farmers and landowners has been facilitated by the appointment to the trusts of staff seconded from the Ministry of Agriculture Fisheries and Food, and a Groundwork Nature Conservation Advisory Service advises on protecting and promoting the wildlife interest of the area.

Wider interest in the approach resulted in the government establishing a Groundwork Foundation in 1985 to promote the concept nationally. Fifteen trusts have been established, another four per year are expected to emerge, and a Groundwork Foundation co-ordinates their development.

A decade into the programme, effectiveness is hard to measure, and little monitoring data has been published. The appeal of the concept to the Countryside Commission and to local authorities can be seen in its ready adoption in so many places, but tensions remain. For local authorities there is the incentive of enhanced grant aid for derelict land reclamation, yet the possible disincentive of losing local control to wider area priorities. Financial strictures make it difficult for local authorities to make the necessary scale of commitment needed for the programmes, and in many areas local industry is struggling to survive, let alone find cash to spare for environmental enhancement. In 1988, recognizing that, for the time being at least, it was unrealistic to expect the trusts to be completely self-financing, the Department of the Environment took over from the Countryside Commission in providing direct grant aid.

Designing for visitors

Many facets of site design have a direct and immediate impact upon user satisfactions. *Rutledge (1971)*, writing of parks, advocated three key design principles: design with purpose; design for people; and design for both function and aesthetics. Designing with purpose ensures the appropriate relationships between different parts of the site, and takes into account the natural environment, built facilities, people's activities and needs, their relationship to each other, and to weather conditions. Designing for people moves away from technical standards of provision and management convenience, towards identifying and meeting people's needs. Designing for function and aesthetics seeks to achieve site efficiency combined with site attractiveness.

Design should begin with known user preferences. Ancillary facilities and support services should relate to the activities on offer and to the characteristics of the users. Facilities should be located in sensible functional relationships to each other, and in a sequence that matches normal behaviour patterns, minimizes confusion or conflict, and makes for easy flows of movement within a site. Indeed, circulation systems are not only crucial to site efficiency, but they can also be used as a powerful management tool for influencing visitor dispersion. Circulation systems should enable people to get to the places they want along pleasant routes which are safe and which avoid interference with other activities. They can be designed and routed to protect sensitive areas and to encourage visitor flow to particular areas (and hence away from others).

Patterns of visitor movement can be influenced in other ways. Chapter 5 noted the relationship between visitor distribution and site configuration, including the effect of 'edges', boundaries, and facilities. Fences and other barriers can be used as 'people-sifters' *(Miles and*

Seabrooke 1977), but the same effect can be achieved more subtly by the judicious planting of vegetation such as thorn bushes. Movable facilities, such as refreshment kiosks, seating and picnic tables, can be located to attract crowds to resilient areas, or they can be relocated from time to time to allow repair in heavily used areas. Vegetation can be planted to create more 'edges'. *Van Lier (1973)* noted the effect of such borders in increasing the capacity of beaches in the Netherlands.

There are arguments in favour of dispersion and concentration. Dispersion spreads the load, and prevents particular sites from carrying a disproportionate share of the total impact. It also, of course, spreads the impact, so that no area is completely spared. For that reason, the alternative strategy, of concentrating use into a few 'honeypot' locations has much to commend it. It concentrates use in areas capable of sustaining it, and concentrates the need for management and support services. Site management requires detailed monitoring of changes, and especially of any adverse impacts. Positive management action can then be taken before degradation becomes detrimental to the user experience, or more costly or impossible to repair.

Breaking down barriers

Proactive marketing is less common in the promotion of countryside recreation than in sport, but there are notable exceptions. One is Operation Gateway, a joint scheme of the Countryside Commission and Nottinghamshire County Council from 1983 to 1988. Adopting the philosophy of a 'Countryside for Everyone', the scheme used three approaches: direct assistance, by working with community groups, accompanying them on introductory countryside visits or arranging for 'host rangers' to receive them; raising awareness, through publicity, events, exhibitions and the media, using multi-lingual materials; and signposting of recreation services. Its aims were fourfold: firstly, to promote awareness of countryside recreation opportunities and an ability to take advantage of them through self-help; secondly, to create new interests among participants; thirdly, to provide unemployed people with a sense of satisfaction and purpose they would otherwise derive from work, and to provide employed people with satisfactions that may be lacking in their jobs; fourthly, to create a continuing awareness among county council staff of the needs of special groups.

Two temporary staff were employed to work in the community, identifying potential trip organizers and helping them to establish a programme. Provisions included day trips, farm visits for disabled groups, awareness events (slide shows and meetings), and production of literature in English, Urdu, Punjabi and Gujerati on countryside recreation sites and public transport services, and special activities for the over 50s *(Countryside Commission 1989j).*

Catering for special needs

For reasons of design, access or lack of promotion, countryside recreation resources are not always readily available to people with disabilities. Some providers, however, have paid particular attention to their needs. At Flamborough Headland a path has been installed for wheelchair users, and for the visually handicapped there are guide rails, foliage to touch, textural variations, and a mixture of fragrances. The Greater Manchester Countryside Unit has placed considerable emphasis on developing opportunities for disabled people to have access to the countryside. In conjunction with voluntary sector bodies, disabled groups and the district councils the Unit co-ordinated a major survey of the main countryside sites throughout the county, highlighting problems and opportunities for disabled people and identifying the need for improvement works. Special Water Activity Days have been held, together with training days for groups of mixed able-bodied and handicapped school children, including environmental problem-solving games. A Braille trail has been established at Etherow Country Park, with related cassette tapes, and tactile maps are in preparation for several key sites.

The Wildfowl and Wetlands Centre at Slimbridge also takes particular care of visitors with special needs. A recent initiative was the launch of a tape-guided tour for the visually handicapped. The tape guides visitors around the site, gives information on the collection of wildfowl, provides instructions on where to walk, and warns of any obstacles or potential hazards.

Prominent among voluntary sector interests in this area is the Fieldfare Trust, a limited company and registered charity which aims to promote enjoyment and education in the countryside for all sectors of the community, particularly those who are disabled or disadvantaged. It promotes the philosophy of Countryside for All, and seeks to operate in a participative way, working with people rather than for them. It seeks to build bridges between the urban community and countryside managers, between people with and without disabilities, and between the environmental heritage and those who are handicapped in enjoying it. It offers training and technical, managerial and development advice to public authorities, private firms and voluntary bodies. It also undertakes fundraising, to obtain grants, sponsorship and donations.

One of its major projects is the Kielder Challenge, sponsored by British Telecom. This is an adventure project for integrated teams of teenagers with and without disabilities which seeks to promote enjoyable countryside activities, social integration, personal confidence and broader horizons. The Challenge began in 1985 with six teams from the north of England. By 1988 the event covered the whole of the UK, with heats in twelve or more locations, and now up to 96 teams can enter. The finals take place in a two day event at Kielder Adventure Centre in September. Activities are judged on teamwork and endeavour, placing the emphasis on abilities rather than disabilities. As well as providing activities directly, the Challenge aims to encourage individuals, schools and clubs to develop outdoor activities of their own.

To create an environment for integration, the Challenge is structured into teams of eight, each including four youngsters with disabilities, typically two electric wheelchair users, one manual wheelchair user, and one ambulant disabled person. Teams generally comprise a mixture of boys and girls. Activities are devised with four themes in mind. Firstly, all members of the team should be actively and positively involved as much as possible; individuals have to consider their own circumstances and those of other people. Secondly, this should not restrict the range of activities available for more mobile members of the team. Thirdly, no one should be asked to undertake an activity which is inappropriate to their physical capabilities or inclination. Fourthly, all activities must be safe for all participants. Points are scored not only for performance, but also for team work in helping each other out, communicating well to agree the approach to an activity, effort and initiative. The rules of each game are devised to ensure that the best way to tackle it does not leave disabled people behind while others race ahead; indeed, it is often the youngsters with disabilities who take the lead in decision making. Sometimes the activities put team members without disabilities at a disadvantage, for example crossing an acid marsh so that the body does not come within two inches of the ground; here able-bodied youngsters have to rely on wheelchair users to take the lead role.

Recreation and conservation

Much of the need for management in countryside recreation relates not to welcoming visitors but to controlling their impact, or preventing and solving conflicts that arise between recreation and other uses.

The effects of recreation on flora, fauna and landscape more readily engender emotion and assumption than hard evidence. All too often the mere existence of recreational activity or the fact of temporary disturbance are taken to infer inevitable adverse impact. However, as *Watmough (1983, p.3)* plainly put it, in the context of recreation and waterfowl, 'It is a truism that birds will fly away when disturbed; for the successful management of enclosed waters it is necessary to know if this matters to the birds'.

Sidaway (1988) identified a range of possible recreational effects on fauna, vegetation and geological features (Table 6.1). These are discussed further in *Talbot-Ponsonby (1988)* and *Swinnerton (1989)*.

In the uplands the main concern is the erosion of hill paths. Once worn, the combination of repeated use, poor surface drainage and severe winter weather, compounds the problem, leading to gullying and preventing the recovery of vegetation. In peaty and poorly drained areas in particular, walkers will then avoid the boggy or muddy areas by walking on adjacent ground, effectively widening the path, and creating further damage. The physical effects of trampling have been extensively researched *(Bayfield and Barrow 1985, Wall and Wright 1977)*. The problems vary with the resistance of the site and the nature and intensity of the activity. On steep terrain erosion problems can be compounded by further gullying caused by rainfall. Activities such as

Table 6.1 Recreation and conservation: possible impacts

Disturbance of Fauna	Activity
Birds	
Disturbance to nesting species	
cliff breeding, eg auks, peregrine, chough	climbing, sub-aqua, canoeing, pleasure boating
moorland, eg grey plover, raptors	public access
woodland, ground-nesting species	orienteering, public access, scrambling
coastal beaches, eg little tern	public access
waterside, eg wildfowl	windsurfing, angling, public access
rare species, eg osprey	collecting, birdwatching, public access
Disturbance to moulting wildfowl	windsurfing, angling
Disturbance to over-wintering wildfowl and migratory waders	water recreation, notably, sailing, windsurfing, water-skiing, angling
Disturbance generally	birdwatching, wildfowling, grouse and rough shooting, clay pigeon shooting, public access
Lead poisoning in swans and wildfowl	angling, wildfowling
Mammals	
Disturbance to breeding/hibernating bat colonies	caving, canal boating
Disturbance to breeding seal colonies	sub-aqua, pleasure boating, canoeing
Insects	
Disturbance to dragonflies (aquatic vegetation)	propeller-driven canal boats
Invertebrate Marine species	collecting, sub-aqua, bait-digging
Damage to Vegetation	
aquatic macrophytes	propeller-driven canal boats
canal bank vegetation, algal growth	canal management: eg dredging, use of herbicides
alpine/arctic flora	climbing, skiing, sightseeing
moorland	long-distance routes, motor sports, horse riding
heath/grassland	sightseeing, motor sports, off-road vehicles, cross-country running, orienteering, horse riding
dunes	motor sports, beach access, horse riding
Damage to Geological Features	
sandstone cliffs	climbing
limestone caves, eg sediments, decorations	caving

Source: Sidaway 1988

ghyll-scrambling can therefore have a significant impact, not least as ghylls and gullies often support important relic flora *(Edwards et al 1989)*.

For repair of physical damage, site closure is clearly the most drastic form of management action. It may also be the most effective, allowing rejuvenation through natural processes or specialist treatment, and minimizing site recovery time. These benefits must be weighed against the disadvantages of diverting or frustrating demand in the period of closure, and the chances of winning back that demand when the site reopens. Another approach is the rest and rotation of sites, or of areas within sites. This allows at least some use to continue. A third approach is to keep the site open while undertaking rehabilitation works. This allows use to continue uninterrupted, but is only possible if remedial action starts before the damage is substantial.

Solutions are mainly technical, including for example soil treatments, ground cover improvements, fertilizing, reseeding and replanting, introduction of more resilient species, selective thinning of vegetation, removing harmful species, and installing hard surfacing in intensively used areas.

Problems are not limited to the land. *Tanner (1979)* examined the importance of the reservoirs of England and Wales for waterfowl, adopting a fivefold site classification system developed earlier by *Atkinson-Willes (1969)*. Of the 254 sites included in the Tanner study, 17 were Class I sites, of national importance because they accommodated a defined percentage of the total British population of particular species. Eleven reservoirs were Class II sites, holding a peak population of 1,000 or more wildfowl, and deemed to be of regional significance. Fifty-five were of local importance, with 250–1,000 wildfowl. Class IV sites were regarded as of minor importance, and the remainder were placed in Class V; numbers in these categories were 31 and 140 respectively. The major concentrations of significant wildfowl populations were thus concentrated into a relatively small number of large lowland reservoirs. Many of these, by their nature and location, are popular sites for recreation. Furthermore, the potential for conflict has increased with the extension of many sports into the winter months; hitherto, a degree of natural time zoning prevented major clashes of interest, as the presence of the peak over-wintering bird populations coincided with the close season of many sports. National reviews of the effect of recreation on waterfowl *(Tanner 1979, Tuite 1983)* concluded that, while recreation may affect the distribution of birds locally, there was no evidence that it caused population declines nationally.

The evidence available suggests that on large enclosed water sites, such as Rutland Water *(Appleton 1982)* and Grafham Water *(Cooke 1977)* the effective zoning of water space has enabled intensive recreational use and large populations of waterfowl to co-exist happily. On smaller sites, findings are mixed. Locally, birds may respond to recreation in a variety of ways. They may ignore it and continue undisturbed; they may stay in the same place but alter their behaviour; they may temporarily or permanently go elsewhere; and they may avoid completely any areas with recreational activity. As *Watmough (1983)* showed at Staunton Harold and Foremark Reservoirs in the Trent Valley, the response varies between different species and with different volumes and types of recreational activity. Three approaches were used. Firstly, the distribution of birds between the many water sites in the region was examined from national wildfowl counts, to see whether the birds were avoiding sites with recreational use. Secondly, levels of recreational activity (fishing and sailing) were increased experimentally at the two main sites. Thirdly, detailed studies were made of the behaviour of birds when disturbed, and the energy costs incurred.

Not surprisingly, the effects of recreation were more the greater the level of use. Of particular significance was the area of water in use for recreation. As expected, effects varied between bird species, with coot particularly tolerant, and wigeon and goosander the most sensitive. With weekend-only recreation and no refuge for waterfowl, most duck left the site, but returned the next day, incurring a 20 per cent increase in energy costs. With weekend-only recreation and a refuge, birds redistributed on-site during recreational activity, incurring five to ten per cent additional energy costs; depending on the pattern of recreation, the more sensitive species sometimes left the site. With continuous recreation and no refuge for waterfowl there were few waterfowl present at all. With continuous recreation and provision of a refuge there was no apparent change in wildfowl numbers. Watmough therefore concluded that the most effective way to reduce the effects of recreation was to provide a suitable refuge, of adequate size and habitat, and located at a suitable distance from recreational activity.

A similar zoning approach is adopted for land based recreation in the Peak District National Park. To ensure that recreational disturbance does not impede the breeding success of the declining populations of moorland birds, the Peak Park Joint Planning Board seeks to negotiate 'access corridors', which allow walkers access to the most popular areas, but maintain a wildlife reserve in the remaining one-third. Such an agreement is being negotiated on part of the Chatsworth estate.

Several studies *(Owens 1977, Batten 1977, Cooke 1977)* have investigated the distance at which birds take flight in response to recreational activities, and this assists the design of appropriate sanctuary areas. Watmough compared the effects of different activities. Mallard, for example, allowed walkers to within 260 metres before flying away, fishing boats within 250 metres, but yachts only within 400 metres, and shooting only within 725 metres. The length of flight of those disturbed ranged from 0.4 kilometres at times of low intensity recreation to 4.3 kilometres on busy Sunday afternoons.

Conservationists sometimes contribute to the problem. Virtually half of the reservoirs in the UK having a water surface of two hectares or more have hides or other facilities for birdwatching *(George 1980)*. Birdwatching was found to be causing a significant decline in bird numbers at Titchfield Haven, Hampshire *(Owen and Williams 1976)*.

Sidaway (1988) identified many examples of positive action and co-operation between recreation and conservation. Concern about the deterioration of the underground environment, for example, led the *National Caving Association* to initiate various conservation measures. The Association *(1972)* found evidence of damage to geological formations, or disfigurement with litter and graffiti in four-fifths of the most popular caves in the country. Measures taken included the establishment of conservation and access committees, new cave management systems, close liaison with the Nature Conservancy Council, co-operation in the management of cave SSSIs, and the publication of conservation leaflets and a code of practice for cavers. Management systems generally take the form of controlling access. Ogof Ffynnon Ddu, South Wales, a National Nature Reserve and Britain's deepest and second longest cave system, is a case in point. Access is controlled by the South Wales Caving Club on behalf of the Nature Conservancy Council. The system has three gated entrances. One gives access to a fine section of 'sporting streamway', and can only be entered with a leader agreed by the Club. A second may be used by clubs affiliated to the Regional Councils of the National Caving Association, who must apply for permits in advance. The third entrance is also controlled by permit. Within the cave access to some of the most spectacular but fragile formations, in Column Hall, is restricted to about four visits a year, accompanied by South Wales Caving Club leaders. Other types of management schemes used elsewhere include the taping of routes to prevent the trampling of ground formations, controlling by permit the use of explosives for exploration, and 'Adopt a Cave' projects in which clubs are asked to take on the responsibility of caring for particular sites.

Collaboration between sport and conservation is evident too in the example of climbing and cliff-nesting birds, where the focus of concern is the impact on specially protected species such as the peregrine falcon. The British Mountaineering Council (BMC) estimates that between five and ten per cent of the cliffs used by nesting peregrine are used for climbing. To avoid conflict, the BMC has agreed with the Nature Conservancy Council and local conservation groups a series of voluntary restrictions on climbing, which are well publicised and generally adhered to. These now apply to twelve nesting sites throughout England and Wales. The BMC embodies a number of conservation objectives within its own policies, and employs a full time Access and Conservation Officer.

The British Orienteering Federation invests considerable effort in working with conservation bodies and landowners in preparing its venues and maps, and planning its events. *Sidaway (1988)* concluded that in practice the impact of orienteering on vegetation is minimized to acceptable levels even on sensitive sites. However, the nature of orienteering is not widely understood, and many conservation bodies are prone to reacting on the basis of their perceptions of the sport as hordes of runners trampling over the same ground. In fact the organization of the activity is such that, in a typical event with 1,000 competitors, a maximum of 500 are likely to be spread around the competition area at any one time, and of course each participant takes a route of his or her choice. The likelihood of damage is therefore confined to the assembly and parking areas, and a small number of control points across the site.

Rather less success has been evident to date in reconciling the interests of waterway restoration and aquatic plant life. Sidaway cited the case of the restoration of the Basingstoke Canal, a joint initiative by Surrey and Hampshire County Councils as owners of the canal, and the Surrey and Hampshire Canal Trust. When disused, parts of the canal had dried out, and it held little scientific interest. Now, however, its water content, which flows through chalk in the west and acidic heathlands in the east, supports an unusually rich flora. This in turn supports several rare species of dragonfly. The canal has other conservation value too: the collapsed Greywell Tunnel supports several species of bats. Consequently, the Nature Conservancy Council has notified the owners of the scientific importance of four sites along the canal, and advocates 'quiet use' only, including canoes and rowing boats, with the number of motorized craft restricted to about 1,000 boat movements a year. This conflicts with the wishes of the county councils and the Canal Trust, whose prime reason for investing in the restoration has always been the use of the canal by pleasure craft of all types. Research is in progress to identify 'critical traffic ranges' with regard to the vegetation of the canal, and the Joint Management Committee of the project has established a conservation working party. Other issues arising include the impact on waterside vegetation of the wash from larger craft, and the effect on the diversity of the aquatic vegetation of homogenizing the water by working the canal.

Clearly motorized activities evoke the staunchest resistance but rather less research. The recent Royal Society for Nature Conservation (RSNC) report on damage to wildlife sites by off-road motor vehicles *(RSNC 1987)*, for example, claimed a need for tighter planning control but gave little information on the criteria used for measuring damage or evidence gained directly from the range of sites where damage is deemed to have occured.

Overall, *Sidaway (1988, p.97)* concluded that:

> Conflicts between recreation and conservation can be solved by sound management and planning. There are plenty of examples to prove the point . . . . . What does seem likely, however, is that conflicts of interest are likely to increase as environmental concerns and standards of protection are raised while recreation pressures grow.

These conflicts are greatest where the respective parties have markedly divergent philosophies; lack understanding of the relationships between species, habitats and human activity, or make assumptions about that relationship; are unwilling to respond to change, such as the onset of decline of a prized species; and have failed to communicate and collaborate regularly.

Sometimes the development and management of recreation facilities brings conservation gains instead of costs. Rutland Water, of international conservation significance and supporting a wide range of recreational use, is an outstanding example, albeit exceptional in scale. But good conservation practice can be applied to much more modest sites. *Marshall and Green (1984)*, for example, demonstrated the wildlife potential of golf courses.

Conflicts within recreation

Some forms of recreation can co-exist happily in the same space; others result on conflict. *Goodall and Whittow (1975)* produced a 'compatibility matrix' based on the resource requirements of particular pursuits. Compatibility of resource requirements, however, is no guarantee of compatibility of activities for different users may want to use the resource in quite different ways. Without effective management, noisy activities such as those involving power boats, motorbikes and other off-road vehicles can conflict with quieter pursuits such as fishing and bird watching. The problems tend to be greatest on constricted linear resources such as trails, rivers and canals.

The arise more from the actors than the activities, as *Jacob and Shreyer (1980)* make plan. In addition to the activity itself, they identified four further factors conducive to conflict. The first was activity style. This referred to the personal meanings which participants brought to their activities. Some may be dabblers, who enjoy participating at a casual level. Others may be much more intense, with the activity as a focal life interest, and a source and expression of status. The latter are particularly prone to conflict with other recreationists, as they regard few people and places as matching their high standards. The second factor was resource specificity. Some users attached particular importance and special qualities to particular sites, and developed possessive and protective attitudes, resisting the intrusion of others. The third factor was mode of experience, which Jacob and Shreyer referred to as focused or unfocused. The 'focused' user seeks an intimate association with specific aspects of the natural environment, whereas the 'unfocused' user simply enjoys the general experience of being in the countryside. The fourth factor was tolerance of lifestyle diversity. This suggested that people deliberately choose recreation sites and settings which accord with their social outlook and position, and are unhappy about sharing resources with people whose lifestyles they regard as inferior, deviant or merely different.

Angling sometimes coexists uneasily with other activities. According to the *1970 National Angling Survey* (NERC 1971), over half of all anglers felt that other users affected their fishing, and this was especially so of coarse anglers. Thirty per cent felt that their enjoyment was impaired by disturbances to the fish, 29 per cent by stirring up the water, 21 per cent by noise and seven per cent by damage to their fishing tackle *(Blenkharn 1980)*.

O'Riordan and Paget (1978) identified three levels of interaction between angling and boating. Most severe was direct physical contact between the parties involved. The second was verbal abuse and frustration. The third, and most widespread, was a more subtle feeling of nuisance and annoyance. In terms of physical interaction, there was no appreciable conflict between the two groups. However, passing boats were certainly noticed by the anglers, and regarded by many as an intrusion: 'the passing boat is still largely viewed as a "tolerable nuisance", but a nuisance nonetheless' (p.13). Anglers varied in their perceptions of the effect of boats on their chances of catching fish. Approximately equal numbers thought that boats did and did not drive fish away, did and did not kill fish with discharges, and did and did not stir up the fish and improve the catch. Boat users were generally unaware of the possibility that they may affect fishing prospects. The majority respected the need for courteous navigation, and requested that information be posted or leaflets be distributed to inform them of angling matches, so that they could anticipate the need for extra care, and adjust their speed or line of navigation accordingly.

Catching fish proved not to be the prime motive of the anglers, although luring fish to the hook was an important challenge. Most enjoyed fishing as a form of peaceful relaxation in a pleasant setting, and poorly handled boats were a cause of upset. Most anglers took steps to avoid boats in deciding when and where to fish, and those who had experienced most contact with boat users were rather more critical of them. Few boat users planned their trips to avoid anglers.

Anglers generally wished to see a voluntary restriction on the movement of boats at certain times, though this view was not widely shared by boat users. Neither group wanted stricter control over the timing of angling matches, but both favoured measures to improve communication. Overall, *O'Riordan and Paget* concluded that, despite the evident occurrence of thoughtless or abusive behaviour by a minority of those taking part in both activities, there were few signs of serious conflict between them, so long as each adhered to a minimum code of conduct expected by the other. With the increasing boat traffic likely to place additional pressure on constricted resources, however, it was felt that the prevailing goodwill should be harnessed before frustration levels rose, and that the formation of local users' groups representing both sets of interests should be encouraged; these could act as a mechanism for fostering communication and respect between the two groups, and co-ordinating their programmes to minimize conflict.

Angling and canoeing are not always the happiest companions. Anglers consider themselves longer in existence, with rights established over time and those rights paid for directly. Canoeists, they claim, disturb the water and the fish, interfere with fishing lines, and hit and damage the banks.

The mutual perceptions of the participants play a strong part in the interaction between motor sports and other users. Motor sports are often judged to be incompatible both with existing land uses and other forms of recreational activity, and many therefore suffer from problems of site availability. *Elson et al (1986a)*, concentrating on activities which do not depend substantially on purpose-built permanent facilities, identified no less than 19 different motor sports disciplines, including motor car hill climbs, sprints, Autocross, Rallycross, four-wheel drive sprints and trials, trail driving, motor cycle grass track racing, motor-cross scrambling, enduros, and kart racing. These vary enormously in nature and resource needs. Indeed, being subsumed under the 'motor sports' umbrella creates inaccuracies of public perception for some of them.

Estimates of participation by *Elson et al* suggest that there are approximately 200,000 motor sports participants in Britain, including 40–50,000 active competitive motor cyclists, and 102,000 active motor car and kart participants. Total motor sport club membership is of the order of 650,000. Outside the formality of organized clubs there exists a large but unquantifiable informal sector:

> Informal riders may vary considerably in motivation and attitude, from highly proficient adults who seek opportunities for off road riding with the minimum of disturbance to others..... to "cowboy" teenage riders using stolen and stripped down machines on rough land with little obvious concern for the impact of their activities on the environment or neighbouring site occupants. *(Elson et al 1986a, p.40)*

The activities of the latter can provoke antagonism against the entire sector, from both public and site owners alike. Motor activities generally, and the specific disciplines individually, suffer from problems of noise, image and land availability.

The governing bodies of motor sports are acutely aware of the noise issue. Most enforce their own noise controls at competitions, and the maximum permitted noise levels have been progressively reduced. If anything, public antagonism has grown, fuelled apparently by the intolerance of recent in-migrants to rural areas who see motor sports as urban, deviant, and at odds with their new-found rural tranquillity. The growth of the informal sector compounds the aggravation. Away from the public highway there is no statutory noise control. Where informal users misbehave on sites used by formal clubs, the clubs may be penalized or evicted. Informal use also leads to more frequent use of sites which clubs may wish to use sparingly in order to prevent the build up of public opposition. Similar problems on green lanes, where motor sports share with walkers and horse riders, have led highway authorities to seek to prohibit vehicular rights of way, thus denying access to legitimate motor sports users as well as the unruly fringe.

The image problem is essentially that of an urban activity making inappropriate claims upon the countryside. It is most acute on small rural sites, accessible only by narrow country roads, where events generate noise, smoke, fumes, erosion, traffic congestion and large numbers of people. Such problems indeed occur, but isolated incidents swiftly engender blanket opposition, and an assumption that any motor sports activity will inevitably cause the full range of impacts.

The noise and image issues give rise to the third problem of motor sports, that of site availability. Research by the *South West Sports Council (1976)* showed that, in a five year period, 34 out of 46 motor cycle clubs had lost at least one private site, and this of course compounds the pressure of use on remaining and unauthorized sites. Furthermore, many motor sports sites are temporary uses of land in transition from one use to another. Local authority response to the need for sites has been hesitant in all but a few cases, as many tarnish the organized sports with any problems of trespass, illegal riding, noise and damage that they have confronted among informal participants. *Elson et al (1986a, p.261)* make plain the inappropriateness of so doing:

> Organised motor sports have . . . . . existed in England for nearly 100 years. They constitute a set of legitimate activities whose attributes fall clearly within any commonly-held definition of sport. They involve the practice of skill, the measurement of performance, competition and, in many cases the development of responsibility and self-reliance. In addition, they perform a valuable training function at youth level and constitute social and community activities valued by club members.

Yet, 'Little has been done to counteract the orthodoxy, prevailing in many quarters, that motorsport interests are unprincipled, uncontrolled and immune to outside pressures'. The remedy rests largely with the motor sports organizations themselves, to be less introspective and defensive, more actively involved in forums which deliberate on access, rights of way, and land use issues, and more positive in promoting a responsible and professional image, eg by disseminating codes of practice and strongly promoting their training benefits. To achieve this, *Elson et al* proposed the formation of a national motor sports pressure group as advocate and consultee on all aspects of provision and control for the sports, and underpinned with regional motor sport liaison committees to promote action on the ground. Guidance for provision addressed to local authorities, land owners and motor sports clubs, setting out the site requirements and management considerations pertaining to the different sports, is given in *Elson et al (1986b)*.

Image and control problems are not confined to activities on dry land, as parallel studies of water sports and air sports by *Elson et al (1989a, 1989b)* have shown. The water sports study focused on the major activities of water-skiing and power boating, but with reference also to hovercrafting and the more recently established activity of jet-skiing. All are relatively new sports, and as such have experienced difficulty in gaining access to sites, most of which are already in recreational use by long established, and non-motorized activities. Inland sites are especially scarce. Sometimes the resistance is from residents rather than other recreationists. Initial plans for the Pugneys Water Area near Wakefield, for example, included provision for water skiing, but as the development progressed, it was excluded due to pressure from local residents. Proposals for the Wanlip site near Leicester changed from water skiing to conservation for the same reason. Air sports, notably gliding, parachuting, hang gliding, parascending and microlight flying, share some of the same problems. They are marginalized in the allocation of air space, and misunderstood by local authorities and rural residents.

Zoning

One way of preventing conflict between different activities is simply to keep them apart. Zoning, in effect, is management by separation. It allocates incompatible uses to different sites or different times. The introduction of time zoning on the Great Ouse and Norfolk Broads in the late 1970s succeeded in separating anglers and boat users, yet allowing each activity access to the whole resource. *Parry (1987)* advocated the use of time zoning at Ladybower Reservoir to protect the common sandpiper. Restrictions on angling for the critical first three weeks after hatching, in June, would provide protection for the young birds.

Spatial zoning is a common element in National Park planning, and the recent reviews of park plans have reiterated its value and effectiveness. In the Peak District, for example, proposals for recreation are considered in relation to five zones:

1 *Wild areas* with a general absence of human influence. Access will normally be allowed on foot. The only facilities provided will be footpaths and wildlife hides which cannot be located in other zones.
2 *Remoter areas of farmland and woodland* with generally poor vehicular access. Low impact recreation will normally be allowed, such as walking, riding, and cycling. Back pack campsites, hostels and farmhouse accommodation may be provided.
3 *The majority of the Park*, where recreation facilities of modest scale will be permitted or welcomed, such as small car parks, small farm based caravan sites, and facilities linked to riding, walking and cycling.
4 *Specific locations* particularly suited to a modest scale of recreational use. These may contain car parks and picnic sites linked to informal recreational use, or provide particular concentrations of facilities for overnight accommodation.
5 *Areas of highest intensity recreational use* and the major visitor facilities such as large car parks, visitor centres and caravan sites.
These will be robust landscape settings capable of absorbing heavy use, such as parkland and reservoir margin woodland. *(Peak Park Joint Planning Board 1988, p.110)*

The conversion of disused field barns provides low key and low cost accommodation compatible with the quieter areas of the Park. Camping barns (or 'bunkhouse barns') have been promoted by the Countryside Commission, and are found mainly in the Peak District and Yorkshire Dales. The drystone barns offer inexpensive overnight shelter, and generate a modest income and social contact for the owners. Typically they offer a communal sleeping platform for up to twelve people, a toilet, water tap and cooking area. There is no electricity or heating. The Peak District camping barn scheme started in 1983; by 1987 20,000 bednights had been recorded.

Zoning of water activities is widespread. At Langstone Harbour intensive recreational use — sailing, angling, boardsailing, pleasure boating and water-skiing — co-exist with significant conservation interests. Water-skiing is allocated a zone for use between March and October in which the general ten knots speed limit of the harbour does not apply. Skiers must obtain a licence, become members of the Langstone Harbour Water-Skiers Association, and display the licence on the towing boat. As well as minimizing conflict, the scheme ensures that all skiers understand the extent of the skiing zone, the location of the nature reserve areas, the directions of skiing, and the speed limits.

At site level, zoning for multiple use is only successful on larger areas, such as Rutland Water. *Newbould (1976)* suggested that a minimum size of water area for effective zoning is 200 hectares. For smaller water bodies, the more effective approach if possible is to allocate separate water bodies to separate functions. This has been possible, for example, in several gravel pit restoration schemes, including the Cotswold Water Park, Kingsbury Water Park in Warwickshire, and Great Linford at Milton Keynes.

Recreational carrying capacity

The capability of a resource to support recreational use is important both for the maintenance of the resource itself and for the recreational experience of the user. The concept of recreational carrying capacity is therefore, at first sight, a key management tool. The *Countryside Commission (1970c, p.2)* defined the concept as 'The level of recreation use an area can sustain without an unacceptable degree of deterioration of the resource or of the recreation experience'.

In addition to the generic concept, definitions of capacity from more specific perspectives have also been developed. The simplest is physical carrying capacity, literally the maximum number of people (or cars) that can be accommodated physically in a given area. As such, physical capacity is clearly a useful design concept for facilities such as tennis courts which, if the rules of tennis are to be upheld, have a fixed and absolute capacity. It is less useful, and less sensible, to apply to more open and extensive areas such as a countryside site, a lake or beach. Admittedly, such areas do indeed have a physical capacity, but most people would find the quality of the recreation experience insufferable long before it were reached, quite apart from the impact on the resource itself. In the countryside context, the concept of physical capacity is applied most usefully to ancillary facilities, such as car parks, whose capacity will in turn influence levels of use of the wider resource. It may also relate to safety limits, such as the maximum number of skiers permitted on a slope at a given time.

Economic carrying capacity may be defined in two senses. One has to do with the relationship of recreation to other uses, such as farming.

In this sense, the economic carrying capacity may be defined as the maximum level of recreational use a resource can sustain without imposing economic harm to other uses. The other approach uses economic carrying capacity not as a maximum level of use to be avoided, but as a minimum ideally to be exceeded: it is defined as that minimum level of use required in order to achieve a required financial return. Given that many forms of countryside recreation are available free of direct charge to the user, this latter use of the concept is of limited application in a countryside context, but it applies to any facilities, such as stately homes, where a charge is imposed and a defined financial target must be met. It may even be said to apply where no charge is made, but a defined level of use is deemed essential to justify the costs of providing and managing the resource for recreation.

Ecological carrying capacity concerns the maximum level of recreational use that a resource can sustain without an unacceptable or irreversible decline in ecological value taking place. Definitions can be deceptively simple, however, and this particular aspect of capacity exemplifies the difficulty of translating principle into practice. Who is to judge what is unacceptable decline, and by what criteria? How are we to recognize irreversible decline before it has taken place? It might be argued that ecological carrying capacity is reached when further recreational use would cause a degree of impact beyond the ability of the site to restore itself by natural means. However, such a stance ignores the role of good management and advancing technology in improving site restoration prospects.

Ecological capacity is itself a composite concept, and the notion of a precise or fixed capacity appears meaningless. The biological and ecological components of a site are manifold. Species vary in sensitivity, rarity and recoverability, and therefore in tolerance to human impact. Impact and capacity may also vary between the seasons, as *Mitchell (1979)* has shown in comparing the impact of the same volume and type of recreational activity in winter and summer. Ecological impact varies too with the characteristics of the recreational activity, as the relative effects of rambling and a rugby match would show. Impact varies also with equipment used, with activities such as trail biking, power boat racing, and model aircraft flying causing distinctive forms as well as levels of degradation.

While the foregoing facets of carrying capacity address aspects of the resource, the final approach views it as an attribute of the user. Perceptual carrying capacity (sometimes referred to as social carrying capacity *Stankey and McCool 1989*) relates to people's perceptions of the presence (or absence) of other users and its effects on their enjoyment of the site. It may be defined as the maximum level of recreational use above which there is a decline in the quality of the recreation experience from the point of view of the participant. More plainly, it measures the point at which new arrivals to a site perceive it to be 'full' (or overfull) and go elsewhere. Focussing on the user, perceptual carrying capacity is perhaps the most crucial yet most complex facet of capacity. It varies between individuals, according to their attraction or aversion to crowds, and it varies for the same person from time to time and from place to place. Being the sole visitor on the summit of Snowdon might be a richly rewarding (and rare!) experience; being the sole visitor to Center Parcs might be strangely unnerving.

Reaction to crowding is largely self-regulating, as several studies have shown *(Burton 1974, US Bureau of Outdoor Recreation 1977, Glyptis 1981a, 1981b)*. As Burton explained *(1974, p.155)*:

> Almost half of those who visit what is already the most crowded part of the Chase would not enjoy their visit any less if the intensity of use increased, and some would even enjoy it more. On the other hand, those who prefer to spend their time in the less crowded areas would appear to be far more sensitive to any increase in the level of recreational use. In brief, visitors sort themselves spatially on the basis of their sensitivity to crowding.

In management terms, therefore:

> A somewhat paradoxical situation exists: in fact there is 'spare capacity' in the areas which are already very intensively used, but the visitors frequenting the less intensively used parts may already consider existing levels of use to be too high and the area over used. (p.180).

Reactions to the presence of others depend not just on numbers present but also on the activities they are doing and the types of people they are. Real or perceived contrasts in social status and behaviour can become a source of frustration or conflict:

> 'Crowding'..... either for the member or the observer of the crowd is not simply a matter of the density of persons in a given space. For the crowded person, at least, the experience of 'being crowded' depends also to some degree on the people crowding him, the activity going on, and his previous experience involving numbers of people in similar situations. *(Proshansky et al, 1970, p.9)*.

A less used but no less useful concept is landscape carrying capacity. Site features, such as size, configuration, terrain and vegetation, affect the distribution of visitors and 'absorb' them to greater or lesser extents. Fifty people in an open park are readily visible as fifty people; fifty people in a wooded area are much less evident. In general, woodland, scrub and sand dune environments are high-capacity landscapes in this respect, and open moorland, downland and beaches low capacity. As far as perceptual carrying capacity is concerned, out of sight is out of mind; visitors react to what they see, not necessarily to what is there.

The most thorough and insightful study of recreational carrying capacity remains that of *Burton (1974)*. Her study of Cannock Chase embraced both ecological and perceptual capacity, with the rationale that 'they describe both the level of use the resource itself can bear, and how much the individual user can tolerate. The physical capacity of the ancillary facilities like road capacity or parking can then be used as a management tool to help regulate the use of the recreational resource itself' *(p.9)*. The study tested two hypotheses: firstly, that the quality of the recreational experience was related to prevailing conditions of crowding; and, secondly, that different intensities of recreational use caused proportional degrees of ecological damage. Perceptual capacity was examined by a combination of visitor interviews and observational mapping, while ecological capacity was investigated by means of detailed site studies of areas of known levels of recreational use.

Burton found that while sensitivity to crowding was not correlated with age, sex, or frequency of visiting, it did vary with social class and, all the more, with educational background. The higher the social class and educational background of people, the less likely were they to be found in the most crowded conditions. A more modest study by *Dodd (1985)* at Box Hill reached similar conclusions.

Burton's work, with other studies, led to the Countryside Commission using Cannock Chase as an experimental site for developing and testing of a Country Park Plan *(Rodgers et al 1982)*. The process of preparing the plan generated a wealth of technical guidance on many aspects of site management, including repairing eroded hill slopes, reclaiming semi-colonized heathland, parking provision on acid soil, and visitor redistribution.

Cannock Chase Country Park is part of the much larger Cannock Chase Area of Outstanding Natural Beauty. Four million people live within 50 kilometres, and the Country Park attracts half a million visitors a year. The agreed policy for recreation was to constrain public recreation as little as possible, but to maintain the overall level of use at or slightly below its existing level. Informed by the earlier capacity study, the plan sought to offer a broad spectrum of recreation opportunity, catering for the tastes of the 'gregarious', 'solitary' and 'specialist' visitors. Further goals were to extend recreation provision in parts of the site not optimally used, to improve information services, and minimize conflict between different types of users. To achieve these aims alongside the nature conservation and landscape objectives of the site, the policy adopted was a 'moderate degree of redistribution of use, coupled with a degree of segregation of user-types, so that particular sites and areas fulfil specific roles' *(Countryside Commission 1985c, p.14)*.

The plan proposed that the park should be divided into three areas, each with a distinct management policy. The main aim was to redistribute visitors from two of the zones to the third. One area was heavily used for recreation, and the plan sought to maintain its prime recreational purpose, enhance the visitor experience (by providing refreshments, more toilets, waymarking and improved parking), but create only a modest increase in use. The second area was of greatest conservation importance. The plan therefore proposed to minimize recreational use, by limiting parking and vehicle access. The third area was under-used by the public, and of limited conservation value. The plan therefore sought to divert visitors into this area and away from the first two, by providing additional parking, attractive sites, toilet facilities, waymarked walks, interpretative centres, picnic areas and horse-riding.

The plan was adopted in 1979, and implemented over the ensuing five years. It sought to determine whether visitor redistribution could be achieved by providing information and interpretative services and only modest parking restrictions; whether severe erosion around the main car park could be repaired without inconveniencing visitors; and whether improved techniques could be found for restoring vegetation and managing weed invasion.

The aims of the redistribution scheme were largely achieved. At the outset the ratio of parking in Zones I, II and III was 64: 14: 22; in 1984 it was 57: 10: 33, although on the busiest days it reverted to the original imbalance. To be confident of continuing success, the redistribution needed reinforcing with the provision of more events and facilities in Zone III. More specific goals were met to varying degrees. The proposals for overall levels of use, and catering for a variety of tastes were well met. Less progress was made regarding provision for elderly and disabled people, and many of the facilities intended, such as benches and barbecues did not materialize during the five year trial. Overall, however, significant progress was made, the plan provided a focus and a mechanism for drawing together the disparate aims of the many organizations involved in managing and using the area, and the systematic monitoring of the implementation process provided lessons applicable to site management elsewhere.

A proper approach to capacity thus entails resource and user aspects. Well used, the concept balances the protection of the resource with satisfying the needs of the users, and it can be an effective aid to site management. Defining and striking that balance, however, must begin with a definition of management objectives. Capacity limits, even when numerically expressed, are subjectively defined: they depend on management setting its aims for a site, and then assessing the relative importance of protecting particular habitats, accommodating particular activities, reaching particular income targets, and so on.

Ranger services

Ranger services are widely used in the National Parks and elsewhere to care for both the countryside and its users. Rangers are essentially fieldworkers who establish close contacts with visitors and with those who live and work in the countryside. They identify and manage practical works needed to improve the appearance of the landscape and help to maintain recreation facilities, especially footpaths. They establish close working links with farmers, gamekeepers and bailiffs, and develop contacts with parish councils, schools and local communities. They provide information and friendly advice to visitors, and maintain a presence in popular areas to resolve any immediate problems caused by visitor pressure. By agreement with landowners and tenants they help with the general protection of property and livestock, advise visitors of the Country Code, and help to enforce bylaws. They undertake waymarking and footpath maintenance, and the interpretation of wildlife and heritage conservation. In many cases, they also provide a search and rescue service, in conjunction with the emergency services.

The training needs of rangers, and of other countryside staff including planners, land agents, conservation advisers, national park staff, rights of way officers, site managers and interpretation staff, have been extensively reviewed and provided for *(Countryside Staff Training Advisory Group 1989)*.

Traffic and transport schemes

In a recreational context, transport can be a means to an end or an end in itself. The means is that of enabling people to reach the destinations they seek. With continuing declines in public transport services and increasing costs to passengers, non car owners have become progressively more disadvantaged as regards access to countryside recreation opportunities. An investigation in the Greater Manchester area in 1986–87 showed clearly the effects of the deregulation of public transport services. Bus services to countryside facilities on Saturdays and Sundays had declined markedly: 'the overall picture was gloomy. Even in those areas where frequency of service had improved, the overall level of service was still depressingly low and clearly a perceived barrier to public access to the countryside' *(Greater Manchester Countryside Unit 1988, p.22)*. Equally, the hordes of car-borne visitors to the countryside have caused concern in many areas about traffic congestion and overcrowding. These two concerns, sometimes separately and occasionally in tandem, have given rise to many public transport schemes for countryside recreation. Some involve the co-ordination of timetables so that people may travel out into the countryside, then walk to connect with another bus or rail service *(Grigg and Smith 1977)*. The Hadrian's Wall Bus Service, introduced by Northumberland National Park Authority, enables non car owners to get to the Wall, and car owners to leave their cars, walk, and then return to their cars by bus. The Snowdon Sherpa, run by Gwynedd County Council, offers a similar service. Gwynedd County Council also supports the Conway Valley Sunday Shuttle, a Sunday rail link from Conway to Blaenau Ffestiniog. Nottinghamshire County Council's Sherwood Forester offers a bus service linking the city of Nottingham with five country parks, Newstead Abbey and Cresswell Crags; 40 per cent of its users are car owners. The Heart of Wales Rambler, promoted by the Sports Council for Wales as a Sunday service using the Swansea–Shrewsbury rail link, attracts around 75–85 users per day, four-fifths of them car owners; 40 per cent of passengers combine use of the service with going for a walk in the countryside *(Lee 1990)*. In many cases success has been more modest than was hoped for. Indeed, schemes which have tried to gauge demand before provision started have found usage to be far less than expressed interest *(Greening and Slater 1981)*. The more successful schemes, such as the Wayfarer in West Yorkshire and Greater Manchester, rely on energetic marketing *(Speakman 1984)*.

First of the transport schemes designed to alleviate the pressure of motor traffic was the Goyt Valley Traffic Experiment *(Countryside Commission and Peak Park Planning Board 1972)*, initially a park-and-ride scheme, whereby car users were required to park in defined car parks, and given the opportunity to continue their journey by free minibus. In the event, few people made use of the minibus, and so the service was withdrawn and the park-and-ride project became a successful park-and-walk scheme.

Another approach to reducing motor traffic in the countryside is to promote cycling. Cycle hire schemes, such as those at the Tissington and High Peak Trails in the Peak District, have the added benefit of making use of disused railway routes. Their potential was first outlined by *Appleton (1970)*, and their particular suitability for walking, riding and cycling was assessed by the *Department of Transport (1982)*. In 1976 in the Peak District scheme Parsley Hay cycle hire centre had 50 cycles and generated 13,000 hirings. By 1986 the scheme had expanded to 324 cycles at four centres, with 39,000 hirings *(Peak Park Joint Planning Board 1988)*. Networks of cycle routes, both within the countryside and from town to country, have been evaluated by the *Countryside Commission (1989k)*.

Transport is in many cases not merely the facilitator of a recreation experience, but the very focus of it. Steam railways have long been a major attraction, harnessing both volunteer commitment and widespread nostalgia to good effect. The earliest were the narrow gauge lines of upland Wales, most notably the Talyllyn Railway, run by voluntary effort since 1951. The widespread closure of standard gauge lines after the Beeching Report of 1963 and the withdrawal of steam traction in 1968 lent new impetus to the cause, and opportunities to preserve additional lines. Prominent among them is the Severn Valley Railway, preserved since 1965. *Wooldridge (1984)* charted both the success of the Severn Valley Railway Company and its financial strictures: in the early 1980s the company had an annual turnover approaching one million pounds, but a profit of under £80,000.

Information and interpretation

Information is an important element of visitor services, and a powerful tool of visitor management. It contributes to visitors' enjoyment by raising their awareness of things to see and do, and at a more basic but equally important level, it helps them to find their way around a site. By providing information on certain aspects and not on others, visitor behaviour can be influenced; people will go to some places and not to others, unaware that their freedom of choice has been curtailed. Interpretation takes many forms. Some involve the provision of personal services, such as talks, guided walks and demonstrations. Others are self-directed, involving the provision of written materials or audio-visual media such as listening posts for visitors to use themselves. The Countryside Commission, for example, designed a series of self-guided trails around forests, farms, ancient monuments, other countryside sites, and urban centres, aimed at increasing people's understanding and cultivating respect for the environment. Various media are used for imparting information, some low-key, some capital intensive and some labour intensive. They include signposting, maps, display boards, nature trails, brochures and guide books, audio-visual displays, wardens, guides, and visitor centres.

The latter media, in particular, reflect a growing trend toward the provision not merely of information but of interpretation. Interpretation seeks to stimulate interest and awareness, and not simply convey information. Interpretation is more user-centred and experiential, demonstrating relationships and meanings in nature through first hand contact with original objects and examples. *Aldridge (1975)* described it as the art of explaining the past in relation to social conditions; the character of an area through the interrelationship of geology, soils, plants, animals and human activity; and the people–environment relationship in more general terms. Interpretation also plays a significant management function. It explains the significance of a site or area, and identifies what is valuable in it and worthy of conserving. By promoting public understanding and encouraging appreciation of the environment, it seeks to cultivate caring and co-operative visitor behaviour. The assumption is that an informed public is a caring public.

The effect of interpretation on visitor behaviour is poorly understood. Little is known about how far the users of a visitor centre are influenced in what they do for the rest of their stay (or thereafter) by the displays they have seen, or of how often something on site prompts visitors to make use of the centres. As *Orrom (1978)* stressed, visitor centres act as 'thresholds' to the sites that contain them, and should be positively linked with the sites. *Smith (1982)* found that visitor behaviour generally accorded with management objectives, but whether this resulted from the provision of interpretative services was unclear.

Many sites use a combination of techniques *(DART/University of Surrey 1978)*. Croxteth Country Park, Merseyside, for example, focuses around a stately home with a range of static exhibits, but also has a working farm run by the local authority.

The use of information and interpretative services as a management device was central to the Cannock Chase Management Plan, referred to before, which sought to redistribute visitors from over-used to under-used parts of the site by means of persuasion rather than restriction. The scheme aimed to increase visitor awareness of the extent of public access and facilities on the site, create new attractions, and promote them to achieve redistribution of existing visitors rather than to attract an entirely new market. The range of methods and media used are summarized in Table 6.2. and evaluated by *Daniels (1985)*.

Table 6.2   Information and interpretative services at Cannock Chase
Country Park

---

* Standard name signs at each major car park.
* Refurbished existing information centre.
* Series of 'Discover Cannock Chase' leaflets.
* Signposts at critical track junctions.
* Country park leaflet with map and description of facilities.
* Theme based trail (the Great War Trail) to encourage visitors to go to
    southern part of site.
* Leaflet describing walks from main car parks.
* Self-guided and waymarked trails.
* Guided walks programme, with topics including pond dips, fungi, and
    military camps.
* New interpretative and schools centre.
* Information packs and teachers' packs.
* Summer Sunday bus service.
* Trail boards in car parks, giving routes and distances.
* Exhibition of topography and habitats of the Chase through time, using text,
    video and tape recordings, photographs, items which could be handled
    (rocks, skins, antlers), movable displays, listening plates, drawings, trans-
    parencies, models, display items and play items (eg sandpit).
* Variety in mood as well as media: use of humour, mood changes in different
    audio-visual programmes, inclusion of occasional less palatable items (eg
    threats to deer).
* Slide-tape presentations, with varying slide change effects, and mixture of
    prose, rhyme, male and female talk-overs, animal calls, silence, music and
    other sound effects.
* Publications for sale.
* Off-site distribution of information and posters.

Source: Information from Daniels 1985

Some schemes are area rather than site based. The benefits of planning interpretative services on an area basis were first demonstrated on Exmoor (*Countryside Commission 1979b*). Another notable scheme was the experimental Tame Valley Interpretation Project in Greater Manchester, co-ordinated by the North West Civic Trust. The experiment, in an area where substantial environmental improvements had been achieved, aimed to stimulate the interest and involvement of local people, create a sense of identity for the valley, and create communication links between local authorities, user groups and other interested parties. Interpretative materials were aimed at both users and non users of the area, and many experimental projects were undertaken. These included a mobile information caravan, nature and environmental studies packs for school children, an outdoor pursuits scheme offering camping, canoeing, fishing and other activities, farm open days, and practical conservation projects with schools. The experiment did little to attract new users to the area, but visits by existing users increased by 40 per cent (*Civic Trust for the North West 1979*).

In a study of the provision of countryside interpretation by the

Forestry Commission, *Uzzell (1985)* identified four main visitor groups: middle class visitors, tourists, specialists, and local people. The last group were often forgotten by interpreters, yet they made up a substantial share of the visitors to Forestry Commission properties. To many interpreters, who tend to regard visitors as passive recipients of the information and services offered, local people pose something of a problem, for they are likely to be frequent visitors, whose interest will only be engaged if there are frequent changes of interpretative display. *Uzzell (1985, p.162)*, however, sees them as an opportunity, and urges a more participative approach to interpretation:

> The presence of a local population with whom one can form a continuous relationship offers many advantages. They can be drawn into the planning of interpretation so that they become not only users but also providers. They can stage exhibitions, devise a lecture programme and even be involved in defining interpretive goals and objectives..... organisations and societies may already exist to provide a focus for such activities. The visitor centre can become not just an exhibition building but rather a local resource centre for continuous and ever-changing countryside and forest interpretation, with a social as well as educational function.

Overview

The informality and spontaneity of much countryside recreation might at first sight imply that there is little need for positive planning and management. However, obtaining and maintaining access, enhancing the quality of the visitor experience, protecting the resources on which it depends, and enabling recreation to coexist with other interests pose planning and management issues of considerable complexity. Some approaches address them singly, others as a system. In all cases, success depends not only on diagnosing a problem, but also on identifying objectives to be achieved, and mechanisms for achieving them. Strategic planning approaches have been adopted both at national and regional levels, most notably by the Sports Council and in the regional strategies of the Regional Councils for Sports and Recreation. Implementation is impeded by the fact that the organisations devising the strategies have neither powers nor resources to translate them into reality directly, but the plans nonetheless provide an important framework for prioritisation and provision.

Several areas have benefitted from integrated management schemes, notably the Colne Valley, the Greater Manchester river valleys, and the Lee Valley. Progress and prospects vary with the different mechanisms for coordination adopted in the three projects. Management schemes using project officers, such as the UMEX, UFEX, Heritage Coast management and Groundwork schemes, have shown how modest means and low-key practical works can significantly enhance the landscape, visitor enjoyment, and landowner-visitor relations.

Other management approaches are used to address specific issues. At site level, much can be achieved, both for visitor enjoyment and resource protection, by good design and attractive facilities. Where recreation and conservation come into conflict they can usually be resolved, whether by separation or conciliation, and there are many examples of positive cooperation between them. The same is true of conflicts between different recreational activities seeking to use the same resource. Where opportunity allows, they can be separated spatially. Where it does not, time-zoning, or voluntary access arrangements or codes of practice may be possible. For some sectors of the population the problem is not what to do in the countryside, but how to get there. Schemes such as Operation Gateway can help to generate interest and confidence among people unfamiliar with the countryside, and special transport schemes can facilitate access. The Countryside Commission's proposal for town-based countryside information services should enhance awareness. Within the countryside itself, information and interpretative services help to enhance not only visitor enjoyment, but also public care and concern for the countryside. Ranger services likewise can combine visitor care and resource protection.

Many forms of countryside management are neither vigorous nor visible, and this is entirely appropriate. Most are concerned with local problems amenable to local solutions and low-key approaches. High profile management and deterrent styles are rarely necessary or appropriate for protecting the resource or enlisting the goodwill of the visitor. Much more can be achieved by more modest, subtle, participative and positive means.

7 Conclusions

The preceding chapters have ranged widely, for countryside recreation poses important resource, policy, management and demand issues. To do justice to them in brief compass is challenge indeed, and to distil key issues and opportunities all the more so. By way of brief conclusion, this final chapter reviews the achievements of recent decades, and the opportunities and threats for countryside recreation in the 1990s.

The achievements may be summarized as attention, access and action. Attention to the wider environment lies at the forefront of the government White Paper *This Common Inheritance (1990)*, referred to more fully below. Attention to countryside recreation came first in response to the access campaigners of the inter-war years, but legislative and policy attention are much more recent. The *1949 National Parks and Access to the Countryside Act* signalled the first tangible step towards protecting areas of high scenic value, and its legacy makes a strong imprint on the countryside today. The *1968 Countryside Act* brought a necessary broadening of perspective, to encompass the whole of the countryside and the transformation of demand and use by mass car ownership. The establishment of the Countryside Commission to promote countryside conservation and recreation provided a focus for countryside interests and policy development. The vision of the countryside in the 1968 Act as an integrated system, rather than a collection of special areas, has been strongly reiterated by the Countryside Commission in its policies to the year 2000.

Linked with that breadth of concern is access. Again, the 1949 Act, though far short of meeting the campaigners' wishes, paved the way for considerable improvements. The production of definitive maps of legal rights of way has proved a protracted business, but the Countryside Commission has injected new impetus into the process, and identified the management need for different parts of the paths hierarchy. The powers of National Park Authorities and local authorities to enter into access agreements and management agreements afford opportunities to negotiate the public use of private land, although the energy invested in reaching such agreements varies from place to place. Proposals for the future management and use of common land will enhance access further if they reach the statute book.

Action to facilitate access has taken a number of forms. The development of information and interpretative services has fostered public awareness and understanding of the countryside and its recreational opportunities. Special transport schemes to and within the countryside have had modest success in affording access for non car owners, and rather more success in encouraging car users to leave their cars once they arrive in the countryside. The provision of ranger services, country parks, picnic sites, car parks and signposting have enhanced recreational opportunities. Countryside management schemes have demonstrated that recreation, conservation and farming can co-exist to mutual benefit in the uplands and lowlands alike, and that conflicts can be reconciled.

Success has been tempered with frustration. Despite the growing adoption of strategic policy planning approaches, provision on the ground remains much more attuned to historic legacy than contemporary need. Access to countryside recreation resources remains imbalanced, both geographically and socially, and there is evidence of genuine latent demand, not merely non-use by those who are not interested. Barriers of access, mobility, awareness and confidence continue to stifle the recreational aspirations of many people. Proactive encouragement of participation, backed with the practical removal of barriers, is still all too rare. Fears of hordes of urban invaders wreaking havoc across a fragile countryside remain firmly entrenched in the mythology of countryside management, but do little justice either to the motives of the visitors or the ingenuity of planners and managers to cope with them.

For the future there are both opportunities and threats for countryside recreation. First and foremost among the opportunities is the firm government commitment to environmental protection. As the Director-General of the Countryside Commission remarked, 'The past year marked a watershed in the history of the environmental movement. In Britain, as elsewhere, the environment moved to the top of the list of public concern and began to influence the politics of the nation as never before' (*Countryside Commission Annual Report 1989–90*). The outcome is the 1990 White Paper, *This common inheritance. Britain's environmental strategy,* a comprehensive survey of all aspects of environmental concern. The White Paper places British issues in the context of broader European and world concerns, and embraces issues of global warming, pollution and waste, land use, water resources, the rural economy, landscape and wildlife, towns and cities, and protecting the heritage. Many of its provisions are relevant to countryside recreation. Firstly, district councils will be required to produce detailed land use plans, leaving counties to concentrate on more strategic issues. Secondly, efforts are to be made to bring more vacant land into use. Thirdly, new community forests are to be encouraged, along with environmentally friendly tourism. Fourthly, the White Paper pledges a national countryside initiative, to be discussed with the Countryside Commission, to encourage landowners and farmers to manage and protect key landscape features under pressure from visitors, such as the flower-rich chalk grasslands of the North Downs and the lowland heaths of Dorset and Suffolk. Fifthly, it endorses the Countryside Commission's proposals for the rights of way system, and for better access and management arrangements for commons. Sixthly, heritage sites are to be better protected, a new heritage forum to be convened, and a register of historic landscape sites compiled. In addition to these specific proposals, many of the more general concerns of the White Paper, such as air pollution, noise and the quality of bathing waters, also have important ramifications for recreation.

Related opportunities for countryside recreation arise from the re-use of agricultural land, the expansion and diversification of woodland, and the Countryside Commission's proposals for common land and new country parks. Overall, the greater people-orientation of the Commission will be vital in ensuring that recreation opportunities develop in ways which combine the protection and enhancement of the environment with the meeting of real public needs.

Possible threats to countryside recreation are numerous. The implications of water privatization for public access and pricing systems have yet to be evaluated. A second threat to recreation is elitism, both on the part of affluent rural in-migrants towards recreation opportunities for the town dweller, and on the part of some recreational activities towards others. Some activities, most notably motor sports, endure considerable public hostility, partly of their own making. Unless they act swiftly to create a more positive and representative image they could suffer still further. Indeed, the strength of political and public commitment to environmental issues could work to the detriment of all but the quietest and most contemplative recreational pursuits. The amenity interest in countryside recreation is well organized and well heard; the more passive and active forms of countryside recreation, such as sightseeing and sporting activities, are much less strongly voiced. Without stronger advocacy they could lose out increasingly — and unnecessarily — to powerful and articulate protectionists.

Protection and positive use are not incompatible. To combine them effectively requires a four pronged approach. The first is to undertake comprehensive resource appraisals to identify sites and areas of crucial importance for conservation *or recreation* reasons. There is no reason for recreation to be relegated entirely to set-piece attractions such as country parks and visitor centres, important though they are as part of a full spectrum of opportunity. The second need is to evaluate demand, addressing not merely the volume of demand for particular activities, but also the needs of particular minority groups and minority activities. The third need is for partnerships between those who share an interest in, or use, the same resources. Separation leads to extreme claims, entrenched views, and a polarization of interests; joint working can usually reach honest appraisals of need, minor concessions, mutual respect, and a sensible sharing of resources. The fourth need is to understand public interests and facilitate access. Even among frequent countryside users, patterns of activity are habitual and unadventurous. Among non users there is lack of awareness of opportunities and lack of confidence in using them. Lack of knowledge is no less a discriminator than lack of transport or finance. Public motivations for visiting the countryside, and satisfactions derived from doing so, are still poorly understood and worthy of systematic appraisal, for in countryside recreation as in many fields it is all too easy for providers to impose upon people the opportunities they would choose for themselves.

Paradoxically, the key to the systematic provision of countryside recreation opportunities lies in flexibility: flexibility, on the one hand, to identify people's varying needs and acknowledge their varying interests; flexibility, on the other hand, to review resources roundly, not with partisan interests to the fore. All too often the debate is *between* recreation and conservation, or *between* angling and canoeing, when in reality the needs of all can probably be met. The countryside is a finite and priceless asset, but with good management it can absorb greater use and new uses. As *Sidaway and O'Connor (1978, p.131)* concluded, 'capacity ..... is what we care to make it'. What we care to make it should be guided by the quality, scarceness and sensitivity of the resource, and the recreational needs of the public.

References

Aldridge D 1975 *Guide to countryside interpretation. Part one: Principles of countryside interpretation and interpretive planning.* HMSO.

Allison L 1986 Do we all have a right to the countryside? In Countryside Recreation Research Advisory Group *New approaches to access in the countryside.* Proceedings of CRRAG conference: 108–119.

Appleton J 1970 *Disused railways in the countryside of England and Wales.* HMSO.

Appleton J 1975 Landscape evaluation: the theoretical vacuum. *Institute of British Geographers Transactions* **66**: 120–123.

Appleton T 1982 Rutland Water Nature Reserve: concept, design and management. *Hydrobiologia* **88**: 211–24.

Atkinson-Willes G L 1969 Wildfowl and recreation: a balance of requirements. *British Water Supply* **11**: 5–15.

Batten L 1977 Sailing on reservoirs and its effects on water birds. *Biological Conservation* **11**: 49–58.

Bayfield N G, Barrow G C (eds) 1985 *The ecological impacts of outdoor recreation on mountain areas in Europe and North America.* Recreation Ecology Research Group Report No. 9.

Bell M 1986 Changing contexts in agriculture and rural life. In Countryside Recreation Research Advisory Group *New approaches to access in the countryside.* Proceedings of CRRAG conference: 54–69.

Bell M 1987 Five ways out of the countryside crisis. *Town and Country Planning* **56** (2): 36–37.

Bell S 1986 Tree talk — what others are saying: precursors of the CLA Working Party on forestry expansion. *Country Landowner* **39** (8): 18–19.

Blacksell M, Gilg A W 1975 Landscape evaluation in practice: the case of south-east Devon. *Institute of British Geographers Transactions* **66**: 135–140.

Blacksell M, Gilg A W 1981 *The countryside: planning and change.* George Allen and Unwin.

Blenkharn A 1980 Conflicts and reconciliation of casual recreational and other uses of rivers. In Council of Europe *Proceedings of International Workshop on Access to Nature*: 33–37. Council of Europe, Strasbourg.

Blunden J, Curry N (eds) 1985 *The changing countryside.* Open University.

Bouquet M, Winter, M (eds) 1987 *Who from their labours rest? Conflict and practice in rural tourism.* Avebury.

British Travel Association, University of Keele 1967 *Pilot National Recreation Survey Report No. 1.* British Travel Association.

British Waterways 1988 *British Waterways national count 1988.* British Waterways Research and Planning Unit.

British Waterways 1989 *Leisure on the inland waterways.* British Waterways Research and Planning Unit.

British Waterways 1990a *Report and accounts of the British Waterways Board 1988–89.* British Waterways.

British Waterways 1990b *Research Matters* **1**. British Waterways.

Bureau Européen de Recherches 1990 *Environmental incentives for farmers in selected European countries.* Countryside Commission.

Burton R C J 1974 *The recreational carrying capacity of the countryside.* Keele University Library Occasional Publications No. 11.

Burton T L, Wibberley G P 1965 *Outdoor recreation in the British countryside.* Wye College, University of London.

Cairns C 1983 *A management plan for the green belt management area in Barnet and South Hertfordshire 1982–1987.* CCP 147 Countryside Commission.

Carruthers S P (ed) 1986 *Alternative enterprises for agriculture in the UK.* University of Reading Centre for Agricultural Strategy.

Cartwright F F 1977 *A social history of medicine.* Longman.

Chadwick G F 1966 *The park and the town.* Architectural Press.

Chairmen's Policy Group 1983 *Leisure Policy for the Future.* Sports Council.

Cherry G E 1975 *Environmental Planning Vol. II. National Parks and recreation in the countryside.* HMSO.

Cherry G E 1985 Scenic heritage and national parks lobbies and legislation in England and Wales. *Leisure Studies* **4** (2): 127–39.

Civic Trust 1964 *A Lea Valley Regional Park.* Civic Trust.

Civic Trust for the North West 1979 *The Tame Valley Interpretation Project.* Civic Trust for the North West.

Clawson M, Knetsch J L 1963 Outdoor recreation research: some concepts and suggested areas of study. *Natural Resources Journal* **3** (2): 250–75.

Clawson M, Knetsch J L 1966 *Economics of outdoor recreation.* Johns Hopkins Press.

Coalter F, Long J, Duffield B S 1986 *Rationale for public sector investment in leisure.* Sports Council/Economic and Social Research Council Joint Panel on Leisure and Recreation Research.

Collins V 1984 *Recreation and the law.* E & F N Spon.

Colne Valley Standing Conference 1983 *Draft proposals for the Regional Park.* CVSC.

Cook D 1974 The battle for Kinder Scout. *Mountain* **32**: 30–32.

Cooke A 1977 *The birds of Grafham Water.* Huntingdon Local Publications.

Cooper C P 1981 Spatial and temporal patterns of tourist behaviour. *Regional Studies* **15** (5): 359–71.

Council for National Parks 1984 *Know your National Parks.* CNP.

Council for National Parks 1986a *50 years for National Parks.* CNP.

Council for National Parks 1986b *National parks: the celebration and the challenge.* Proceedings of the 50th anniversary conference. CNP.

Council for National Parks 1990 *A vision for national parks. Evidence to the National Parks Review Panel.* CNP.

Council for the Protection of Rural England 1990 *Our finest landscapes. CPRE submission to the National Parks Review Panel.* CPRE.

Countryside Commission 1970a *The planning of the coastline.* HMSO.

Countryside Commission 1970b *The coastal heritage.* HMSO.

Countryside Commission 1970c *Countryside Recreation Glossary.* Countryside Commission.

Countryside Commission 1974a *Country park plans.*

Countryside Commission 1974b *The use of site surveys in countryside recreation planning and management.* Countryside Commission.

Countryside Commission 1974c *Upland management experiment.* CCP 82 Countryside Commission.

Countryside Commission 1976 *The Lake District upland management experiment.* CCP 93 Countryside Commission.

Countryside Commission 1977 *SIRSEE: Study of Informal Recreation in South East England: the demand report.* Countryside Commission.

Countryside Commission 1979a *The Snowdonia upland management experiment.* CCP 122 Countryside Commission.

Countryside Commission 1979b *Exmoor National Park interpretive plan study.* CCP 123. Countryside Commission.

Countryside Commission 1989 *Countryside management in the urban fringe.* CCP 136 Countryside Commission.

Countryside Commission 1983a *The changing uplands* CCP 153. Countryside Commission.

Countryside Commission 1983b *Our programme for the countryside 1983–88.* Countryside Commission.

Countryside Commission 1985a *National countryside recreation survey: 1984* CCP 201. Countryside Commission.

Countryside Commission 1985b *Annual report 1984–85.* Countryside Commission.

Countryside Commission 1985c *Cannock Chase 1979–84: a country park plan on trial.* CCP 181 Countryside Commission.

Countryside Commission 1986 *Common Land. The Report of the Common Land Forum.* CCP 215 Countryside Commission.

Countryside Commission 1987a *New opportunities for the countryside* CCP 224. Countryside Commission.

Countryside Commission 1987b *Policies for enjoying the countryside* CCP 234. Countryside Commission.

Countryside Commission 1987c *Forestry in the countryside* CCP 245. Countryside Commission.

Countryside Commission 1987d *Enjoying the countryside. Priorities for action.* CCP 235 Countryside Commission.

Countryside Commission 1987e *The National Park Authority* CCP 230 Countryside Commission.

Countryside Commission 1987f *National parks: our manifesto for the next five years.* CCP 237 Countryside Commission.

Countryside Commission 1988 *Paths, routes and trails: policies and priorities.* CCP 266 Countryside Commission.

Countryside Commission 1989a *Incentives for a new direction for farming* CCP 262 Countryside Commission.

Countryside Commission 1989b *The Countryside Premium for set-aside land* CCP 267. Countryside Commission.

Countryside Commission 1989c *Planning for a greener countryside.* CCP 264 Countryside Commission.

Countryside Commission 1989d *National Parks review: a discussion document.* CCD 56 Countryside Commission.

Countryside Commission 1989e *Areas of Outstanding Natural Beauty in England and Wales.* CCP 276 Countryside Commission.

Countryside Commission 1989f *Paths, routes and trails: policies and priorities.* CCP 266 Countryside Commission.

Countryside Commission 1989g *Managing rights of way: an agenda for action.* CCP 273 Countryside Commission.

Countryside Commission 1989h *Common knowledge ?* CCP 281 Countryside Commission.

Countryside Commission 1989i *A new National Forest in the Midlands.* CCP 279 Countryside Commission.

Countryside Commission 1989j *A countryside for everyone.* CCP 265 Countryside Commission.

Countryside Commission 1989k *Recreational cycling in the countryside.* CCP 259 Countryside Commission.

Countryside Commission 1990a *Ten critical years: an agenda for the 1990s.* CCP 282 Countryside Commission.

Countryside Commission 1990b *Training of public rights of way officers.* CCP 298 Countryside Commission.

Countryside Commission News 1989 **39** September/October.

Countryside Commission, Forestry Commission 1989 *Forests for the community.* CCP 270 Countryside Commission.

Countryside Commission, Ministry of Agriculture, Fisheries and Food, Welsh Office 1986 *Ploughing and rights of way.* CCP 214 Countryside Commission.

Countryside Commission, Peak Park Planning Board 1972 *The Goyt Valley traffic experiment.* Countryside Commission.

Countryside Commission 1990c *Annual Report 1989 – 90* Countryside Commission.

Countryside Recreation Research Advisory Group 1976 *Digest of Countryside Recreation Statistics.* CCP 86 Countryside Commission.

Countryside Recreation Research Advisory Group 1980 *Digest of Countryside Recreation Statistics 1979.* CCP 86 Countryside Commission, Countryside Commission for Scotland and Sports Council.

Countryside Review Committee 1977 *Leisure and the countryside. A discussion paper.* Department of the Environment. HMSO.

Countryside Staff Training Advisory Group 1989 *Training for tomorrow's countryside.* CCP 269 Countryside Commission.

Crowe S 1966 *Forestry in the landscape.* HMSO.

Cullen P 1982 *An evaluation of the Heritage Coast Programme in England and Wales.* CCP 155 Countryside Commission.

Daniels J L 1985 *Encouraging visitor redistribution.* Cannock Chase Country Park Project Technical Report 3. CCP 184 Countryside Commission.

Darby H C (ed) 1951 *An historical geography of England before 1800.* Cambridge University Press.

Dartington Amenity Research Trust, University of Surrey 1978 *Interpretation in visitor centres.* Countryside Commission.

Davidson J 1970a *Outdoor recreation information: suggested standard classifications for use in questionnaire surveys.* Countryside Commission.

Davidson J 1970b *Outdoor recreation surveys: the design and use of questionnaires for site surveys.* Countryside Commission.

Davidson J 1974 Recreation and the urban fringe *The Planner* **60**, 9: 889–934.

Davidson J 1976 The urban fringe *Countryside Recreation Review* **1**: 2–7.

Dearden P 1980 Towards protection of scenic resources. *Environmental Conservation* **7** (2):153–8.

Department of the Environment 1972 *The planning of the undeveloped coast.* Circular 12/72 HMSO.

Department of the Environment 1975 *Sport and Recreation.* Cmnd 6200 HMSO.

Department of Transport 1982 *Study of disused railways in England and Wales. Potential cycle routes.* HMSO.

De Selincourt E (ed) 1970 Wordsworth's *Guide to the Lakes* Oxford University Press.

Dodd A M 1985 *Box Hill. The recreational use of a country park.* Unpublished MSc Recreation Management project Loughborough University of Technology.

Donnelly P 1986 The paradox of the parks: politics of recreational land use before and after the mass trespasses. *Leisure Studies* **5**: 211–31.

Dower J 1945 *National Parks in England and Wales.* Ministry of Town and Country Planning Cmnd 6628. HMSO.

Dower M 1965 *The challenge of leisure.* Civic Trust.

Dower M 1986a Feedback from the case studies. In Countryside Recreation Research Advisory Group *New approaches to access in the countryside.* Proceedings of conference: 88–97.

Dower M 1986b National Parks: perceptions and practice. In Council for National Parks *National Parks: the celebration and the challenge.* Proceedings of 50th anniversary conference: 6–17.

Dower M 1989 The countryside: access — a National Park perspective. In Sports Council *Recreation Management 1989 The Challenge of Countryside and Water Recreation*: 58–62.

Duffield B S, Owen M L 1970 *Leisure + countryside = : a geographical appraisal of countryside recreation in Lanarkshire.* University of Edinburgh.

Edwards A 1986 *An agricultural land budget for the United Kingdom.* Wye College, University of London.

Edwards J R Piggott C Cope R 1989 An appraisal of the ecological impacts of 'ghyll scrambling' in the English Lake District. In Brown B J H (ed) *Leisure and the environment.* Leisure Studies Association Conference Papers **31**: 198–216.

Elson M J 1977 *A review and evaluation of countryside recreation site surveys.* Countryside Commission.

Elson M J 1979 *The leisure use of green belts and urban fringes.* Economic and Social Research Council/Sports Council Joint Panel on Leisure and Recreation Research.

Elson M J 1986 *Green Belts: Conflict mediation in the urban fringe.* Heinemann.

Elson M J 1989a The urban fringe — will less farming mean more leisure? A critical review of recent events. In Brown, B J H (ed) *Leisure and the environment.* Leisure Studies Association Conference Papers **31**: 164–173.

Elson M J 1989b *Recreation and community provision in areas of new private housing.* Housing Research Foundation.

Elson M J 1990 *Negotiating the future. Planning gain in the 1990s.* ARC Limited.

Elson M J, Buller H, Stanley P 1986a *Providing for motorsports. From image to reality.* Study 28 Sports Council.

Elson M J, Buller H, Stanley P 1986b *Motorsports and motor recreation. A handbook for providers.* Study 29 Sports Council.

Elson M J, Lloyd J, Thorpe I 1989a *Providing for motorised water sports.* Study 36 Sports Council.

Elson M J, Lloyd J Thorpe I 1989b *Providing for air sports.* Study 35 Sports Council.

English Tourist Board 1987 *A vision for England.* English Tourist Board.

English Tourist Board, Countryside Commission 1989 *Principles for tourism in the countryside.* Countryside Commission.

Fairbrother N 1972 *New lives, new landscapes.* Penguin.

Fedden R 1968 *The continuing purpose: a history of the National Trust, its aims and work.* Longman.

Fedden R 1974 *The National Trust, past and present.* Jonathan Cape.

Ferguson M J, Munton R J C 1978 *Informal recreation in the urban fringe: the provision and management of sites in London's Green Belt.* Working paper no. 2 Land for informal recreation. University College London Department of Geography.

Ferguson M J, Munton R J C 1979 Informal recreation sites in London's green belt *Area* **11**: 196–205.

Fines K D 1968 Landscape evaluation: a research project in East Sussex. *Regional Studies* **2** (1): 41–5.

Fitton M 1976 The urban fringe and the less privileged *Countryside Recreation Review* **1**: 25–34.

Forestry Commission 1985 *The policy for broadleaved woodlands.* Forestry Commission.

Forestry Commission 1987 *The Forestry Commission and recreation.* Policy paper 2 Forestry Commission.

Forestry Commission 1988 *Forest Life* 4, August.

France L 1984 The recreational potential of Kielder Water. *Leisure Studies* **3** (1): 15–33.

General Household Survey Office of Population Censuses and Surveys. HMSO.

George M 1980 Natural values of wetlands. In Council of Europe *Proceedings of International Workshop on Access to Nature.* Council of Europe Strasbourg.

Glyptis S A 1981a Room to relax in the countryside *The Planner* **67** (4): 120–122.

Glyptis S A 1981b People at play in the countryside *Geography* **66** (4): 277–85.

Glyptis S A 1987a *Sport and recreation in rural areas. A sample study of Ryedale and Swaledale.* Yorkshire and Humberside Council for Sport and Recreation.

Glyptis S A 1987b *Recreation in expanding residential areas.* Report to Newbury District Council and The Sports Council. Loughborough University.

Goodall B, Whittow J 1975 *Recreation requirements and forest opportunities.* Geographical Papers **39** University of Reading.

Greater London Council 1972 *The Colne Valley Park —a new prospect.* Colne Valley Regional Park Standing Conference.

Greater London Council 1975 *Greater London Recreation Study. Research report 19.* GLC.

Greater Manchester Countryside Unit 1988 *Annual report 1987/88.* Association of Greater Manchester Authorities.

Greater Manchester Countryside Unit 1989 *Annual report 1988/89.* Association of Greater Manchester Authorities.

Greening P A K, Slater P 1981 *Rural recreational transport: the Sunday bus experiment.* Research report 1026 Transport and Road Research Laboratory.

Grigg A O, Smith P G 1977 *An opinion survey of the Yorkshire Dales rail service in 1975.* Transport and Road Research Laboratory.

Hansard 1948–49 Parliamentary Debates House of Commons 5th series **463**

Harrison C M 1980–81 Recovery of lowland grassland and heathland in southern England from disturbance by seasonal trampling. *Biological Conservation* **19**: 119–30.

Harrison C M 1981a A playground for whom? Informal recreation in London's Green Belt. *Area* **13**: 109–114.

Harrison C M 1981b *Preliminary results of a survey of site use in the South London Green Belt.* Working Paper 9, University College London Department of Geography.

Harrison C M, Burgess J, Limb M 1989 Popular values for the countryside. In Brown B J H (ed) *Leisure and the environment.* Leisure Studies Association Conference Papers **31**: 43–57.

Hertfordshire County Council 1986 *County Structure Plan Approved 1986 Review.* Hertfordshire County Council.

Hill H 1980 *Freedom to roam.* Moorland Publishing.

Himsworth K H 1980 *A review of Areas of Outstanding Natural Beauty.* CCP 140 Countryside Commission .

Hirst M, Coleman A 1983 Indecent exposure on the beach. *Justice of the Peace*, 10 September: 579–81.

Hockin R, Goodall B, Whittow J 1977 *The site requirements and planning of outdoor recreation activities.* Geographical Papers No. 54, University of Reading.

Hogg D 1977 The evaluation of recreational resources. In Mercer D (ed) *Leisure and recreation in Australia.* Sorrett, Melbourne.

House of Commons Papers 1983 *Access to the Countryside (Northern Ireland Order.* HMSO

House of Lords Select Committee on Sport and Leisure 1973 *Second Report.* HMSO.

Jackson G A M 1982 *Countryside trip making. The role of awareness levels and decision mechanisms.* Unpublished MSc Recreation Management project Loughborough University of Technology.

Jacob G, Shreyer R 1980 Conflict in outdoor recreation: a theoretical perspective. *Journal of Leisure Research* **12**, 4: 368–80.

Kaplan S, Kaplan R, Wendt J S 1972 Rated preferences and complexity for natural and urban visual material. *Perception and Psychophysics* **13**: 354–56.

Lake District National Park Authority 1986 *The Lake District National Park plan. Introducing the Lake District National Park.* LDNPA.

Lake District National Park Authority 1990 *National Parks Review. Comments by the Lake District National Park Authority.* LDNPA.

Landscape Research Group 1987 *Looking at the landscape: a review of recent practice and research in landscape assessment.* Countryside Commission.

Lean G 1989a Green and ruined land. *Observer Magazine* 4 June 1989: 20–24.

Lean G 1989b A land set in cement. *Observer Magazine* 11 June 1989: 45–47.

Lee R 1990 *Recreational transport schemes: two Sports Council for Wales initiatives.* Unpublished MSc Recreation Management project Loughborough University of Technology.

Lee T 1990 What kind of woodland and forest do people prefer? In Countryside Recreation Research Advisory Group *People, trees and woods.* Proceedings of CRRAG conference: 37–51.

Lee Valley Regional Park Authority 1969 *Park plan and proposals.* Lee Valley Regional Park Authority.

Lee Valley Regional Park Authority 1986 *Lee Valley Park Plan.* Lee Valley Regional Park Authority.

Linton D 1968 The assessment of scenery as a recreation resource. *Scottish Geographical Magazine* **84** (3): 219–38.

Locke S 1985 *Country park visitor surveys: lessons from a study at Sherwood Forest and Rufford Country Parks, Nottinghamshire.* CCP 180 Countryside Commission.

Lowe P, Goyder J 1983 *Environmental groups in politics.* Allen and Unwin.

Lowenthal D, Prince HC 1965 English landscape tastes. *Geographical Review* **55**: 186–222.

Lowerson J 1980 Battles for the countryside. In Gloversmith F (ed) *Class, culture and social change.* Harvester Press.

MacEwen A, MacEwen M 1982 *National Parks: conservation or cosmetics?* Allen and Unwin.

MacEwen A, MacEwen M 1987 *Greenprints for the countryside?* Allen and Unwin.

Margetson S 1969 *Leisure and pleasure in the nineteenth century.* Cassell.

Marshall I C, Green B H 1984 *An appraisal of semi-natural ecosystems on golf courses in Kent.* Occasional paper 12, Department of Environmental Studies and Countryside Planning, Wye College.

Maund R 1982 The Greater Manchester Adventure: an exercise in strategic environmental improvement. *Environmental Education and Information* **2**: 79–86.

McIntosh P, Charlton V 1985 *The impact of Sport for All policy 1966–1984 and a way forward.* Study 16 Sports Council.

McLaughlin B 1989 The future of recreation—agriculture and landscape change. In Sports Council *The challenge of countryside and water recreation.* Recreation Management conference 1989: 77–81.

Mercer D 1980 *In pursuit of leisure.* Sorrett, Melbourne.

Mercer I 1990, quoted in Morrison J Military called to account. *National Parks Today* **27** summer: 1.

Miles C, Seabrooke W 1977 *Recreational land management.* Spon.

Minister of Land and Natural Resources/Secretary of State for Wales 1966 *Leisure in the countryside: England and Wales.* Cmnd 2928. HMSO.

Ministry of Agriculture, Fisheries and Food 1972 *Forestry policy.* HMSO.

Ministry of Housing and Local Government 1955 *Green Belts.* Circular 42/55. HMSO.

Ministry of Housing and Local Government 1962 *Green Belts.* HMSO.

Ministry of Town and Country Planning 1947 *Conservation of nature in England and Wales: Report of the Wild Life Conservation Special Committee (England and Wales)*. Cmnd 7122. HMSO.

Ministry of Transport 1967 *British Waterways: Recreation and Amenity* Cmnd 3401. HMSO.

Mitchell B 1979 *Geography and resource analysis*. Longman.

Munton R J C 1983 *London's Green Belt: containment in practice*. Allen and Unwin.

National Caving Association 1972 *Caves and conservation*. National Caving Association.

National Parks Commission 1952 *Third Report*. HMSO.

National Parks Commission 1967a *The coasts of Kent and Sussex*. HMSO.

National Parks Commission 1967b *The coasts of Hampshire and the Isle of Wight*. HMSO.

National Parks Commission 1967c *The coasts of South-West England*. HMSO.

National Parks Commission 1967d *The coasts of South Wales and the Severn Estuary*. HMSO.

National Parks Commission 1968a *The coasts of North Wales*. HMSO.

National Parks Commission 1968b *The coasts of North-West England*. HMSO.

National Parks Commission 1968c *The coasts of North-East England*. HMSO.

National Parks Commission 1968d *The coasts of Yorkshire and Lincolnshire*. HMSO.

National Parks Commission 1968e *The coasts of East Anglia*. HMSO.

National Parks Commission 1969a *Coastal recreation and holidays*. HMSO.

National Parks Commission 1969b *Nature conservation at the coast*. HMSO.

National Rivers Authority undated *National Rivers Authority. Guardians of the water environment*. National Rivers Authority.

National Rivers Authority 1990 *Annual report and accounts 1989–90*. National Rivers Authority.

National Trust 1977 *A fourth progress report on Enterprise Neptune*. National Trust.

National Trust 1990 *Annual report 1989*. National Trust.

Natural Environment Research Council 1971 *National Angling Survey 1970*. NERC.

Nature Conservancy Council 1984 *Nature conservation in Great Britain*.

Nature Conservancy Council 1987 *13th report. 1 April 1986–31 March 1987*. Nature Conservancy Council.

Nature Conservancy Council 1989 *15th report. 1 April 1988–31 March 1989*. Nature Conservancy Council.

Newby H 1988 *The countryside in question*. Hutchinson.

Newbould C 1976 Wildlife conservation — the role of the NCC. In Royal Society of Arts *Recreation and conservation in water areas*: 27–49.

Nichols G S 1986 *A user survey of the Tissington Trail*. Unpublished MSc Recreation Management project, Loughborough University of Technology.

North Regional Planning Committee 1969 *Outdoor leisure activities in the Northern Region*.

Northumbrian Water Authority 1978 *The Kielder water scheme*. NWA.

Open Spaces Society undated *Our common right*. Open Spaces Society.

O'Riordan T, Paget G 1978 *Sharing rivers and canals*. Study 16 Sports Council.

Orrom M 1978 The interpretive policy and visitor centres of the Forestry Commission. *Museums Journal* **77**, 4: 171–73.

Owen M, Williams G 1976 Winter distribution and habitat requirements of wigeon in Britain. *Wildfowl* **27**: 83–90.

Owens N W 1977 Responses of wintering Brent Geese to human disturbance. *Wildfowl* **28**: 5–14.

Parry M L 1987 Multi-purpose use of waters. In Institute for Terrestrial Ecology *Angling and wildlife in fresh waters.* ITE Symposium 19: 66–71.

Parry M L, Bruce A, Harkness C E 1982 *Changes in the extent of moorland and roughland in the North York Moors.* University of Birmingham Department of Geography.

Patmore J A 1972 *Land and leisure.* Pelican.

Patmore J A 1983 *Recreation and resources.* Blackwell.

Patmore J A 1987 Surplus agricultural land: agricultural change and recreation in National Parks. *Tarn and Tor* **11**: 6–7.

Peak Park Joint Planning Board 1988 *Peak National Park plan. Draft 1st review.* Peak Park Joint Planning Board.

Penning-Rowsell E C 1975 *Alternative approaches to landscape appraisal and evaluation. Supplement.* Middlesex Polytechnic.

Phillips A, Ashcroft P 1987 The impact of research in countryside recreation policy development. *Leisure Studies* **6**, 3: 315–28.

Pigram J J 1983 *Outdoor recreation and resource management.* Croom Helm.

Pimlott J A R 1947 *The Englishman's holiday.* Faber and Faber.

Porchester Lord 1977 *A study of Exmoor.* HMSO.

Proshansky H M, Ittelson W H, Rivlin L G 1970 *Environmental psychology: man and his physical setting.* Holt, Rinehart and Winston, New York.

Ramblers Association 1980 *A policy for footpaths.* Ramblers Association.

Ratcliffe D (ed) 1977 *A nature conservation review.* Cambridge University Press.

Report of the Committee on Land Utilization in Rural Areas 1942 Ministry of Works and Planning Cmnd 6378. HMSO.

Report of the National Parks Committee 1931 Cmnd 3851. HMSO.

Report of the National Parks Committee (England and Wales) 1947 Cmnd 7121. HMSO.

Report of the National Parks Policy Review Committee 1974 Department of the Environment. HMSO.

Richardson S D 1970 The end of forestry in Great Britain. *Advancement of Science* **132**: 153–63.

Robinson D, Laurie J, Wager J, Traill A 1976 *Landscape evaluation.* University of Manchester.

Rodgers H B, Burton R C J, Shimwell D W, Bostock J L 1982 *Cannock Chase—the preparation of a country park management plan.* CCP 154 Countryside Commission.

Rodgers H B, Patmore J A (eds) 1972 *Leisure in the North West.* North West Sports Council.

Royal Commission on the Distribution of Income and Wealth 1979 *Report number 7.* Cmnd 7595. HMSO.

Royal Society for Nature Conservation 1987 *Damage to wildlife sites by off-road motor vehicles.* RSNC.

Rutledge A 1971 *Anatomy of a park.* McGraw-Hill, New York.

Sandbach F R 1978 The early campaign for a National Park in the Lake District. *Institute of British Geographers Transactions* **3** (4): 498–514.

Scott A 1990 The changing forestry scene in Britain. In Countryside Recreation Research Advisory Group *People, trees and woods* Proceedings of CRRAG conference: 15–18.

Sheail J 1975 The concept of National Parks in Great Britain 1900–1950. *Institute of British Geographers Transactions* **66**: 41–56.

Shercliff W H 1987 *Nature's joys are free for all. A history of countryside recreation in North East Cheshire.* Shercliff.

Shoard M 1980 *The theft of the countryside.* Temple Smith.

Shoard M 1987 *This land is our land.* Paladin.

Sidaway R M 1986 Towards a new understanding of access and accessibility. Action, policy and implementation. In Countryside Recreation Research Advisory Group *New approaches to access in the countryside.* Proceedings of CRRAG conference: 25–40.

Sidaway R M 1988 *Sport, recreation and nature conservation.* Study 32 Sports Council.

Sidaway R M 1990 Environmental Protection Bill: implications for sport and outdoor recreation. *Sports Update* 4, January 1990, Sports Council for Wales.

Sidaway R M, Coalter J A, Rennick I M, Scott P G 1986 *Access study. Summary report.* Sports Council and Countryside Commission.

Sideaway R M, O'Connor F B 1978 Recreation pressures in the countryside. *Countryside for all?* Proceedings of Countryside Recreation Research Advisory Group Conference. CRRAG.

Sillitoe K K 1969 *Planning for leisure.* HMSO.

Small D 1979 *Forest for all seasons.* Geographical Magazine L1: 620–8.

Smith D J 1982 *Evaluating the effectiveness of countryside interpretation in achieving site management objectives.* Unpublished MSc Recreation Management project Loughborough University of Technology.

South West Sports Council 1976 *A regional strategy for sport in the South West.* Sports Council South West Region.

Speakman C 1984 Public transport and the countryside. In Bannister C, Groome D (eds) *Out and about.* Department of Town and Country Planning Manchester University.

Sports Council 1972 *Provision for sport: indoor swimming pools, indoor sports centres, golf courses.* HMSO.

Sports Council 1982 *Sport in the community. The next ten years.* Sports Council.

Sports Council 1986 *A digest of sports statistics for the UK,* 2nd edition, Sports Council Information Series No. 7.

Sports Council 1988 *Sport in the community. Into the 90s.* Sports Council.

Sports Council undated *What is the Sports Council?* Fact sheet. Sports Council.

Standing Committee on National Parks 1938 *The case for National Parks in Great Britain.* SCNP.

Standing Conference for London and South East Regional Planning 1979 *Policy for recreation in London's Green Belt.* SCIIIR. SCLSERP.

Stankey G H, McCool S F 1989 Beyond social carrying capacity. In Jackson E L and Burton T L (eds) *Understanding leisure and recreation.* Venture Publishing Pennsylvania: 497–516.

Stansfield K 1982 Turning the black belt green. *Local Government News* July–August: 30–31.

Steers J A 1944 Coastal preservation and planning. *Geographical Journal* **104**: 7–27.

Stoakes R 1979 Oil prices and countryside recreation travel. In CRRAG *Digest of Countryside Recreation Statistics 1979* Countryside Commission, Countryside Commission for Scotland and Sports Council.

Swinnerton G S 1989 Recreation and conservation. In Jackson E L and Burton T L (eds) *Understanding recreation and leisure.* Venture Publishing Pennsylvania: 517–65.

Talbot-Ponsonby H (ed) 1988 *Recreation and wildlife: working in partnership.* Proceedings of Countryside Recreation Research Advisory Group Conference 1987 CRRAG.

Tanner M 1977 *The recreational use of water supply reservoirs in England and Wales.* Report no. 3 Water Space Amenity Commission.

Tanner M F 1979 *Wildfowl, reservoirs and recreation.* Research report 5 Water Space Amenity Commission.

Telling A, Smith R 1985 *The public right of navigation.* Study 27 The Sports Council.

This common inheritance. Britain's environmental strategy. 1990 Cm 1200 HMSO.

Thompson A E 1971 The Forestry Commission: a reappraisal of its functions. *Three Banks Review* **91**: 30–44.

Thorpe H 1949 The village greens of County Durham. *Institute of British Geographers Transactions* **15**: 153–80.

Tourism and Recreation Research Unit 1983a *Urban parks and open spaces — a review.* Economic and Social Research Council/Sports Council Joint Panel on Leisure and Recreation Research.

Tourism and Recreation Research Unit 1983b *Recreation site survey manual: methods and techniques for conducting visitor surveys.* Countryside Commission for Scotland.

Travis A S 1976 Urban fringe recreation in other countries: some examples. In Travis A S and Veal A J (eds) *Recreation and the urban fringe.* Proceedings of CRRAG conference: 31–43.

Travis A S 1990 Recreation in the woods today: a United Kingdom review. In Countryside Recreation Research Advisory Group *People, trees and woods.* Proceedings of CRRAG conference: 19–36.

Tuite C H 1983 *The impact of water-based recreation on the waterfowl of enclosed inland waters in Britain.* Wildfowl Trust, Nature Conservancy Council and Sports Council.

UK Centre for Economic and Environmental Development 1990 *Military live firing in National Parks.* UK CEED.

Unwin K 1975 The relationship of observer and landscape in landscape evaluation. *Institute of British Geographers Transactions* **66**: 130–4.

US Bureau of Outdoor Recreation 1977 *Guidelines for understanding and determining optimum recreation carrying capacity.* US Bureau of Outdoor Recreation, Washington DC.

Uzzell D L 1985 Management issues in the provision of countryside interpretation. *Leisure Studies* **4**, 2: 159–174.

Van Lier H 1973 *Determination of planning capacity and layout criteria of outdoor recreation projects.* Institute for Land and Water Management Research, Wageningen.

Wall G, Wright C 1977 *The environmental impact of outdoor recreation.* Department of Geography, University of Waterloo, Canada.

Watmough B 1983 *The effects on wildfowl of recreation at reservoirs in the Mid-Trent Valley.* Severn-Trent Water Authority.

Webster P 1976 Local authority action in the urban fringe. *Countryside Recreation Review* **1**: 13–20.

Williams A T, Howden J C 1979 The search for a coastal ethos: a case study of one of Great Britain's Heritage Coastlines. *Shore and Beach* **47**: 17–21.

Wooldridge Z J 1984 *The Severn Valley Railway*. Unpublished MSc Recreation Management project Loughborough University of Technology.

Zimmerman E W 1951 *World resources and industries*. Harper, New York.

Index